NEW MEXICO
CULTURAL RESOURCES
DIRECTORY

Typeset by Copygraphics, Santa Fe.

Printed at University Printing Services, Albuquerque.

Bruce King, Governor
Helmuth J. Naumer, Cultural Affairs Officer
Doug Svetnicka, Project Director

New Mexico Office of Cultural Affairs
La Villa Rivera Building
228 E. Palace Avenue
P.O. Box 2087
Santa Fe, New Mexico 87504-2087
(505) 827-8233, or 827-6364

Museum of New Mexico Press
P.O. Box 2087
Santa Fe, New Mexico 87504-2087
(505) 827-6454

ISBN 0-89013-223-2

On the cover:

Nativity. By Helen Cordero of Cochiti Pueblo.
Slipped and painted earthenware, c. 1964.
Girard Collection of the Museum of International Folk Art
of the Museum of New Mexico, Office of Cultural Affairs.
Photograph by Michel Monteaux.

NEW MEXICO CULTURAL RESOURCES DIRECTORY

The Complete Guide to Arts, History, and Community Events

Compiled by the New Mexico Office of Cultural Affairs

Museum of New Mexico Press • Santa Fe

Spanish conquistadors and missionaries; Pueblo Indians and American pioneers—New Mexico is able to vaunt the oldest and most prolific history in the nation.

The region's exciting past, its ethnic and cultural diversity, and its colorful life-ways hold a special fascination for we New Mexicans, and for our many guests from throughout the nation and the world. The visible reminders of our unique past and contemporary arts and culture are everywhere—ready to entertain and to educate; to make us joyous and to help us explore.

With the strength and diversity of New Mexico's history and cultures in mind, we in the Office of Cultural Affairs are delighted to present this compendium of our state's distinguished cultural resources. This directory is no less than a celebration...a fitting toast to our historic sites, arts and crafts fairs, literature, visual and performing arts, and community festivals.

Please join us in building upon this directory with suggestions for modifications and additions. We welcome your comments.

Helmuth J. Naumer
Cultural Affairs Officer

The Office of Cultural Affairs is an agency of the State of New Mexico, charged with administering the Museum of New Mexico, Space Center, Museum of Natural History, New Mexico State Library, Arts Division and Historic Preservation Division. The agency's mission is to manage effectively the historical and cultural facilities, sites and programs of the State of New Mexico and to encourage and provide for the research, preservation, public presentation and promotion of the state and region's cultural resources.

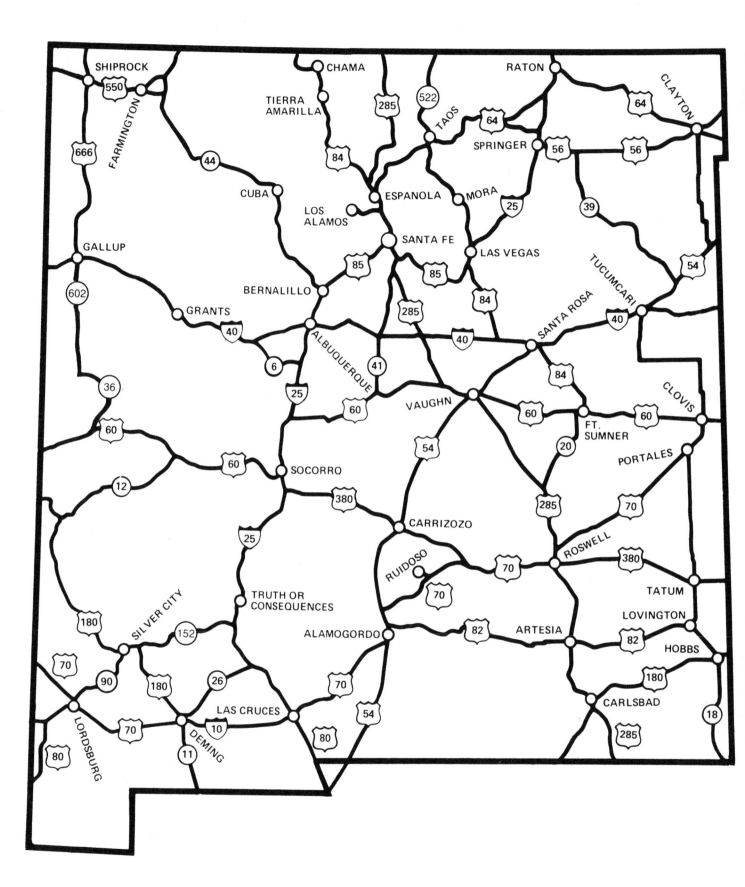

How To Use This Directory

Each listing has been coded with one or more of the following symbols:

Type of Cultural Resource

A Arts Associations

V Arts & Crafts/Visual Arts

E Community Events

H Historic Buildings & Sites

O Historical Organizations

L Libraries

M Museums

P Performing Arts

All telephone numbers in New Mexico have a 505 area code. Please call appropriate resource for dates and times of events—only general time frames are given in the directory. For more information on New Mexico's cultural treasures, contact the Office of Cultural Affairs.

Abiquiu H

Hwy 84, north of Espanola

Once the site of an Indian Pueblo, Abiquiu was settled in the mid-18th Century by a group of Spaniards and genizaros (Hispanicized Indians). In the late 18th Century, explorers Fray Francisco Atanacio Dominguez and Fray Silvestre Velez de Escalante visited here. In 1830, the settlement became one of the stops on the Spanish Trail which linked Santa Fe with Southern California. Today, the town in the bend of the Rio Chama is perhaps best known as the home of the celebrated artist, Georgia O'Keeffe.

Christ-in-the-Desert Monastery H

13 miles off Hwy 84, near Ghost Ranch

The monastery serves as a secluded Benedictine settlement on the banks of the Chama River. The building is considered a piece of architectural excellence—adobe, stone, glass and wood employed to create a pleasing structure in the tradition of early New Mexico religious architecture. The monastery is on the State Register of Cultural Properties.

Dominguez-Velez de Escalante Trail H

Hwy 84, north of Espanola

Their mission was to spread Christianity among the Indians, and to accomplish their goal Fray Francisco Atanasio Dominguez and Fray Silvestre Velez de Escalante opened a trail between Santa Fe and Monterey, California. The two missionaries led a small party northwest in 1776. Abiquiu was the last Spanish settlement they saw in their five-month, 2000-mile journey.

Florence Hawley Ellis Museum of Anthropology M L

Hwy 84
Ghost Ranch Conference Center, 87510
685-4333

Situated amidst the colorful cliffs made famous by Georgia O'Keeffe, this anthropology museum focuses on cultures within a 60 mile radius; historic Navajo, Pueblo, early Spanish-American, and Anglo; prehistoric Gallina and Chama Valley; library.

Ghost Ranch Living Museum M

near Abiquiu
Hwy 84, 87510
685-4312

This is an intriguing outdoor natural history museum, featuring living animals, native botanical specimens, geological collections, as well as paintings and prints related to natural resources conservation. The museum offers lectures and films. Self-guided and guided tours are available.

Old Spanish Trail H

Hwy 84, north of Abiquiu

Antonio Armijo journeyed from Abiquiu to California in 1829-30 in order to trade for mules, thus extending the Old Spanish Trail and opening it to trade between Santa Fe and Los Angeles. His route turned west, near present-day Abiquiu Dam, to Largo Canyon, which led him to the San Juan River.

Acoma Pueblo H

south of I-40 between Grants and Albuquerque
252-1139, 552-6604

Acoma, meaning People of the White Rock, has been inhabited since before the 12th century. The pueblo, called Sky City, is situated on top of a mesa, hundreds of feet above the surrounding countryside. The entire pueblo is a National Historic Landmark. People are known for their fine pottery. Pueblo includes an arts and history museum as well as the Franciscan mission church of San Estevan, established in 1629. Festivals and celebrations include: San Pedro's Day in June, St. James' Day and the Corn Dances of Santa Ana's Day in July, and the feast of San Estevan, patron saint of the pueblo, in September. The pueblo is on both the State and National Registers.

Acoma Arts and Crafts Fair V

252-1139

Held in June.

Acoma Community Library Resource Center L

P.O. Box 469, 87034
552-6604

Acoma Pueblo Christmas Festivals   E

Three days of traditional costumed dances celebrating the birth of Jesus, December 25-27. Held at San Estevan del Rey Mission at Old Acoma Pueblo.

Acoma Pueblo Museum   M

P.O. Box 309, 87034
252-1139

This pueblo-run museum features Indian pottery and history exhibits, 15th Century to present.

Governor's Feast Day   E

Held at Old Acoma Pueblo in February.

San Estevan Feast Day   VE

This popular festival is held September 2 at the old Acoma Pueblo. San Estevan's Harvest Dance and Annual Feast includes a mid-morning mass, procession, afternoon Harvest Dance, food booths and a large arts and crafts fair.

San Estevan de Acoma Mission Church   H

252-1139

Built between 1629 and 1642 and repaired in 1799-1800, San Estevan del Rey Mission Church is among the finest and most impressive of the Spanish Colonial Mission Churches in New Mexico. The unique character of the missions lies in their almost perfect blend of Indian and Spanish influences. The church is on the State and National Registers.

San Juan Feast Day   E

Rooster Pull at Old Acoma Pueblo held on June 24.

San Lorenzo Feast Day   E

Fiesta Day in the neighboring settlement of Acomita on August 10.

San Pedro and San Pablo Feast Days   E

Rooster Pull at Old Acoma Pueblo on June 29.

Santa Maria Feast Day   E

Held on the first Sunday in May at the neighboring settlement of McCartys.

Santiago Feast Day   E

Rooster Pull at Old Acoma Pueblo on July 25.

Alamogordo   H

Two brothers Charles B. and John A. Eddy, promoters of the El Paso and Northeastern Railroad, can be credited with the development of the town in 1898. Alamogordo served as a junction with a railroad line to a nearby lumbering operation in the Sacramento Mountains. The first atomic bomb was exploded 60 miles northwest of Alamogordo on July 16, 1945.

Alamogordo Cultural Center   P

P.O. Box 1782, 88310

Alamogordo Public Library   L

920 Oregon Ave., 88310
437-9058

Dog Canyon/Oliver Lee Memorial State Park   MH

Hwy 54, 8 miles south of Alamogordo,
then 5 miles east on County Road A-16
437-8284

This historical State park commemorates the life and times of an important New Mexico pioneer. The earliest occupation of Dog Canyon, south of Alamogordo, began more than 5,000 years ago. Several groups of Apache Indians first came to the Dog Canyon area about 500 years ago, and continued to inhabit the canyon as recently as the late 19th Century. A museum in the park records the area's history.

Flight Fest   E

Space Center in Alamogordo
437-2840

Amateur model rocketry competition and show on the grounds of the Space Center, edge of Sacramento Mountains in Alamogordo. Held annually in June.

Holloman Air Force Base Library   L

Holloman Air Force Base, 88310
479-6511

New Mexico State University/ Alamogordo Library   L

2400 N. Scenic Drive, 88310
434-0840

Saturday in the Park VE

434-2867

Held in Washington Park in mid-May, featuring arts & crafts booths as well as demonstrations from the Holloman Air Force Base.

Space Center M

P.O. Box 533, 88311-0533
437-2840

Celebrating the history, technology and daring of space exploration with facilities including the International Space Hall of Fame (museum with extensive collection of artifacts and interpretive programs), Clyde W. Tombaugh Space Theater (OMNIMAX projector system and planetarium); John P. Stapp Air and Space Park, Astronaut Memorial Garden, and Shuttle Camp summer program for kids. The Space Center is a division of the New Mexico Office of Cultural Affairs.

Space Center/International Space Hall of Fame Induction E

Space Center
437-2840

Each year the Space Center selects a handful of individuals who have made major contributions to space research and exploration and honors these people with induction into the International Space Hall of Fame (a part of the Center). Induction ceremonies take place each year during late September.

Toy Train Depot M

1991 White Sands Blvd., 88310

Hundreds of model and toy trains in this 90 year-old train depot. An HO layout of 1000 square feet depicts the railroad in the Alamogordo area in the 1940's. Displays of engines, cars, cabooses and other nostalgic models line the walls.

Trinity Site H

85 miles from Alamogordo on the White Sands Missile Range

Site of the first atomic bomb explosion. Site open to the general public annually on the first Saturday in April and October. The site is on the National Register of Historic Places.

Tularosa Basin Historical Museum M

P.O. Box 518, 88310
437-6120

History museum; Mogollon Indian artifacts; cloud climbing railroad pictures; fossils and displays of clothing; mining and farm tools; Casas Grandes pottery exhibit.

White Sands National Monument MH

15 miles southwest of Alamogordo
U.S. 70-82, 88310
479-6124

Sprawling spectacular white sands and dunes, located near the site of the explosion of the first atomic bomb. A natural history museum is located on the grounds of the monument.

Albuquerque H

Spanish settlers called the Duke City home long before the Pueblo Revolt of 1680, but the town had been resettled when the "Villa de Alburquerque" was founded in 1706. The new town promoted colonization, but it was also aimed at providing protection from attacks by Indians in Rio Abajo, or lower Rio Grande Valley.

Action Arts A

Old Town Station
Box 7443, 87194
243-1673

A non-profit literary, media and performing arts corporation that sponsors Palomita Productions (one woman and small production theater), Folktales and Tales for Folks (a story theater duo), and Tapestry Players (multi-ethnic theater company).

Albuquerque Arts Alliance A

P.O. Box 40154, 87196-0154
243-4971

This is a non-profit membership organization which advocates, educates, provides technical assistance and information, and facilitates programs for all the arts. The Alliance provides services, including information and referral, to artists, arts organizations and art supporters.

Albuquerque Children's Theater P

4139 Prospect NE, 87110
888-3644

Albuquerque Civic Light Opera Association P

4201 Ellison NE, 87109
345-6577

Now in its third decade, ACLOA brings Broadway-style musical theater to the Popejoy Hall stage at the University of New Mexico. ALCOA is one of the largest community producers of musical theater in the nation.

Albuquerque Community Foundation AVP

6400 Uptown Blvd. NE
Suite 500W, 87110
883-6240

Among other activities, the Foundation organizes each year's Arts Alive! showcase of the performing arts (late August), as well as Magnifico! Albuquerque's Festival of the Arts (May).

Albuquerque Little Theater P

224 San Pasquale SW, 87104
242-4750

Now in its seventh decade of continuous production, this group performs plays in one of Albuquerque's most charming and historic facilities. The intimate-sized theater, built in 1936 and designed by famed southwestern architect John Gaw Meem, includes an art gallery in addition to a lobby and lounge. As a nonprofit community theatre, the company combines local volunteer talent with a staff of theatre professionals to produce a popular entertainment series of comedies, dramas, musicals and mysteries. The theatre is located across from Albuquerque's historic Old Town.

Albuquerque Municipal Airport Building (old) H

Yale Blvd. SE

This building is located near the current Albuquerque International Airport on Yale Blvd. S.E. Airports from the 1930s and earlier periods are rare survivors in the United States. And WPA constructed airports are even rarer. This building preserves a central time in Albuquerque's history, the boom era of the war years. It also symbolizes a critical time in U.S. aviation history. The airport began operation in 1928 and was used for passenger and freight transport until 1942. The $875,000 facility is also considered a good example of an institutional use of the Pueblo Revival architectural style. The old airport building is on the State Register of Cultural Properties.

Albuquerque Museum ML

2000 Mountain Road NW
P.O. Box 1293, 87103
243-7255

This is a major, nationally accredited museum featuring decorative arts, fine arts and crafts, costumes, photographs, and artifacts of cultural history from 20,000 B.C. to the present. The museum features four centuries of Spanish Colonial artifacts, from arms used during the Spanish conquest to 18th century Spanish coins. The museum, which was established by the City of Albuquerque in 1967, also has an extensive library.

Albuquerque Philharmonia Orchestra P

265-0283

Albuquerque Public Library L

501 Copper NW, 87102
768-5100

Albuquerque Public Library (old) H

423 Central Ave. NE

Located at Edith and Central, the library was constructed in 1925 and is considered an excellent example of 20th Century Revival of Pueblo-Spanish architecture. The interior of the building was decorated by prominent Taos artist Gustave Bauman. The fireplaces are beautiful. Building is on the State Register.

Albuquerque United Artists A

P.O. Box 1808, 87103
243-0531

This is a non-profit contemporary arts organization composed of local artists. The group promotes several visual arts activities throughout the year in various locations.

Albuquerque Women's Ensemble P

242-6454

American Indian Week E

Indian Pueblo Cultural Center
2401 Twelfth Street, NW
843-7270

This is a week-long tribute to the American Indian focusing on cultures and traditions as well as major concerns. Held during the third week in April.

Armijo School ⒣

1021 Isleta Blvd. SE

Built in 1914 and located in one of Albuquerque's oldest communities, the Armijo School has always served as an unmistakable South Valley landmark. Building is on both the State and National Registers.

Artists of Indian America, Inc. ⒜⒫

6636 Mossman Place NE, 87110
881-4093

This is a non-profit performing arts organization designed to stimulate social and cultural improvement among American Indian people. The group brings top Indian talent to schools and communities in New Mexico through concerts, workshops, performances and personal contact.

Arts Alive ⒫

6400 Uptown Blvd. NE
Suite 500W, 87110
883-6240

The Albuquerque Community Foundation organizes this annual event to showcase the upcoming performing arts seasons in the area. Held in late August, the evening includes several live performances being conducted simultaneously. Albuquerque restaurants participate in "A Taste of New Mexico" which provides food for the event. Performing arts groups also have booth displays to promote their organizations and sell tickets for their seasons. Proceeds from Arts Alive benefit the Art Endowment Fund of the Albuquerque Community Foundation.

Arts and Crafts Fair, Indian Pueblo Cultural Center ⓥ

2401 Twelfth Street NW
843-7270

Annual arts and crafts fair at the Indian Pueblo Cultural Center. A large assembly of Native American artisans, special activities and Indian dances.

ARTSPACE Magazine ⒜

P.O. Box 4547, 87196
266-1507

Atchison, Topeka & Santa Fe Railway Depot - Albuquerque ⒣

314 First Street SW

This depot was constructed in 1902 in the unusual California Mission style of architecture. The style is indicative of the Santa Fe Railway's intent to impress its travelers with the unique quality of Southwestern architecture. The depot is all that remains of a complex that was the heart of Albuquerque. Its complimentary Alvarado Hotel —a Harvey House—was torn down several years ago. Depot is on the State Register.

Ballet en Fuego - Latin Dance Revue ⒫

156 Calle Arroyo Seco NW, 87105
836-7579

This is a professional, Albuquerque-based dance company offering an extensive Mexican, Spanish, and contemporary Latin dance repertoire in full, colorful costume. The company has performed regionally, nationally as well as internationally.

Bill Evans Dance Company ⒫

P.O. Box 2815
Corrales, 87048
898-1531

This company, founded in 1975, moved to Albuquerque in 1988 and is now the professional contemporary dance company in residence at the University of New Mexico. The company, under the direction of Bill Evans, performs an original repertory of modern dance and jazz/tap choreography. Three to four performances per year are offered at the KiMo Theatre, as well as UNM's Rodey and Popejoy Halls. The company also presents the Bill Evans Summer Institute of Dance, an intensive workshop for dance students and professionals from throughout the nation. During the institute, several performances are open to the public. In addition to its Albuquerque performances, the company regularly tours to other New Mexico communities.

Center for Anthropological Studies Library ⓛ

P.O. Box 14576, 87191
296-4836

Chamber Orchestra of Albuquerque P

P.O. Box 35081, 87176
881-0844

Conducted by music director David Oberg, this chamber orchestra presents a variety of concerts each season. The 31-musician professional orchestra routinely performs six classical subscription concerts, an all Baroque concert, a joint concert with the University of New Mexico Chorus, several ensemble programs, and concerts for children and seniors. Major soloists of national and international reputation regularly appear with the group. Most concerts are performed at St. John's United Methodist Church.

Contemporary Dance Alliance P

877-7153

Danse Classique Theatre P

4616 Jupiter NW, 87107
345-0795

This group features ballet concerts.

Danzantes P

P.O. Box 4613, 87196
247-9640

This company presents dance dramas and other works of dance at the KiMo Theatre in Albuquerque.

Ernie Pyle Home/Library H

900 Girard SE
265-2065

This memorabilia-filled home of the beloved Pulitzer Prize-winning war correspondent is now a public library.

Experimental Theatre P

Fine Arts Center
UNM campus, 87131
277-4402

A 120-seat facility, this black-box venue houses experimental plays, dance and performance art.

Fine Arts Music Series P

P.O. Box 1638, 87103
243-5646

Folktales and Tales for Folks P

Old Town Station
Box 7443, 87194
243-1673

A two women performance duo; story theatre, family and adult audiences. In town and touring group.

Fourth Ward Historic District H

west of downtown

This area is significant for its architecture, and its great variety of fine homes built between 1880 and about 1930. This was Albuquerque's prime residential neighborhood during the period 1905 through 1923. It is also culturally significant as the home of many of the city's most influential citizens. Architectural styles include bungalow, Queen Anne, hipped box and Spanish Pueblo Revival. District is on both the State and National Registers.

Gathering of Nations Powwow V E

University Arena
University and Stadium SE
836-2810

Dance competitions, arts and crafts, 5K run, 10K walk, Miss Indian World contest. Held in mid-April.

Geology and Meteoritic Museums M

Northrop Hall
UNM campus, 87131
277-4204

These unusual museums take the visitor on a tour of the geology of our Solar System. Samples of rare meteorites from Mars and the Asteroids sit side by side with diverse and colorful examples of minerals, rocks and fossils, including dinosaur bones, from our own planet, Earth. Several special exhibits are devoted to aspects of the geology of New Mexico and meteorites recovered from within the state. Geology Museum hours: 8 a.m.-5 p.m. (7:30 a.m.-4 p.m. summers). Meteoritics Museum hours: 9 a.m.-12 noon and 1 p.m.-4 p.m.

Governor's Festival of the Arts E

New Mexico State Fairgrounds
265-1791

Held in May.

Grecian Festival   V E

St. George Greek Orthodox Church
308 High St. SE
242-2212

This festival features Greek food, dancing, as well as an arts and crafts fair. Held the first weekend in October.

Guerreros de Chicomostoc   P

157 Willow Road NW, 87107
247-4119

This group of Aztec dancers presents pre-Columbian warrior ritual dances from central Mexico, complete with authentic vestments and musical instruments.

Hilton Hotel (old)   H

125 Second Street NW

Built in 1939, this building is significant as the last of Albuquerque's great "southwestern" hotels. The facility reflects the modern building techniques of the time while displaying traditional New Mexico decor. Property is on both the State and National Registers.

Hispanic Culture Foundation   A

P.O. Box 7279, 87194
831-8360

Historic Residences of Downtown Albuquerque   H

Central Avenue

Located adjacent to historic Old Albuquerque—Spanish community founded in 1706—this area is primarily residential, characterized by a variety of architecture, with good representation of practically every style found in the city between 1860 through 1930. District is on both the State and National Registers.

Huning Highlands Historic District   H

Grand Ave area

This area represents predominant turn-of-the-century building styles, ranging from Queen Anne to Italianate. Huning Highlands was named for Franz Huning, a German immigrant who made New Mexico his home in the mid-1800s, and who by the 1880s had become a prominent Albuquerque citizen. District is on both the State and National Registers.

Indian National Finals Rodeo   V E

Tingley Coliseum, State Fairgrounds
255-1791

American Indian rodeo riders from the U.S. and Canada compete for prize money and the title of World Champion Indian Cowboy. Indian arts and crafts, Powwow and ceremonial dance competition. Miss Indian Rodeo Pageant. Held in late November.

Indian Petroglyph State Park   H

West of Coors Road on Unser Boulevard

Five extinct volcanoes stand silhouetted against the western sky above Albuquerque. For thousands of years their lava flows were a hunting ground for ancient man who camped along the hard, dark rock. They left behind a record of their lives and the beliefs that sustained them in the form of an estimated 15-17,000 rock drawings (petroglyphs) chipped out of the rocky formations of what is now Indian Petroglyph State Park. Site is on the State Register of Cultural Properties.

Indian Pueblo Cultural Center   M V P

2401 Twelfth St. NW, 87102
843-7270

The Indian Pueblo Cultural Center houses a 260-seat theater. Many ceremonies and dances are adapted to stage presentation, particularly during the winter months; others are held in the open in the central plaza. The Pueblo Indian Museum is also housed at the Center. The Center is governed by the 19 Pueblo Governors of New Mexico. In October there is an Indian Crafts Fair and dances are held on the weekends.

International Balloon Fiesta   E

Balloon Park
821-1000

Annual festival held the first full week of October. It is one of the largest air shows in the world, with up to 500 participants and thousands of spectators. Features an opening day parade, daily air shows, precision parachute teams, an evening balloon glow, marching bands, balloon souvenirs, ethnic foods.

Jonson Gallery of Contemporary Art   Ⓜ

UNM campus
1909 Las Lomas NE, 87131
277-4967

A branch of the University Art Museum, offering changing exhibitions of work by contemporary artists and continuous exhibitions of works by Raymond Jonson (1891-1982), a prolific artist and teacher in New Mexico for more than 60 years. Collections include 2000 works by Jonson and other modern artists. The gallery's stated mission—"to exhibit the work of significant artists deserving more exposure."

Journal/Tribune Library   Ⓛ

Albuquerque Publishing Company
P.O. Drawer J-T, 87103
823-3493

June Music Festival of Albuquerque   Ⓟ

P.O. Box 35081, 87176-5081
888-1842

Kearny's Route   Ⓗ

I-25, between Santa Fe and Albuquerque

Brigadier General Stephen Watts Kearny led a group of U.S. forces on an invasion into New Mexico in 1846. On August 8 of that year, he raised the U.S. Flag in Santa Fe. Following his conquest of Santa Fe, he marched unopposed into Bernalillo and Albuquerque. As a result of this occupation, New Mexico passed from the control of Mexico into that of the United States.

Keller Hall Series   Ⓟ

Fine Arts Center on the UNM campus
277-4402

Numerous musical concerts throughout the year, including a distinguished faculty and guest artist series. Also, student recitals and concerts.

Keystone Theater   Ⓟ

3211 Central NE
255-6819

KiMo Theater   ⓋⓅ

423 Central NW
848-1370

One of the gems of the historic Route 66 is the KiMo Theater. Built in the 1920s, the KiMo is an art deco interpretation of American Indian motifs. Inside the lobby are murals by Carl von Hassler depicting various Indian Pueblos of the area, and flamboyant decorations that include wrought iron wild turkeys, and buffalo skulls with illuminated eye sockets. Renovated in 1980, the 750-seat theatre now hosts a full schedule of theatrical events. The theatre and adjoining art gallery are open 9 a.m. to 5 p.m. Monday through Friday as well as during scheduled performances. Theater is on both the State and National Registers.

Kirtland Air Force Base Library   Ⓛ

Kirtland AFB, 87117
844-0795

Kiva Auditorium   Ⓟ

Albuquerque Convention Center
842-8565

La Compania de Teatro de Alburquerque   Ⓟ

P.O. Box 884, 87103
242-7929

One of ten major Hispanic theater companies in the nation, La Compania is a community based theater offering four plays per season. The plays are chosen from the modern and classical repertoire of both English and Spanish.

La Zarzuela de Alburquerque   Ⓟ

3301 San Rafael SE, 87106
265-0821

This is a volunteer community organization that performs Zarzuela, the traditional Spanish folk operetta or musical comedy.

Las Posadas de Barelas   Ⓔ

Barelas Community Center
848-1343

Annual event—Christmas Eve walk enacting the night of Jesus' birth. Singing through the streets, ending in the church with a celebration, and then later, refreshments and a celebration at the Barelas Community Center.

Los Griegos Historic District   H

Los Griegos Area
Three miles north of downtown

This old Spanish agricultural community is the only 19th Century village in Albuquerque's North Valley which has retained its architectural continuity and cultural traditions. The buildings are the embodiment of a unique culture that has its base in 18th Century Spanish custom. District is on both the State and National Registers.

Los Poblanos Historic District   H

Rio Grande Valley north of Albuquerque

This district is located in one of the few remaining stretches of uninterrupted farmland and riverside cottonwood bosque in the Rio Grande Valley north of Albuquerque. Its architectural structures date from 1850. The district also includes three 1930s houses designed by famed architect John Gaw Meem. Area is on both the State and National Registers.

Magnifico! Albuquerque's Festival of the Arts   VP

6400 Uptown Blvd. NE
Suite 500W, 87110
883-6240

Held each year in May, this is a city-wide celebration encompassing the visual, literary, performing and culinary arts. More than 150 events are featured throughout the two-plus weeks of the festival. Highlights include the Art of Albuquerque Show, a juried and invitational exhibition of the city's visual artists; The Tastes of Albuquerque, a culinary offering; an outdoor sculpture show viewed from tethered hot air balloons; a Spanish Market; An Intimate Evening With An Artist series, informal discussions with Albuquerque's noted artists; and an Indian Festival with traditional dances and Pueblo cuisines, Indian fashion show, as well as Indian jewelry and pottery. Other events include musical and dance performances, children's performances and workshops, art demonstrations, gallery and museum shows, artist studio tours and wine tastings from New Mexico's vineyards.

Manzano Day School (La Glorieta)   H

1801 Central Avenue

La Glorieta, a focus of Albuquerque life and history for more than a century, is among the most important historical residences in the city. Two wings of the building date to the Civil War period, and two of the city's most influential families—the Hunings and Fergussons — lived in the house. It is a four-sided adobe building with a placita in the center. Today, the Manzano Day School occupies the facility. Building is on both the State and National Registers.

Maxwell Museum of Anthropology   M

UNM campus, 87131
277-4404

Exhibiting collections that are international in scope, the Maxwell Museum's special emphasis is on materials from native cultures of the American Southwest. Objects such as Mimbres and Pueblo pottery, American Indian baskets, jewelry, and Navajo weaving are on display.

Menaul Historical Library of the Southwest   L

301 Menaul Blvd., NE, 87107
345-7727

Monte Vista Fire Station   H

3201 Central Ave NW

The building is of the Spanish Pueblo Revival style of architecture built with WPA funds in 1936. Building is on both the State and National Registers.

Mother's Day Festivities   E

Indian Pueblo Cultural Center
2401 Twelfth St. NW
843-7270

Indian dances are held each year in May to commemorate Mother's Day.

Mother's Day Concert at the Rio Grande Zoo   P

Rio Grande Zoological Park
903 10th Street SW
842-8565

By the New Mexico Symphony Orchestra. Picnic baskets welcome. Zoo admission.

Museum of Southwestern Biology Ⓜ

UNM campus, 87131
277-5340

This museum features the plants, mammals, birds, reptiles, amphibians and fish of the Southwest. In addition to its education programs—affiliated with the University's Biology Department—numerous temporary exhibits are offered. It is open to the public by appointment.

Musica Antigua de Albuquerque Ⓟ

1017 Roma NE, 87106
842-9613

This is an ensemble of five professional musicians, specializing in the performance of medieval, Renaissance and Baroque music using voices and authentic period instruments. The group's early music repertoire includes such instruments as the viola da gamba, recorder, crumhorn, vielle, medieval harp, shawm and harpsicord. Subscription series concerts are offered in both Albuquerque and Santa Fe, with four different programs throughout the season.

NM Folk Music Society Ⓟ

Heights Community Center
823 Buena Vista SE
256-1998

National Atomic Museum ⓂⓁ

Kirtland Air Force Base
P.O. Box 5400, 87115
844-8443

Starting with a copy of a letter written by Albert Einstein to President Franklin Roosevelt encouraging the development of the atomic bomb, this museum traces the history of the top-secret Manhattan Project. A 53-minute film, "The Ten Seconds That Shook the World," is shown three times daily at 10:30 a.m., 2 p.m. and 3:30 p.m. The museum also offers full-scale models of missiles, a B-52 bomber, and the F-105D fighter bomber. A library is also available. Visitors must obtain a pass at the Wyoming Gate entrance to the base.

New Mexico Arts & Crafts Fair/ Summer Festival of the Arts Ⓥ

State Fairgrounds
550 San Mateo, NE
Suite 111, 87109
884-9043

More than 200 New Mexican artists display and sell juried original arts and crafts including: calligraphy, ceramics, jewelry, leatherwork, macrame, drawing, painting, prints, sculpture, stitchery, weaving and woodworking. Open-air festival atmosphere offers entertainment, demonstrations, children's activities, concessions, and special events. Held the last full weekend in June.

New Mexico Ballet Company Ⓟ

P.O. Box 21518, 87154
299-7798

This is a major, resident ballet company with a season running October through April, featuring four performances at UNM's Popejoy Hall. Artistic Director David Chavez choreographs original works in addition to presenting classical repertory.

New Mexico Historical Review Ⓞ

1013 Mesa Vista Hall
University of New Mexico, 87131
277-5839

Founded by Lansing Bloom under the auspices of the Historical Society of New mexico and the Museum of New Mexico, the "New Mexico Historical Review" began publication in Santa Fe in 1926. The review has and continues to provide a forum for high-quality research and writing on the Southwest, it peoples, and their cultures. The review is published through the sponsorship of the History Department in the University of New Mexico.

New Mexico Jazz Workshop Ⓟ

P.O. Box 1925, 87103
255-9798

New Mexico Museum of Natural History ML

1801 Mountain Road NW
P.O. Box 7010, 87194
841-8837

This museum is a high-tech masterpiece that many visitors have likened to Disneyland. The museum contains permanent and changing exhibits on zoology, botany, geology and paleontology. Exhibit environments are arranged in a time-line fashion and feature a walk-through volcano, ice-age cave, live sharks and other sea animals, and the "Evolator," a time machine that transports passengers on a 38 million year ride into New Mexico's past. The facility also offers a large format theater experience. Special events include lectures, summer camps, field trips, workshops and seminars. The museum is state operated, administered by the Office of Cultural Affairs.

New Mexico Repertory Theatre P

P.O. Box 789, 87103
243-4500

New Mexico Repertory Theatre is Albuquerque's resident professional theater company. The mainstage season of six productions runs from October to May and features an eclectic repertoire of classical as well as adventuresome contemporary plays. NMRT consistently presents the world premieres of Tony Award-winning Mark Medoff's new plays. A new, forward-looking program is The Millennium Project: a retrospective of 20th Century American theater during the ten seasons of the 1990s. Special programs include The Humanities and the Stage, the Student Matinee series, and statewide tours. For group rates, contact the Box Office Manager. Performances take place at the historic KiMo Theater in downtown Albuquerque. The Rep also maintains a Santa Fe address at P.O. Box 9279, 87504, telephone 984-2226.

New Mexico State Fair EVP

State Fairgrounds
P.O. Box 8546, 87198
265-1791

Eighth largest in the nation with thoroughbred and quarter-horse racing, PRCA rodeo, entertainment by recording stars, midway, Indian and Spanish villages, livestock shows, arts and crafts. Begins the Friday after Labor Day and runs for 17 days.

New Mexico State Fair Fine Arts Gallery V

State Fair Grounds, Gate 3
P.O. Box 8546, 87198
265-1791

This gallery showcases the permanent collection of fine arts of the New Mexico State Fair. The facility features the annual State Fair Juried Art Exhibit, temporary exhibits throughout the year, and a sales gallery.

New Mexico Symphony Orchestra P

P.O. Box 769, 87103
842-8565

Under the direction Neal Stulberg, this is one of the most prestigious orchestras in the Southwest. Its 40-plus orchestra concerts offer a variety of musical fare—from classical concerts with world renowned guest artists, to lively Pops concerts, to the Symphony in the Sunshine chamber orchestra series (featuring the silent film classic, Metropolis, with live orchestra accompaniment), and performances of The Nutcracker over Thanksgiving weekend. Most take place at the University of New Mexico's Popejoy Hall; others at a restored vaudeville theater and the Rio Grande Zoo bandshell.

New Mexico Women Composers Guild P

9704 Aztec Road NE, 87111
292-0253

The Guild was founded in 1980 to pursue creative expression in music and to extend professional status for women composers through providing opportunities for exposure and performance of their works. The group currently has about 15 members throughout New Mexico. Public performances include a yearly concert in UNM's Keller Hall, as well as several others in communities, retirement centers, schools and hospitals throughout the state.

New Mexico Woodwind Quintet, Inc. P

7450 Prairie Rd. NE, 87109

Nob Hill Business Center H

3500 Central Ave SE

Built just after World War II, the Nob Hill Business Center was Albuquerque's first drive-in shopping facility—located in the old East Heights area along E. Central Avenue. It's U-shaped drive-in plan, all of its original streamlined moderne detailing and many of its original neon signs are intact. District is on the State Register.

Nutcracker Ballet P

Popejoy Hall, UNM campus
842-8565

Annual performance by the New Mexico Symphony Orchestra, Thanksgiving holiday weekend.

Occidental Insurance Company Building H

119 Third Street SW

Located on the corner of Third and Gold, the Occidental Life Building was considered the most artistic building ever erected in Albuquerque. Opened to the public on August 1, 1917, the facility was designed by architect Henry Trost of El Paso. With its prominent arches, columns and bas-relief terra cotta, the style is an adaption of the Doge's Palace in Venice, Italy. Building is on both the State and National Registers.

Old Town Western Gunfights E

Old Town
842-8838

Held Sunday afternoons throughout the year.

Old Town in Albuquerque H

Central Avenue west to Rio Grande Boulevard
243-7255

Old Town is centered in the tree-shaded Plaza, and is surrounded by charming adobe buildings and a church. Albuquerque began in this historic area when the Royal Villa of San Felipe de Alburquerque was established on the banks of the Rio Grande in 1706 (the first "r" was eventually dropped). Indians and other artisans sell their wares on the streets that line the Plaza. San Felipe de Neri Church is at the center of Old Town Plaza. Built in 1793, the church is still the center of the section's religious life.

Opera Southwest P

515 15th St. NW, 87104
265-8150

The 1988/89 season is the 17th season, and will include three performances each of The Magic Flute, conducted by Richard Bolcrey from Colorado, and Madame Butterfly, conducted by Yoshimi Takeda, former conductor of the New Mexico Symphony Orchestra. Two or three operas are produced each winter season. Local and out-of-town talent are utilized.

Palomita Productions P

Old Town Station
Box 7443, 87194
243-1673

One woman and small production theater adaptable to many spaces and places. In town and touring company.

Partners of the Americas/New Mexico A

P.O. Box 7252, 87106
848-1320

Popejoy Hall P

UNM campus
277-3121

A prime entertainment center of Albuquerque is located in the Fine Arts Center on the UNM campus. Built in 1966, Popejoy Hall is a modern theater facility with 2,094 seats. Popejoy stages 170 professional and local performances each year. Popejoy's Performing Arts Series includes dance, concerts, plays, as well as full-scale ballet, opera and symphonic works. For group rates, contact the marketing director.

Pueblo Indian Museum M

Indian Pueblo Cultural Center
2401 12th St. NW, 87102
843-7270

This unique museum and cultural center features exhibits on the history of New Mexico's 19 Indian Pueblos. The permanent exhibit on the lower level depicts the development of the Pueblo culture from prehistoric times to the present. On the upper level, changing exhibits feature murals and other works of contemporary Pueblo artists. The Center also offer a large gift shop, Indian restaurant, and native dancing and craft demonstrations.

Pueblo Revolt Site H

site off I-25, between Santa Fe and Albuquerque

In 1680, the Pueblo Indians staged a dramatic revolt against Spanish rule. Forced to evacuate Santa Fe by Pueblo bands of Tanos, Tewas and Tiwas, Governor Otermin led the retreating Spanish colonists south through the lands of the Keres pueblos, passing through the Pueblo of Santo Domingo in August of that year.

Quintessence-Choral Artists of the Southwest P

7521 Bear Canyon Rd. NE, 87109
821-0309

An Albuquerque-based ensemble of approximately 30 professional singers under the direction of John Peed of Farmington. Concerts are held throughout the year. The ensemble has a versatile repertoire that includes works from all periods.

Rio Grande Zoological Park

903 Tenth Street SW, 87102
843-7413

This zoological park has a collection of 1200 animals from around the world. They represent a cross-section of mammals, birds, reptiles and amphibians. There is also a children's zoo, snack bars and a gift shop. Guided tours are available on request. The zoo also offers educational programs in the schools and a Zooparents Program.

Rodey Theatre P

Fine Arts Center
UNM campus, 87131
277-4402

This is a 450-seat theatre which serves as the main venue for the UNM Department of Theatre and Dance. Four mainstage theatre productions and three dance productions highlight the department's main season as well as student and community productions. The theatre, completed in 1974, has the capability of either thrust or proscenium seating.

San Felipe de Neri Church H

Old Town Plaza
P.O. Box 7007, 87194
243-4628

More than two and a half centuries of history are contained in this church which was built in 1792. Named for Albuquerque's patron saint, it is a Spanish Colonial style church with enormous adobe walls, and an elaborate and handcrafted interior. Essentially, all of New Mexico's post-Spanish past is contained and synthesized in San Felipe de Neri. It is interesting to note that the parish itself was established in 1706. The original church was destroyed by a flood in 1791. Church is on both the State and National Registers.

San Felipe de Neri Fiesta E

Old Town Plaza
P.O. Box 7007, 87194
243-4628

Three days of food and entertainment in honor of Albuquerque's patron saint. Held on the first weekend in June.

Sandia Cave H

I-40 west to Hwy 14 north, left on Hwy 165

The artifacts found in the cave date back to 23,000 BC and are some of the oldest evidence of human beings found in the United States. The site is on both the State and National Registers. Directions: I-40 west to Hwy 14 north; then left on Hwy 165; turn off on the dirt portion of Hwy 165; Sandia Cave is on the right.

Sandia Mountain Cloggers Dance E

296-0453

Held every Thursday—call for information.

Second Story Theater P

behind Albuquerque Little Theater
224 San Pasquale SW

Small theater facility.

Senior Arts A

P.O. Box 4679, 87196
877-4430

Silver Hill Historic District H

University Boulevard

This is the best preserved example of Albuquerque's first suburban subdivision built up on the mesa just after World War I. It features long rows of regularly spaced houses in a variety of styles along with manicured lawns. This was a middle-class neighborhood, populated mostly with newcomers to the city during the 1920s. District is on both the State and National Registers.

Simms Fine Arts Center   🆅🅿

Albuquerque Academy
6400 Wyoming Blvd. NE, 87109
828-3338

This arts center on the campus of the Albuquerque Academy houses the Simms Gallery, with exhibits highlighting professional artists from throughout the state and city in combination with showings of student and faculty art. Exhibits change about every six weeks. The center is also home to about a dozen theatrical performances each year, ranging from full length musicals to historical plays and contemporary dramas and comedies. Musical performances during the year include eight to ten offerings in jazz, chamber music, vocal presentations and full stage bands, often with guest performers working with students.

South Broadway Cultural Center   🅻🅿🆅

1025 Broadway SE, 87102
848-1320

The Center is operated by the City of Albuquerque as a branch library and part of the Cultural Affairs Program. It is a multicultural meeting place where art exhibits, films, classes and performing arts as well as books and magazines can be enjoyed. A gallery features monthly exhibits and several workshops per year, most with a cultural or educational nature. A small performing space, complete with technical lighting and sound system is available for performing artists and groups of both local and national touring fame. The Center also has a film and video rental program available to individuals and organizations. The Center is supported in part by the Friends of the South Broadway Cultural Center, a non-profit organization.

Southwest Arts and Crafts Festival   🆅

Exhibit Hall, State Fairgrounds
262-2448

More than 150 entrants from across the nation compete in this invitational, juried show. Held in mid-November.

Southwest Ballet Company   🅿

670 Juan Tabo NE, 87123
294-1423

The Southwest Ballet is a professional ballet company resident in Albuquerque and serving the state of New Mexico and the Southwest. The company which was founded in 1980 by Edward Androse presents a winter/spring subscription series in Albuquerque and a soon to be summer season in Santa Fe. The company performs lecture-demonstrations in the public and private schools, tours throughout the state and also performs with other organizations such as the NMSO and the Albuquerque Opera Theater. The dance company has a well developed repertoire, which includes three Balanchine works, including the hard to obtain "Concerto Barocco." Other works include the Eugene Loring/Aaron Copland "Billy the Kid," and Vincente Nebrada's "Romeo and Juliet." Southwest Ballet performs for audiences in Albuquerque at the KiMo Theater and Popejoy Hall.

Spanish History Museum   🅼

2 blocks south of UNM
2221 Lead SE, 87108
268-9981

Current exhibits—New Mexico: From Kingdom to Statehood, 1598-1912; Spanish Aid to George Washington during the American Revolution; Spanish Heraldic Coats of Arms; Founding Families of New Mexico. Special programs include frequent lectures on historical topics.

Spruce Park Historic District   🅷

University Ave. area

Located just west of the University of New Mexico, this district contains the greatest concentration and widest variety of 1920s and 1930s residential architectural styles in Albuquerque. In a single block, one can find red-tiled roofs on Mediterranean style homes, Gothic cottages, Spanish Pueblo Revival and streamlined moderne. This area is still a thriving, well-preserved neighborhood. Area is on both the State and National Registers.

Storytellers International   🅰

4703 Club House Lane NW, 87114
897-0713

Summerfest   🅴

Civic Plaza, 3rd and Marquette NW
768-3490

Every Saturday in July, from 5-10 p.m., showcasing the culture and cuisine of Albuquerque's numerous ethnic groups.

Sweet Adelines P

12216 Casa Grande NE, 87112
296-6496

The Enchanted Mesa Chapter of Sweet Adelines, Inc. belongs to Sweet Adelines, an international organization of 24,000 women, who are part of a Women's Barber Shop Chorus. The group rehearses weekly and performs by request for conventions, organizations, churches, women's groups, etc. They offer an annual Fall show in September or October. Women who sing are invited to join the group.

Tapestry Players P

P.O. Box 7443, 87194
243-1663

This is a multi-ethnic theatre company performing original and innovative theatre pieces that examine how culturally diverse people relate. Tapestry Players is associated with Action Arts, a non-profit organization.

Teatro Consejo P

1710 Centro Familiar SW, 87105
873-1604

Telephone Pioneer Museum M

1209 Mountain Road Place NE, 87110
256-2105

This is a communications museum with telephones, switchboards, teletypes, tools, equipment and other artifacts unique to communication.

UNM Theater Arts Department P

Rodey Theater, UNM campus
277-4402

Four mainstage theatre productions and three dance productions highlight the department's main season as well as student presentations.

University Art Museum M

Fine Arts Center
UNM campus, 87131
277-4001

Art museum—19th and 20th Century American and European art, including major collection of photographs and prints; also paintings, sculpture, and other works on paper. Has a changing exhibition program, with both a contemporary and historical focus on the visual arts; also hosts lectures and gallery talks.

Very Special Arts New Mexico A

P.O. Box 7784, 87194
768-5188

This organization, which is an educational affiliate of the John F. Kennedy Center for the Performing Arts, develops accessible arts programs for children and adults throughout the state. These include Very Special Arts Festivals, and a number of special projects such as ENABLED, an annual series of exhibitions of the work of artists with disabilities; and the BUEN VIAJE DANCERS, a troupe of multiply-handicapped dancers who tour throughout the state and region.

Viva Zarzuela! P

4708 Douglas McArthur NE, 87110

Vortex Theatre P

2004 ½ Central Ave. SE
247-8600

An 14 year-old community theater known for producing some of the most innovative theater in Albuquerque. The Vortex presents ten shows each year and is open year-round. Productions range from classical to modern and also world premieres.

Watson Historic District H

Lomas Blvd. & Mountain Rd.

This area is a 1940s subdivision of Pueblo Revival style adobe homes north of Old Town. Famed Albuquerque designer and builder Leon Watson is credited with judicious use of native materials and crafts, as well as wise planning. District is on the State Register of Cultural Properties.

Weekend Indian Dances and Craft Demonstrations E

Indian Pueblo Cultural Center
843-7270

Pueblo dances every Saturday and Sunday 11 a.m. and 2 p.m. from mid-April through mid-October.

Weems Artfest V

State Fairgrounds
2801 Eubank NE, 87112
293-6133

This annual event, held during the first week in December, features about 200 artisans from throughout the Southwest with an emphasis on originality and affordability—holiday shopping at its best.

Wool Warehouse Dinner Theater   P
518 First Street NW
764-WOOL

Albuquerque's only dinner theater is listed in the state and national registers; the building was once a wool warehouse, and was renovated in 1984. Comedies are performed Wednesday-Saturday, as a dinner show. Sunday brunch has a matinee performance. Many award winning plays are performed; actors are drawn from the local community.

Zimmerman Library/ University of New Mexico   L
UNM campus, 87131
277-4241

Alcalde

Los Luceros Hacienda   H
Hwy 68, vicinity of Alcalde

Historic residence and grounds of early New Mexican settler and leader Don Juan de Onate. The property enjoys a place on both the State and National Registers.

Alma   H
Hwy 180, north of Silver City

This small community, once a stop on the "outlaw trail" from Mexico, was used as a refuge by such men as Butch Cassidy and his gang.

Ancho

Ancho Railroad Depot/ My House of Old Things   MH
north of Carrizozo, off Hwy 54
437-6120

This is the original depot building constructed in 1902 when the railroad made its way into Ancho, which is now a ghost town. The depot is now home to a museum, My House of Old Things. The Ancho Depot is on the State Register of Cultural Properties.

Angel Fire

Angel Fire Artsfest   V
377-3765

Display and sale of fine arts and traditional crafts. Juried show with cash awards for best of show in categories. Other activities include foods bazaar, children's activities. Held in mid-September.

Angel Fire Bluegrass Festival   P
377-6353

Held in early August.

Angel Fire Repertory Theater Society   P
377-6724

Light comedy, melodrama, and reviews on weekends during the summer.

DAV Vietnam Veterans National Memorial   M
six miles northwest of Angel Fire
via Hwys 434 and 64
377-6900

This chapel was erected in 1968 by Dr. Victor Westphall in memory of his son and all other U.S. personnel killed in the fighting in Vietnam. It was first dedicated as the Vietnam Veterans Peace and Brotherhood Chapel, and on May 30, 1983, it was rededicated as the DAV Vietnam Veterans National Memorial.

Dance at Angel Fire   P
P.O. Box 891, 87710
377-6049

This is a mid-summer four-week series of dance workshops, seminars and performances showcasing all dance forms.

Eagle Nest Artist Showcase   V
377-2420

This is an annual showcase with juried competition in several arts and crafts categories by regionally recognized artists. On site sales by exhibitors, with a limit of 30 booths. The event runs 10 a.m.-4 p.m. Held last weekend in July.

Memorial Day Activities, Angel Fire   E
DAV Vietnam Veterans National Memorial
377-6900

Activities include bike tour and fitness walks.

Moreno Valley Arts Council   Ⓐ

P.O. Box 355, 87710
377-3765

Music from Angel Fire   Ⓟ

P.O. Box 502, 87710
377-6353

This is a classical and jazz music series featuring internationally famous artists. The series offers performances in Angel Fire, Taos and other Northern New Mexico communities. Performances runs mid-August through early September.

**Northern New Mexico
Cultural Arts Center**   Ⓥ Ⓟ

377-6049

Paul Bunyan Days   Ⓔ

Olympic Park
377-6401

Annual lumberjack competition: log rolling, buck saw, axe throw, tug-o-war, chainsaw skills. Also includes demonstration-equipment, sales booths, picnic, organized children's games, etc. Held in early September.

Winterfest at Angel Fire   Ⓔ

377-6353

Events include balloon rallies, ski racing, softball on skis, torchlight parade and the Bob Harney Memorial shovel races. Held in early February.

Anton Chico   Ⓗ

Hwy 119

Located in the Anton Chico Land Grant, which was established in 1822, and situated along the northern portion of the Pecos River, the village of Anton Chico includes 72 standing and ruined historic buildings. The well-preserved village is a good example of the traditional central plaza community design. Most structures are connected and face the plaza, and so provided protection against Indian attacks. Established in the early 1830s the villages of Anton Chico Abajo and the nearby Colonias de San Jose and La Placita de Abajo are unique examples of early to late 19th Century Hispanic frontier communities that have changed little over the years. Anton Chico is on both the State and National Registers.

Artesia   Ⓗ

Hwy 285, between Roswell and Carlsbad

This town, named for the region's many artesian wells, lies on the route of the Pecos Valley cattle trails once used by cattlemen such as Charles Goodnight, Oliver Loving and John S. Chisum. Artesia, established in 1903, is located in what was once part of Chisum's vast cattle empire.

Artesia Arts Council   Ⓐ

P.O. Box 782, 88210
748-3012

This is a non-profit corporation aimed at aiding, encouraging, advising and correlating activities dedicated to the promotion of cultural arts. Activities sponsored are varied in the visual and performing arts, including the annual "Art in the Park," held the third Saturday in October.

Artesia Museum and Art Center   Ⓜ Ⓗ

505 W. Richardson Avenue, 88210
748-2390

This museum features exhibits of arrowheads, pottery, pioneer medical displays, history of Artesia's oil industry, a mineral collection, early newspaper press, early cooking utensils, and a good pictorial history of Artesia. Local artists provide many exhibits for the art center. Housed in historic S.S. Ward Home, built 1904-05.

Artesia Public Library   Ⓛ

306 W. Richardson, 88210
746-4252

Aztec   Ⓗ

334-9551

Aztec, which lies near an important National Monument, was founded in 1876 when portions of the Jicarilla Apache Reservation were opened for non-Indian settlement. It is now the seat of San Juan County, developed in 1887 as a response to the desire of local residents to be free from the powerful political forces of Rio Arriba County.

Altrurian Public Library   Ⓛ

201 W. Chaco, 87410
334-9456

Aztec Fiesta Days   ▣
334-9551

Parades, booths, carnival, regional tug-o-war competition, barbecue and entertainment on the first weekend in June.

Aztec Founders' Day   ▣
Aztec Museum
334-9829

This Sept. 13th event features music, special exhibits and refreshments in the Aztec Museum. Other activities include a parade, horseshoe tournament and a costume contest.

Aztec Main Street Historic District   ▣
Downtown area
334-9829

A one-half block (one block front) area of commercial buildings, this is a particularly well-preserved segment of typical New Mexican commercial street development, 1900-1915. Interesting properties, a variety of architectural styles on the National Register of Historic Places and the New Mexico State Register of Cultural Properties.

Aztec Museum Association — Aztec Pioneer Museum & Frontier Village   ▣▣
125 N. Main, 87410
334-9551

Museum offers displays on clocks, dolls, quilts, cameras, oil field equipment, farm equipment, china, pioneer rooms, office equipment and many other early pioneer artifacts. Also featured are rocks, minerals and Indian artifacts. The village features a sheriff's office, jail, law office, doctor's office, 1880 log cabin, blacksmith shop.

Aztec Ruins National Monument   ▣▣
1.5 miles north of Aztec
334-6174

Large prehistoric pueblo built by Anasazi people early in the 12th Century. Monument includes restored Great Kiva. Visitor Center contains exhibits of pottery, basketry and other items made and used by the people who lived here.

Festival de los Farolitos   ▣
Aztec Ruins National Monument
334-9551

This event features a luminaria display at Aztec Ruins National Monument prior to Christmas. In addition to the walls of the ruins, many homes and businesses are lighted with thousands of the "little fires."

Bayard   ▣
Hwy 90, east of Silver City

Mogollon Indians settled this area long before the Europeans. During the late 19th Century, this was a stronghold of Apaches led by Victorio and Geronimo. Today, Bayard lies in a great commercial mining region.

Bayard Public Library   ▣
525 Central
P.O. Box U, 88023
537-6244

Fort Bayard   ▣
Hwy 90, east of Silver City

Fort Bayard was one of many posts established on the frontier to protect settlers and miners against Apache attacks. Company B of the Black 125th Infantry served here, as did Lt. John J. Pershing. Created in 1866, the fort became a military hospital in 1900, and today serves as Fort Bayard Medical Center. The post's cemetery, first used in 1866, is still maintained as a National Cemetery.

Fort Bayard National Cemetery   ▣
Hwy 90, east of Silver City

Established in 1866 as the military cemetery for Fort Bayard, many troopers, veterans, and civilians are buried here. It became one of New Mexico's two National Cemeteries in 1973.

Belen   ▣
Spanish colonization began along the Rio Grande south of Albuquerque in the mid-1700s. The Belen land grant was made to encourage this expansion, and colonists from Albuquerque settled here around 1740. Belen is Spanish for Bethlehem.

Belen Harvey House   ▣
104 North 1st Street

Built in 1901, this is a fine example of Mission style architecture erected under the auspices of the Santa Fe Railway in a style which came to symbolize the company's presence in New Mexico and the Southwest. This was easily the most visible and successful public building in Belen which in turn was a major rail center in New Mexico. The building is on both the State and National Registers.

Belen Public Library   ▣
333 Becker Ave., 87002
864-7797

Our Lady of Belen Fiestas E

Our Lady of Belen Church
864-8043

Burning of the devil, parade, games, food booths, carnival. Held in mid-August.

Rio Valley Festival V E

221 E. Main St.
P.O. Box 6, 87002
864-8091

Arts and crafts, food and trade booths in early June.

St. Patrick's Balloon Rally E

Los Lunas
865-1581

Food and trade booths, balloonists in March.

Valencia County Fair E

County Fairgrounds
864-1666

Parade, rodeo, dance, livestock and agricultural displays. Held in late August.

Bernalillo H

The Pueblo Indian province of Tiguex, in the area of Bernalillo, served as winter headquarters for Spanish explorer Coronado in 1540-42 during his explorations of the southwest. Bernalillo was founded after the Spanish reconquest of New Mexico by Diego de Vargas in 1692. De Vargas died here in 1704.

Coronado State Monument M H

one mile west of Bernalillo
Hwy 44 off I-25
867-5351

In the year 1540 Spanish explorer Coronado came to this region near the Rio Grande seeking fabled cities of gold. Instead, he found 200-year old adobe villages inhabited by the native people of the area. The Tiwa pueblo of Kuaua, the site of Coronado's encampment and the present-day State Monument, dates from A.D. 1300. Like many Rio Grande Valley Pueblos, it was deserted by the early 1600s. The site of Kuaua was declared a State Monument in 1935. Pueblo ruins, including a kiva, have been partially reconstructed, and an interpretive trail winds through the site. The Southwest-style visitor center contains exhibits on the prehistory and history of the valley.

Martha Liebert Library L

901 Camino del Pueblo
P.O. Box 638, 87004
867-3311

New Mexico Wine Festival at Bernalillo E

867-3311

Held in early September.

Salazar, Abenicio Historic District H

With buildings dating from 1873, this area accurately presents the rural lifestyle found in earlier years. It also includes many structures of historical and architectural significance. The district is located near Our Lady of Sorrows Church which was built in 1719. The largest and most dominant structure in the district is Our Lady of Sorrows High School, constructed in 1922. The district is on both the State and National Registers.

Bloomfield

Salmon Ruins H

2 miles west of Bloomfield
632-2013

This historic pueblo is one of the largest—600-750 rooms—of the many colonies founded by the Chacoans of the 11th Century. It is considered to be a pre-Columbian stone community. A newly opened Heritage Park at Salmon Ruins features dwelling sites of eight cultures. The site is on the National Register of Historic Places.

San Juan Archaeological Research Center M H L

Salmon Ruins
#975 Hwy 64
Farmington, 87401
632-2013

Research library; permanent and temporary exhibits; guided tours; films; lectures. On-going archeological excavation site; artifacts from Salmon Ruins; photographs; Salmon Brothers manuscripts.

Bosque Farms

Bosque Farms Community Library L

1455 West Bosque Loop, 87068
869-2227

Canjilon   H

Hwy 84, north of Espanola

The town is where the descendants of the Spanish conquistador De Vargas are said to have settled in 1774 and still live.

Capitan   H

The area around Capitan saw a great deal of action during the infamous Lincoln County War, 1876-79. Charles B. and John A. Eddy platted the townsite in 1900, after building a spur of the El Paso & Northwestern Railroad from Carrizozo. The railway was built to open the Salado coal fields, which were abandoned in 1901. In 1950, a little bear cub, his feet badly burned, was rescued from a forest fire near here. The cub was nursed back to health and flown to Washington D.C. to become the living symbol of "Smokey Bear" in the U.S. Forest Service's fire prevention program.

Capitan Depot   H

This depot was built circa 1900 when the El Paso & Southwestern Railway first entered the newly-named village of Capitan (originally called Gray). The depot was opened primarily for shipping coal from the nearby coal fields. There was just one deadend line into Capitan, no way to turn around, so the train had to back in or back out. The depot is on the State Register of Cultural Properties.

Smokey Bear Historical State Park   H

P.O. Box 591, 88316
354-2748

Visitor Center with historical exhibits and grave of Smokey Bear.

Smokey Bear Museum   M

P.O. Box 246, 88316
354-2612

Log museum houses the story and memorabilia of Smokey the Bear.

Smokey Bear Stampede   E

Lincoln County Fairgrounds
354-2224

This tribute to Smokey the Bear features a parade, fun run, barbecue, Western dance and rodeo. Held in early July.

Capulin

Capulin National Monument   M L

3.5 miles from Capulin
State Route 325, 88414
278-2201

Natural history collection; library; natural history park; 1500-foot volcanic cinder cone and related geological phenomena; visitor's center; self-guided tours; interpretive programs.

Goodnight-Loving Trail   H

near Capulin

Charles Goodnight cut this route through Trinchera Pass in 1868. His goal—to bypass the Raton Pass with an easier, shorter, toll-free cattle trail.

Carlsbad   H

Carlsbad was first named Eddy after Charles B. Eddy, pioneer cattleman. However, the little town was later renamed for the famous European resort. In the 19th Century, this part of the Pecos River became the center of a major cattle empire.

Alfalfafest   V E

Carlsbad Civic Center
887-6516

This is Carlsbad's salute to the agricultural community. Events include mud volleyball, horseshoe pitching, giant tug-of-war, lawn tractor obstacle course races, country music competition, a Friday night barn dance, "Best of the Southwest" Burrito Cookoff, food and entertainment, as well as arts and crafts. This is a three-day, weekend event held the second weekend of October at the Carlsbad Civic Center.

American West Celebration   V E

887-6516

Arts shows, music and an arts & crafts fair held in early April.

Bat Flight Breakfast   E

Cave entrance to Carlsbad Caverns National Park
785-2232

Pre-dawn spectacle as thousands of Mexican Free Tail Bats re-enter Carlsbad Caverns National Park. The Bat Flight Breakfast is 5-7 a.m. Held annually in mid-August.

Carlsbad Art-A-Fair   Ⓥ

Lake Carlsbad Recreation Area
885-4591

Art show on the banks of the Pecos River. Works of Southwestern artists and craftsmen are exhibited. Sales, demonstrations and entertainment. Held the first weekend in June at the Lake Carlsbad Recreation Area.

Carlsbad Arts & Humanities Council   Ⓐ

1311 Riverside Dr., 88220

Carlsbad Caverns National Park   Ⓜ

3225 National Parks Highway, 88220
785-2232

This is a major National Park, representing New Mexico's largest single visitor attraction. In addition to the fossil reef cave system, programs include bat flight talks, natural history interpretive programs and museum exhibits.

Carlsbad City Spirit   Ⓐ

P.O. Box 610, 88221
885-4591

Carlsbad Civic Center   Ⓟ

887-6516

This facility is the scene of numerous plays, concerts, revivals, registered Charlois cattle sales, and beauty pageants, as well as conventions.

Carlsbad Museum and Art Center   Ⓜ

101 S. Halagueno, 88220
887-0276

This museum offers a variety of collections and exhibits, such as natural history artifacts—mammoth and camel bones; Western relics—saddle guns, chuck boxes; and fine art displays—McAdoo collection of paintings, Jack Drake bird carvings, other temporary exhibits.

Carlsbad Public Library   Ⓛ

101 S. Halagueno, 88220
885-6776

Carlsbad Western Days and A.J.R.A. Rodeo   Ⓔ

887-6516

Old West comes back to life. Everybody dresses in western clothes and decorates their businesses in western motif. Street dances, barbecue, parade, and rodeo every night. Held at Eddy County Sheriff's Posse arena in mid-July.

Guadalupe Mountains National Park   ⓂⓁ

HC 60, Box 400
Salt Flat, Texas, 79847-9400
915-828-3251

Natural history park; Capitan reef formation formed during the Permian period; library and museum collection.

Mescal Roast   Ⓔ

Living Desert State Park
887-5516

Traditional counselors from the Mescalero Apache Tribe will guide park staff and volunteers in the process of the pit baking New Mexico Agaves. The "Mescal" plants will be harvested from the Guadalupe Mountains, prepared at the Park, and shared with visitors who might like to sample a taste of this native southwestern food source. The Apache Dance of the Mountain Gods is scheduled to be performed on nights during the event. Festivities will conclude with demonstrations at the roasting pit and distribution of food samples. Held annually in mid-May.

New Mexico Art Education Association   Ⓐ

1405 Bryan Circle, 88220

September 16th Celebration   Ⓔ

San Jose Plaza
887-1381

This annual celebration takes place on or near (weekend) Sept. 16. Events include a parade, booths, Mexican rodeo and dances.

Southeastern New Mexico Historical Society   Ⓞ

887-6516

Works to preserve the historic sites in this area.

Carrizozo   Ⓗ

Carrizozo was born in 1899, a new town on the El Paso and Northeastern Railroad. Nearby is the ghost town of White Oaks, once a booming mining camp. The likes of Billy the Kid, Sheriff Pat Garrett, Governor Lew Wallace, and Albert Bacon Fall all figure prominently in the history of the area.

Salinas National Monument   ⊞

Hwy 54, north of Carrizozo

This unique regional complex of prehistoric Indian pueblos and associated 17th century Franciscan mission ruins constitutes a "capsule in time" in which the first century of Native American-European contact in what is now the United States is preserved. The complex includes Abo, Quarai and Gran Quivira Ruins. The central visitor center is in Mountainair's historic Shaffer Hotel.

Cebolleta   ⊞

I-40 west of Laguna Pueblo

A Navajo mission was established at Cebolleta in the mid-18th Century, and by the early 1800s Albuquerque area cattlemen had built a fortified town. During the resulting warfare, the Spanish settlers used nearby Los Portales Cave as a refuge. The cave was later converted to a shrine with an altar carved from the living rock.

Cerrillos   ⊞

Hwy 14, south of Santa Fe

The mineral-rich area around Cerrillos produced turquoise which was traded as far away as the valley of Mexico. An early settlement of Los Cerrillos harbored Spanish refugees from the 1680 Pueblo Revolt. The present community was not founded until the lead strike of 1879. Cerrillos now is a charming, tree-shaded ghost of its former self, where movies and television series are sometimes filmed. It has a small but lively population. The town now features antique stores, a petting zoo, and an interesting church. It is on the State Register of Cultural Properties.

Cerrillos Fiesta   ▣

Hwy 14, south of Santa Fe
983-7317

Held each year on a weekend in June.

Gold and Turquoise Mines   ⊞

south of Santa Fe

This is the site of the first gold placer mining west of the Mississippi. It began with the discovery of the precious metal in the rugged Ortiz Mountains south of here in 1828, 21 years before the California gold rush. Since then, the district has produced more than 99,000 ounces of placer gold. Nearby are the prominent Cerrillos Hills, site of ancient turquoise mines worked by the Indians centuries before the arrival of the Spanish. The Cerrillos ("little hills") are regarded as the oldest mining district in the United States.

Chaco

Chaco Culture National Historical Park   Ⓜ⊞Ⓛ

54 miles west of Bloomfield
Star Route 4
P.O. Box 6500, 87413
786-5384

Major Anasazi cultural center during the 9th and 10th Centuries. Site includes 13 major "Great House" Indian ruins, museum, library and campground. Self-guided tours. Called the "Stonehenge" of the West. Chaco is a World Heritage site, as one of 12 sites in the United States on this United Nations list under the World Heritage Convention.

Chama   ⊞

Hwy 84, near the Colorado border

In its beginnings Chama was just a small crossroads town. But after 1880, the humble town became an important site on the Denver & Rio Grande Western Railroad. The Cumbres & Toltec Scenic Railroad, north of Chama, is an important visitor attraction and the remnant of the San Juan Extension, a narrow-gauge line which once served the mining areas of southwestern Colorado.

Burns-Kelly Store   ⊞

Terrace Avenue & 5th Street

This mercantile building has been a Chama landmark for more than a century. It was built in 1886 by T.D. Burns and later owned by Pat Kelly. The structure is on the State Register.

Chama Days ▣
756-2306

Parade, rodeo and dances. Held in mid-August.

Chama Jail House ▣
This is an original log jailhouse built in 1879. The old jail is on the State Register of Cultural Properties.

Chama Winter Carnival ▣
756-2306

Held each year during February.

Cumbres and Toltec Scenic Railroad ▣
P.O. Box 789, 87520
756-2151

In 1880 the Denver & Rio Grande Railroad built the San Juan Extension to serve the mines of south-western Colorado. The Cumbres & Toltec Scenic Railroad still operates 64 miles of the narrow gauge system between Chama, New Mexico and Antonito, Colorado. It is America's longest and highest steam railroad. Jointly owned by the two states, it is a "living museum" of railway history. The railway is listed in both the State's and National Historic Registers.

Eleanor Daggett Memorial Library ▣
4th and Maple
P.O. Box 786, 87520
756-2388

Foster Hotel (Chama Hotel) ▣
This hotel was built in 1881 to help satisfy a sudden need in Chama to support the Denver & Rio Grande Railway's entry into the area. The Chama Hotel was one of the first community buildings in the town, and is the only community building survivor of several disastrous fires that have wiped out the town. The building is on both the State and National Registers.

Chimayo ▣
New Mexico 76, east of Espanola

Although Chimayo is considered to be a uniquely Spanish settlement, Indians occupied the Chimayo valley centuries before the arrival of the Spaniards. The village of Chimayo, founded in the early 18th century, shortly after the reconquest of New Mexico, has been an important center of Northern New Mexico Spanish tradition for more than 250 years. The village retains the historical pattern of settlement around a defensible plaza.

Plaza del Cerro ▣
Chimayo's old plaza shows the plan of a fortified colonial plaza better than any other location in New Mexico. The plaza—with its surrounding low adobe structures—is thought to date to the 1740s. The original "torreon," or defensive watchtower, still stands near the plaza and remains in good condition. The plaza is on both the State and National Registers.

Santuario de Chimayo ▣
Since its construction in 1817, this church has been the destination of countless pilgrims and visitors who are drawn by testimonies of the curative power of the earth from the anteroom beside the altar. As many as 30,000 people participate in the annual Good Friday Pilgrimage. El Santuario is on both the State and National Registers.

Chloride ▣
42 miles northwest of T or C via I-25 and Hwy 52

Ghost town.

Cimarron ▣
376-2614

Located on the Mountain Branch of the Santa Fe Trail, this truly wild West town was settled around 1844. In 1857 it became the home of Lucien B. Maxwell, and headquarters for the famous Maxwell Land Grant of almost two million acres. An agency for Utes and Jicarilla Apaches was located here from 1862 to 1876. Located just south of Cimarron is the Philmont Scout Ranch.

Black Jack's Hideout ▣
near Cimarron

In Turkey Creek Canyon near here, the outlaw gang of Thomas "Black Jack" Ketchum had one of its hideouts. After a train robbery in July 1899, a posse surprised the gang at the hideout. The outlaws scattered after a bloody battle, and the Ketchum gang was broken up.

Cimarron Days and Oldtimers Reunion ▣▣
P.O. Box 604, 87714
376-2614

This celebration features an arts and crafts fair, entertainment and special events. Held Labor Day weekend.

Cimarron Historic District   H

State Road 21
376-2614

The majority of the buildings that were constructed in the mid-19th century in the town of Cimarron still exist. Built of adobe or stone, the buildings have only undergone minor modifications. The village pattern remains essentially as it was first established during the 1850s. Most were used for commercial purposes. Buildings include the County Courthouse, the Old Stone Jail, the St. James Hotel, and Maxwell's 1864 Stone Flour Mill. Cimarron itself was the local agency for the Ute Indians, and was the cowboy capital of northern New Mexico. The district is on both the State and National Registers.

Cimarron Historical Records   O

376-2614

This group is putting together walking tours, special visiting home tours, and is working with the Santa Fe Trail historical group to write about and mark the historical points in Cimarron.

Clifton House Site   H

Hwy 64, between Cimarron and Raton

Three-quarters of a mile west of here at the Canadian River crossing was the popular overnight stage stop on the Old Santa Fe Trail. Clifton House was built in 1867 by rancher Tom Stockton, and materials were brought here overland from Dodge City. For years it served as headquarters for cattle roundups. After abandonment of the Santa Fe Trail in 1879, it fell into disuse and burned.

Colfax County War   H

Hwy 58, west of Cimarron

For twenty years after the 1869 sale of the Maxwell Land Grant, homesteaders, ranchers, and miners fought the new owners for control of this enormous region. The resulting murders and general breakdown of law and order led to the removal from office, in 1878, of Territorial Governor Samuel B. Axtell.

Ernest Thompson Seton Memorial Library   L

south of Cimarron on Hwy 21
Philmont Scout Ranch, 87714
376-2281

Works and personal collections of Ernest Thompson Seton, author, artist, and naturalist; co-founder of the Boy Scouts of America. 6,000 volume library of natural history and history of the Southwest. Philmont Museum, Kit Carson Museum and Villa Philmonte are also located on the ranch.

Kit Carson Museum   M

south of Cimarron
Philmont Scout Ranch, 87714
376-2281

This history museum focuses on the early settlement of the area, fur trading and the Santa Fe Trail. Also featured is a replica of Kit Carson's adobe home on the spot of his original home (at Rayado). The Philmont Museum, Seton Memorial Library and Villa Philmonte are also located on the ranch. Open June-August.

Old Mill Museum   M H

one block off Hwy 21, 87714
376-2662

Housed in Aztec Mill, built in 1864 to furnish grain to Indians. Regional exhibits of artifacts, memorabilia and early photos. This facility is open May-September.

Philmont Museum   M

south of Cimarron
Philmont Scout Ranch, 87714
376-2281

Art and history museum of Philmont and the area. Also houses the Seton Memorial Library, which contains works and personal collections of Ernest Thompson Seton, author, artist and naturalist; co-founder of the Boy Scouts of America. 6,000 volume library of natural history and history of the Southwest. Villa Philmonte, the restored home of Philmont benefactor, Waite Phillips, is open June through August, as is the Kit Carson Museum.

Philmont Scout Ranch   H

four miles south of Cimarron on Hwy 21
376-2281

Oklahoma oilman Waite Phillips gave this 127,000 acre property to the Boy Scouts of America in 1938 and 1941. The first National Boy Scout Camp ever established, Philmont now hosts young men from all over the world. Kit Carson, Lucien B. Maxwell, and Dick Wooten were important in the history of the area.

Santa Fe Trail H

Hwy 64, between Cimarron and Raton

William Becknell, the first Santa Fe Trail trader, entered Santa Fe in 1821 after Mexico became independent from Spain and opened its frontier to foreign traders. The Mountain Branch over Raton Pass divided here. One fork turned west to Cimarron, then south and joined a more direct route at Rayado. The difficulty of bringing caravans over rocky and mountainous Raton Pass kept most wagon traffic on the Cimarron Cutoff of the Santa Fe Trail until the 1840s. Afterwards, the Mountain Branch, which here approaches Raton Pass, became more popular with traders, immigrants, gold-seekers, and government supply trains.

St. James Hotel H

Hwy 21
Route 1, Box 2, 87714
376-2664

Built in 1875 by Henri Lambert, chef for President Abraham Lincoln and General U.S. Grant, the hotel has had such famous visitors as Zane Grey, Annie Oakley, Buffalo Bill Cody and Billy the Kid. Ten of the rooms have been refurbished in original Victorian splendor. The building is on the State Register of Cultural Properties.

Clayton H

374-9253

Trade caravans and homesteaders traveling the Cimarron Cutoff of the Santa Fe Trail passed near here. Clayton was founded in 1887 and named for the son of cattleman and ex-Senator Stephen W. Dorsey, one of its developers. It became a major livestock shipping center for herds from the Pecos Valley and the Texas Panhandle.

Albert W. Thompson Memorial Library L

17 Chestnut, 88415
374-9423

Public library, including the D.D. and Helen Monroe Special Collection on the Southwest, and specifically on northeastern New Mexico.

Black Jack Ketchum H

Sheriff's office, next to the courthouse

The north wall of the sheriff's office is where Black Jack Ketchum, leader of a notorious band of train robbers, was hanged in 1901 after he was wounded in Folsom and surrendered in 1899.

Clayton Arts Council A

P.O. Box 517, 88415
374-830-536

An umbrella group for other cultural organizations, the Clayton Arts Council hosts the annual Clayton Arts Festival in October.

Clayton Arts Festival V

American Legion Hall
374-9253, 9636

The festival is held during the first weekend in October, and has grown larger and larger over the years. Features a fine arts department with purchase awards, as well as numerous arts and crafts booths—pottery, weaving, lapidary, jewelry. Spanish-American food is also available.

Clayton Independence Day Celebration V E

374-9250

The community's largest annual celebration with art/crafts show, dances, rodeo, barbecue, street parade and fireworks.

Clayton Players, Inc. P

374-8035

Hosts monthly meetings for those interested in theater and music; presents stage plays, periodic dinner theater, and entertainment at various community functions.

Clayton School Museum M

Clayton High School
323 S. 5th Street, 88415
374-2596

This small museum is devoted to local WPA projects from the Great Depression. It is open by appointment.

Dinosaur Days V E

downtown
374-9253

Open air bazaar with many activities, including the Rotary Club's Old Western Dance, with costumes and old-fashioned dance prizes. Tour of dinosaur tracks at Clayton Lake State Park; dinosaur dinner at Clayton Airpark. Usually held last weekend in April.

Dinosaur Tracks at
Clayton Lake State Park   H

15 miles northwest of Clayton via Hwy 370
374-8808

Eklund Hotel   H

15 Main Street

An excellent example of turn-of-the-century architecture using native building materials. The building has been placed on the State Register of Cultural Properties.

Herzstein Memorial Museum   MH

Old Methodist Church
South 2nd & Walnut, 88415
374-9977, 374-9508

Many items and displays pertaining to the early history of the area are exhibited. Included are dinosaur footprints, Indian relics, Santa Fe Trail artifacts, ranching and farming tools, household items, and more.

Old Western Dance   E

American Legion Hall
374-9253

This event features food and entertainment, a children's dance contest as well as prices for the best costumes. Held during the last week in April.

Rabbit Ear Mountains   H

near Clayton

These two striking mounds were the first features to become visible to Santa Fe Trail traffic crossing into New Mexico from Oklahoma, and so became important landmarks for caravans. From here, traffic on this major 19th-century commercial route still had about 200 miles to travel before reaching Santa Fe.

Rabbit Ear Roundup Rodeo   E

374-9253

Parade, barbecue, team roping, novice barrel races, dances, fireworks. Held in early July.

Santa Fe Trail Art Association   A

374-9045

This organization hosts seminars and workshops for area artists and sponsors locals arts shows. It is the prime mover behind the local arts council and the annual arts festival.

Santa Fe Trail in Union County   H

The Dry Cimarron Cutoff of the Santa Fe Trail crosses Union County. The major portion of the route passes north of the Rabbit Ear Mountains. At many points, trail ruts remain clearly visible. One of the important crossings is McNee's Crossing where, in 1831, the first Fourth of July celebration occurred in what is now New Mexico.

Union County Cultural Arts Show   V

374-9693

Held annually during spring, this one day arts and crafts show is sponsored by the Union County Homemakers Council.

Union County Fair   E

Union County Fairgrounds in Clayton
374-9361

This county fair is everything rural America is supposed to be, with exhibits, livestock sale and judging, horse shows, etc. Held in mid-August.

Union County Historical Society   MO

374-9508, 374-8035

Maintains Herzstein Memorial Museum as well as programs on the area's history.

Wagon Ruts at Clayton   H

One mile east of Clayton on Hwy 56

Some local historians contend these are truly Santa Fe Trail ruts, pointing out that until 1828 traffic passed south of the Rabbit Ears. Others say the wagon ruts were created as the Clayton to Kenton, Oklahoma Freight Route.

Cleveland

Cleveland Roller Mill Museum   MH

P.O. Box 287, 87715
387-2645

This three-story adobe roller mill played a major role in the agricultural economy of Northern New Mexico for a period of 80 years. The flour mill was built and equipped in 1877, closed for production in 1957, the last mill to operate in the Mora Valley. In its time, it was one of the two largest mills in the western United States. The mill is fully operable and a permanent exhibit within the structure is being installed by the Historic Mora Valley Foundation. The mill is also the site for the annual Cleveland Roller Millfest, held in early August. It enjoys a place on both the State and National Registers.

Cleveland Roller Millfest V E

P.O. Box 287, 87715
387-2645

This event, held each year in early August at the Cleveland Roller Mill, features arts & crafts booths, historical talks and demonstrations. Sponsored by the Historic Mora Valley Foundation.

Historic Mora Valley Foundation M H O

P.O. Box 287, 87715
387-2645

This organization actively works to preserve, interpret and promote Mora Valley history, specifically the Cleveland Roller Mill Museum—the facility, its exhibits and public programming.

Cloudcroft

Christmas in Cloudcroft E

682-2733

Crowning of Snow Queen, skating party, ice sculpture contest, parade, lighting tours, Santa. Usually held weekend before Christmas.

Cloud-Climbing Railroad H

In order to provide timber for the construction of his El Paso & Northeastern Railroad north of Alamogordo, Charles B. Eddy in 1898 built a spur into the Sacramento Mountains. The line operated as far as Cloudcroft until 1947. The Cloudcroft Trestle is all that remains.

Cloudcroft Community Library L

P.O. Box 125, 88317
682-2733

Cloudcroft Fiesta E

P.O. Box 125, 88317
682-2733

Costumes, music, food on Labor Day weekend.

Cloudcroft Historical Museum M

682-2733

The focus for this small museum is on local Sacramento Mountains pioneer history.

Cloudcroft Lodge H

Set in a scenic location in the Sacramento Mountains, the Cloudcroft Lodge is one of the oldest and most prominent of New Mexico's resort hotels. It was constructed in 1899 by the El Paso & Southwestern Railway as "The Pavilion—The Breathing Spot of the Southwest." In 1909 the original lodge was destroyed by fire, and another was built and opened in 1911, welcoming Pancho Villa as one of its first customers. Today the Lodge is as popular as it was in the early 1900s. The building enjoys a place on the State Register of Cultural Properties.

Cloudcroft Oktoberfest V E

682-2733

This event features Cloudcroft's largest arts and crafts fair, a juried show with more than 60 artists representing as many as 10 states. Artistic fields include pottery, oil, watercolor, leather, wood, photography, textiles, jewelry, etching and sculpture. Other Oktoberfest events include the "Tenderfoot Express" hayride, music, food booths, horseshoe tournament, square dances and guided nature tours. Held in Zenith Park on the first full weekend in October.

July Jamboree V E

Zenith Park
682-2733

Crafts, games, food, hayrides, horseshoe tournament. Held on the weekend closest to the 4th of July.

Mayfair V E

682-2733

Arts and crafts, food booths, and many other activities, including hayrides, horseshoe tournaments. A rodeo is held in Wimsatt Arena. Held annually on Memorial Day weekend.

Railroad Days E

682-2733

This event features miniature railroad displays, lectures, tours and hikes along the old railroad bed through Cloudcroft. Held in mid-September.

Sacramento Mountains Historical Society Museum   Ⓜ Ⓗ Ⓞ

P.O. Box 435, 88317
682-2958

Pioneer Village and Museum. History museum; historical collections of Sacramento Mountain pioneers and early railroad; housed in early pioneer-restored log cabin. Oral history program. Special events include Old-Timers Reunion, honoring special old-timers.

Singing in the Clouds   Ⓟ

High School Gym
682-2733

Groups from three states sing together in the rarified air of Cloudcroft. Held in mid-August.

Clovis   Ⓗ

During the 1700s and early 1800s, Comanche Indian buffalo hunters used trails that passed near here. In 1907 the Santa Fe Railroad established Clovis to serve as the eastern terminal of the Belen Cutoff, which would connect with the transcontinental line at Belen. Formerly the domain of ranchers, the railroad opened the area to farmers.

Blackwater Draw   Ⓗ

Hwy 70, south of Clovis

This archaeological area features famous camp sites for Folsom Man.

Cannon Air Force Base/Clovis Library   Ⓛ

Cannon AFB, 4855 88103-5725
784-2786

Christmas Country Fair   Ⓔ

The Old Gibson Building
West 21st Street
762-0541/1340

Held in early December.

Christmas Market   Ⓥ

Sacred Heart Gym
900 Merriwether
769-1607

Held the first Friday and Saturday in December, booths are rented mostly to local craftpersons.

Clovis Arts and Crafts Show   Ⓥ

North Plains Mall
763-3435

Annual arts and crafts fair held in early November and sponsored by the Clovis Women's Club.

Clovis Central Fire Station   Ⓗ

320 Mitchell Street

Constructed in the "motor age" style of architecture, this was the first modern style building in Clovis. It was built during the Great Depression and reflected the optimism that Clovisites had in their fast-growing community. The building is on both the State and National Registers.

Clovis City Hall and Fire Station, 1908   Ⓗ

308 Pile Street

Clovis was indeed a fast-growing town in the wee hours of the 20th Century. The city hall and fire station—built in 1908—was the first governmental building for the town which began in 1906. The building is on both the State and National Registers.

Clovis Music Festival   Ⓟ

762-0017

Gospel concerts, guided tours, historical presentations, sock hop, 50's rock concerts, parade, barbecue, buy-sell-trade show, block party, 50's car display, etc. In honor of Buddy Holly and Norman Petty. A week of tours of the 7th street Norman Petty studio where Buddy Holly recorded his biggest hits. Features performances by renowned recording artists. Held in mid-August.

Clovis Post Office   Ⓗ

Fourth & Mitchell Streets

This building is significant as the leading federal project in Clovis during the early Depression. Built in 1931, the post office was a blend of Spanish Colonial Revival and Neo-classical styles. The structure is now the Clovis-Carver Public Library. The building is on both the State and National Registers.

Clovis-Carver Public Library   Ⓛ

4th and Mitchell St., 88101
769-1973

Curry County Fair   Ⓔ

763-6505

Large agricultural exhibits, tractor pulls and livestock shows. Held in late August.

Hart Youth Ranch/Pigpin Ranch H
769-0425

Site of the Pigpin Ranch started in 1884. Original ranch house built in 1887, with timbers from Pete Maxwell's home in Fort Sumner in which Billy the Kid was killed by Pat Garrett. Visitors welcome.

High Plains Historical Federation O
763-6361

Editors of a book "High Plains History," profiling more than 100 years of east-central New Mexico history.

Hotel Clovis H
210 Main Street

Built in 1931, at the height of the Depression, the building reflects the rapid growth and optimism of the city of Clovis at that time. It was known as "The Skyscraper of the Plains." The hotel ranks among the two or three most important Art Deco buildings erected in New Mexico. The old hotel is on both the State and National Registers.

Old Lyceum Theatre H
411 N. Main
763-6085

Historic vaudeville theater built in 1919-1920. It has been restored, and is operated by a nonprofit, community supported group, "Old Lyceum Theatre, Inc.". Owned by the city of Clovis and used as a performing arts theater.

Pioneer Days E
763-3435

Recalls the days when homesteaders and ranchers were sinking roots into the fertile soil of Curry County. A parade, rodeo, annual balloon festival, pageants and exhibits honor the pioneers. Held in early June.

Cochiti Pueblo H
30 miles southwest of Santa Fe;
I-25 to Hwy 22
465-2244

Cochiti was established in the 1200s by Keresan speaking Indians who came here from villages located at the present site of Bandelier National Monument. European contact was slight until Juan de Onate's colonization in 1598. In the 1960s, the mission church of San Buenaventura de Cochiti was restored to its 19th Century appearance. Cochiti is on both the State and National Registers. The people of this pueblo have displayed excellence in the crafting of drums and pottery figures, including prized storyteller figures.

Cochiti Pueblo Feast Day E
Morning Mass, procession and afternoon Corn and Rain Dances on July 14.

Dances to Commemorate the Christmas Season E
Traditional dances during Christmas week.

Easter Celebration E
Mass, procession and traditional dances.

New Year's Day Celebration E
Festivities include Mass, procession, and traditional dances on January 1.

Pueblo de Cochiti Community Library L
P.O. Box 70, 87041
465-2244

Santa Cruz Feast Day E
Corn Dance on May 3.

Three Kings Day E
New tribal officers honored on January 6: Transfer of the Canes of Authority.

Colfax H
12 miles northeast of Cimarron via Hwy 64

Ghost town.

Colonias

Colonias de San Jose Historic District ⊞

State Road 329

Located in the Anton Chico Land Grant, which was established in 1822, and situated along the northern portion of the Pecos River, this village includes 23 standing and ruined historic buildings. Located 30 miles downstream from Anton Chico, Colonias de San Jose is an exception to the typical plaza-oriented design, and instead is laid out in a grid. Established in the mid-1860s, the village is one of three on the Anton Chico Land Grant that are unique examples of early to late 19th century Hispanic frontier communities, having been changed little over the years. This district is on both the State and National Registers.

La Placita de Abajo Historic District ⊞

vicinity of Colonias

Located in the Anton Chico Land Grant, which was established in 1822, and situated along the northern portion of the Pecos River, the village includes one standing historic building and 17 sites of ruined historic buildings. Along with Anton Chico Abajo, La Placita de Abajo was built in the traditional central plaza community design. Most structures were connected and faced the plaza, providing protection against Indian attacks. Established in the last quarter of the 19th century, the village is located one mile downstream from Colonias de San Jose. This district is on both the State and National Registers.

Columbus

Camp Furlong ⊞

This is the site of the shattering raid by Pancho Villa and his men on March 9, 1916. It served as a base of operations for the United States retaliation raids into Mexico. It was also the first military air field in the country, home to the 1st Aero Squadron. A few historic buildings remain. Camp Furlong is on both the State and National Registers.

Columbus Historical Museum ⋈⊞

P.O. Box 562, 88029
531-2733

This museum features artifacts of local history in the old Southern Pacific Railroad Depot.

Columbus Village Library ▮

P.O. Box 350, 88029
531-2795

Pancho Villa State Park ⊞

35 miles south of Deming via Hwy 11
531-2711

This is New Mexico's southernmost park, on the Mexican border. The park commemorates the 1916 raid by Pancho Villa on this small border town. Facilities include a campground and cactus garden.

Pancho Villa's Raid ⊞

on the Mexico/New Mexico border near Columbus

In March of 1916, Francisco "Pancho" Villa, a major figure in the Mexican Revolution, crossed the international border with a large force, attacking and looting Columbus, New Mexico. Eighteen U.S. soldiers and civilians, and approximately 100 Villistas were killed. Gen. John J. "Black Jack" Pershing led an expeditionary force into Mexico in pursuit of Villa.

Conchas

Conchas Dam ⊞

vicinity of Conchas

Conchas Dam is the oldest and one of the largest water projects undertaken by the U.S. Army Corps of Engineers in New Mexico. Begun under the Emergency Relief Act of 1935, the dam became operational in the summer of 1939. To date it is a $16 million project. The reservoir protects the Canadian River Valley below the dam from floods. It has controlled several minor floods occurring since the reservoir became operational. The dam provides water storage space for irrigation and conservation. It also is used as a recreational facility, with more than a quarter of a million people making use of the facility each year. The dam is on the State Register of Cultural Properties.

Cordova ⊞

15 miles east of Espanola via Hwy 76

This small community high in the Sangre de Cristo Mountains boasts a healthy tradition of woodcarving. Highly skilled artisans transform the native aspen and cedar into "santos" (carved saints) as well as decorative items.

Corrales   H

Spanish colonization of this region, once the location of many Tiwa Indian pueblos, began in the 17th century. Corrales is named for the extensive corrals built here by Juan Gonzalez, founder of Alameda. In the 18th Century this rich farming area was subject to Comanche attacks, and was raided by Navajos as late as 1851. San Isidro, patron saint of farmers, is the traditional guardian of the valley. The present church is the third to bear his name. Spanish, and later, U.S. garrisons used the valley as a base of defense to protect the river settlements of Albuquerque and Bernalillo, and nearby pueblos and towns from Navajo raids.

Corrales Arts Council   A

P.O. Box 2723, 87048
898-7600

Corrales Community Library   L

La Entrada Road, 87048
897-0733

Corrales Historical Society   O

P.O. Box 1051, 87048
898-7221

This organization promotes a greater appreciation and understanding of the history and tradition of Corrales. The Society's activities include the preservation and maintenance of the Old San Ysidro Church as well as other community landmarks, research into Corrales heritage, and supporting educational and cultural projects.

Father's Day Concert   P

La Entrada Park
897-0502

Picnic and band concerts in June on Father's Day.

Harvest Festival   E

898-9775

Held in mid-October.

International Folk Dancers   A

Star Route, Box 150-I, 87048
898-3206

This is a recreational group which teaches and dances folk movements of various nationalities. Group meets on certain evenings throughout the year at the First Unitarian Church at 3701 Carlisle NE in Albuquerque. (Not a performing group.)

Old San Ysidro Church   H

Old Church Road
P.O. Box 1051, 87048
898-7221

Listed on both the state and national registers of historic places, the church is a classic example of New Mexican Hispanic religious village architecture from the 18th and 19th centuries and one of the few surviving examples in the Albuquerque area. Built in the shape of a cross, the massive adobe masonry walls are three feet thick and hand-plastered with adobe on both the exterior and interior. Hand-hewn corbels support the viga ceiling and hand-adzed lintels are above the doors and windows. The original building had a flat earthen roof with a belfry in the facade over the main entrance. The historic building was purchased from the Archdiocese of Santa Fe in 1974, and today is owned by the Village of Corrales and managed by the Corrales Historical Society.

San Ysidro Fiesta   E

P.O. Box 460, 87048
898-1779

Music, dance, food and entertainment in mid-May.

Crownpoint

Crownpoint Community Library   L

P.O. Box 731, 87313
786-5359

Cuba

Cuba Community Library   L

Route 126
P.O. Box 370, 87013
289-3777

Deming   H

In 1870, Governor Juan Bautista de Anza passed near here while searching for a trade route between Santa Fe and the mines of Sonora, Mexico. Deming was founded in 1881 when the Santa Fe and Southern Pacific Railroads were connected, giving New Mexico its first railway access to both the Atlantic and the Pacific.

Arts in the Park E

Courthouse Park
546-9559

This program of music, dance and free art materials for children runs Sunday afternoons during July.

Butterfield Trail Days V E

Courthouse Park
546-2674

Parade, art show, trading post, flea market, booths, horseshoe tournaments, costume contest. Held in early July.

Cooke's Wagon Road H

I-10, between Deming and Lordsburg

In 1846, while leading the Mormon Battalion to California during the Mexican War, Lt. Col. Philip St. George Cooke blazed the first wagon road from New Mexico to the West Coast. The potential of the route for railroad construction was one of the reasons for the Gadsden Purchase in 1854. Cooke entered Arizona through the Guadalupe Pass.

Deming Armory H

Silver & Hemlock St.

The Deming Armory was built in 1915-16 in response to the Mexican Revolution, fearing invasion by guerrilla raids across the nearby border. This construction was also a response to the growing war in Europe. The structure is now home to the Deming-Luna Mimbres Museum. It is on both the State and National Registers.

Deming Arts Council A

100 S. Gold
P.O. Box 1845, 88031
546-3663

This is a non-profit arts organization governed and operated primarily by volunteer artists and art supporters. The organization sponsors exhibitions, performances and literary events by local and national talent and offers workshops for Luna County residents and visitors.

Deming Arts and Crafts Fair V

546-2674

Local and out-of-town participants display work. Refreshment booths, entertainment in addition to sizeable arts and crafts show. Held annually in early June.

Deming Center for the Arts P

100 S. Gold
P.O. Box 1845, 88031
546-3663

The center is the site for performances by chamber music groups, small dance companies, and readings of poetry and fiction by local writers through the year.

Deming Coaling Tower H

The tower was built in 1926 by the Southern Pacific Railroad and serves as an important remnant of New Mexico's railroading heritage. These were the peak years of coal-fired steam locomotives. The tower is on the State Register.

Deming Public Library L

301 South Tin, 88030
546-9202

Deming Theatre Company P

100 S. Gold
P.O. Box 1845, 88031
546-3663

Deming/Luna Mimbres Museum M H

301 South Silver Avenue
P.O. Box 1617, 88030
546-2382

Large historical museum with more than 22,000 square feet of toys and dolls, 1850 through present; Mimbres pottery and other Indian artifacts; minerals and rocks; artifacts of early settlers; Fort Cummings and Camp Cody military memorabilia; Hispanic display; various collections of antique glass, china and silver; quilts and antique lace; old vehicles; street scene.

Fiddlers' Contest P

Hospitality House, off Rockhound Road
546-2332

Held annually in mid-May.

Fort Cummings H

I-10, between Las Cruces and Deming

Established in 1862, this fort operated until the 1880s, protecting the Butterfield stage route between San Diego, CA and San Antonio, TX. The military post was used as a base of operations for the Apache Wars against Cochise, Victorio and Geronimo.

Great American Duck Races   E

546-2674

Duck races, entertainment, flea market, booths, hot-air balloon races, dances, tortilla toss—one of New Mexico's most unique and well-attended events. Held annually in late August.

Klobase Festival   E

Courthouse Park
546-2674

Feast of Bohemian smoked sausage, barbecued beef, salads, beans, cakes and pies. Sponsored by the Czech community. Held each year in mid-October.

Luna County Community Concerts   P

546-7511

Luna County Historical Society   O

301 South Silver, 88031
546-2382

Open Studio Tour   E

throughout town
546-9625

Tour of studios and galleries near downtown Deming, with artists present. Held during October.

Rockhound Roundup   E

Southwestern New Mexico State Fairgrounds
546-2674

This event draws more than 500 participants from 41 states. Rock trips, snack bar, auctions and judging seminars. Free camping. Held in mid-March.

Silver Avenue Historic District   H

Silver Ave.

This district features buildings—mostly red brick —constructed between 1886-1917. Silver Avenue was the most important thoroughfare for this railroad oriented town, where the Southern Pacific and Atchison, Topeka & Santa Fe Railways met. The district is on the State Register of Cultural Properties.

Southwestern New Mexico State Fair   E

546-2674

Livestock competition, rodeo, parade, carnival. Held in late September, early October.

Dexter

Dexter Public Library   L

115 East 2nd
P.O. Box 249, 88230
734-5482

New Mexico Dairy Day   E

Lake Van
734-5474

This unique event, held each year in early June, features milk carton boat races, a triathlon, and an ice cream eating contest.

Dixon

Open Studio Tours   V

Hwy 68 between Espanola and Taos

The working studios of many of Dixon's artists and craftsmen are open during an annual autumn event sponsored by the Dixon Arts Association. Held in early November.

Eagle Nest

Angel Fire Community Library   L

P.O. Box 223, 87118
377-6180

Eagle Nest Public Library   L

P.O. Box 168, 87718
377-2486

High Country Arts Festival   V

377-2420

Wheeler Peak

near Eagle Nest

Across Moreno Valley stands Wheeler Peak, 13,161 feet, highest peak in New Mexico. Rocks of Wheeler Peak and the Taos Range are highly resistant granites and gneisses of Precambrian age. Moreno Valley is underlain by soft sandstones and shales which are covered by stream and glacial deposits. Placer gold was mined at Elizabethtown north of here during the 1860s.

El Morro

El Morro National Monument   ⊞

43 miles southwest of Grants
783-4226

Inscription Rock where early pioneers beginning with Spanish Conquistadors have left their signatures. Hundreds of visitors, dating from two years before the Pilgrims landed at Plymouth (1605), inscribed their names, the date, or even verses of poetry at the base of the mesa, making El Morro a commanding register of 300 years of European and American exploration and expansion in the southwestern United States. In addition to the historic records are several examples of pre-Columbian petroglyphs. On top of the mesa are two Indian pueblo ruins numbering approximately 250 rooms each, and dating from 1200-1300. Eighteen rooms of one, Atsinna, have been excavated and stabilized. The monument is on both the State and National Registers.

El Rito   ⊞

north of Espanola

This village was settled in the 1830s by residents from the Abiquiu area. The Territorial Legislature of 1909 established the Spanish-American Normal School here to train teachers for northern New Mexico schools. After several changes in name and purpose, the institution is now the Northern New Mexico Community College.

El Rito Public Library   Ⓛ

P.O. Box 237, 87530
581-4728

Elephant Butte

Elephant Butte Dam   ⊞

East of Truth or Consequences, Hwy 51

For more than a half century, the Elephant Butte Dam has provided a dependable water supply for irrigation along the Rio Grande. At the time of its completion in 1916, the Elephant Butte Dam created the largest irrigation reservoir in the world. Located just east of T or C, the dam represents 600,000 yards of concrete, easily making it one of the most massive engineering projects of the early 1900s. It is on both the State and National Registers.

Elida

Ruth McCowen Library   Ⓛ

Elida City Hall, 88116
274-6316

Elizabethtown   ⊞

5 miles north of Eagle Nest via Hwy 38

Ghost town.

Embudo   ⊞

Hwy 68, midway between Espanola and Taos

Located in a narrow canyon of the Rio Grande, Embudo features many historic Spanish structures dating from 1880. Embudo means "funnel" and is a name given to the village by Spanish settlers in the 17th Century. The town was at one time a service stop on the Denver & Rio Grande Railway: the station is now a restaurant. In 1888 the first stream gaging station was established here on the Rio Grande by the U.S. Geological Survey. This district is on both the State and National Registers.

Embudo Stream-Gaging Station   ⊞

Hwy 68, between Espanola and Taos

Established in 1888; site of the first United States Geological Survey training center for hydrographers. Those trained here made some of the earliest hydrological studies in the nation, leading to stream-gaging of many streams throughout the country, and thus providing important evaluations of the nation's surface water resources. It is on the State Register of Cultural Properties.

Musica y Danza Folklorica del Norte   ⒶⓅ

P.O. Box 61, 87531
579-4300

Research and performance of New Mexico folkloric music and dance: Penitente alabado; corrido; ballet folklorico; New Mexico composers.

Espanola

Bond House Museum Ⓜ Ⓗ

710 Bond Street, 87532
753-2377

The Bond House Museum and Cultural Center is located in a home constructed in 1887 by Frank Bond, an important pioneer in the mercantile and ranching history of Northern New Mexico. Exhibits illustrate the unique tri-cultural history of the Espanola valley. Changing shows of local craftspersons and artists expose the public to the deeply rooted artistic heritage of this area.

Espanola Public Library Ⓛ

Richard Lucero Center
314-A Onate St. NW, 87532
753-3860

Espanola Valley Arts Festival Ⓥ

Northern New Mexico Community College
753-2155

Held yearly in October.

Espanola Valley Ⓗ

When it was described by Gaspar Castano de Sosa in 1591, the Espanola Valley contained about ten Tewa-speaking pueblos, several of which are still occupied today. Juan de Onate established New Mexico's first colony here in 1598. Long on the northern frontier of Spanish settlement, the Valley has continuously reflected its Indian and Spanish heritage.

Northern New Mexico Community College Library Ⓛ

P.O. Box 250, 87532
753-7141

Onate Fiesta Ⓔ

753-2377

This annual celebration features a parade, food and entertainment. Held during the second week in July.

Rio Arriba County Fair and Horse Show Ⓔ

Fairgrounds
753-2831

Held each year in mid-August.

San Gabriel—on the Camino Real Ⓗ

Hwy 68, between Espanola and Taos

Governor Juan de Onate set up his headquarters in San Juan Pueblo in 1598, but by 1601 he had moved the Spanish capital across the Rio Grande to Yuque-Yunque Pueblo. Named San Gabriel, it served as the seat of government until 1610, when Onate's successor founded a new capital at Santa Fe.

Santa Cruz Dam Ⓗ

14 miles east of Espanola

Built between 1926 and 1929, the Santa Cruz Dam is the principal feature in the irrigation network created by the Santa Cruz Irrigation District during the 1920s. This district was organized to provide irrigation water for about 5000 acres of land along the Rio Santa Cruz. The dam is on the State Register of Cultural Properties.

Santa Cruz de la Canada Ⓗ

Hwy 76, near Espanola

In 1695, Governor Diego de Vargas funded his first town, Santa Cruz de la Canada, designed to protect the Spanish frontier north of Santa Fe. The church, which still stands, was constructed in the 1730s. In 1837, residents revolted against Mexican authorities, resulting in the death of Governor Albino Perez.

Estancia Ⓗ

Incorporated in 1909 and county seat of Torrance County since 1905, Estancia is located in an enclosed valley or basin. It was ranching country until the early 20th century, when the coming of the railroad opened it to homesteaders and farmers. Pinto beans were the best known local crop until the 1950s.

Estancia Public Library Ⓛ

10th and Highland
P.O. Box 167, 87016-1629
384-2708

Torrance County Fair Ⓔ

Hwy 41, south of Moriarty, east of Albuquerque
384-2372

Held in mid-August.

Eunice

Eunice Public Library   L

10th and N Streets
P.O. Box 1629, 88231-1629
394-2336

Farmington   H

326-7602

Until 1876 this area comprised part of the Jicarilla Apache Reservation. Anglo settlement quickly began at the confluence of the San Juan, Animas, and La Plata Rivers. Farmington became a ranching and farming area and, later, an important producer of oil, gas, coal and uranium.

Anasazi: The Ancient Ones Pageant   P

Lion's Wilderness Park
326-7602

Musical outdoor drama about the area's Navajo and Mormon pioneer heritage. Pageant runs Wednesdays through Saturdays from late June through early September.

Bolack Game Reserve and Wildlife Museum   M

south of Farmington
325-4275

Game reserve and museum owned and operated by former New Mexico Governor Tom Bolack. Tours by appointment.

Farmington Civic Center   P

Downtown
327-7701

Civic Center includes facilities for theatrical and musical productions as well as art exhibits.

Farmington Freedom Days   E

326-7602

This 4th of July weekend celebration features an auction, food fair, street dance, ice cream social, parade, concert, Western-style contests and fireworks.

Farmington Museum   M

302 N. Orchard, 87401
327-7701

This museum offers a wide range of experiences including pioneer and Indian trading post artifacts, San Juan Basin natural history exhibits, New Mexico's first children's experience center, and an historic Farmington frontier town.

Farmington Public Library   L

100 W. Broadway, 87401
327-7701

Library collections and scheduled arts and crafts exhibitions.

Farmington Trade Days/ SummerFun Showcase   V E

Farmington Civic Center
326-7602

Retail trade show for Four Corners merchants includes food, entertainment, fashion shows, arts and crafts. Held on a weekend in late May, early June.

Gathering of the Arts   V P

P.O. Box 2777, 87499
325-1264

Annual mid-June celebration showcasing visual and performing artists and arts groups of northwestern New Mexico. Event is sponsored by the Northwest New Mexico Arts Council.

Holiday Arts and Crafts Fair   V

Garden Room of the Inn
632-2013

This is a benefit arts and crafts fair for the San Juan Archaeological Research Center and Library at Salmon Ruins. Held annually the last weekend in November and the first weekend in December.

Native American Days   V E

Animas Valley Mall
326-5465

This celebration features authentic Native American dancing as well as an arts and crafts fair. Held in September.

Northwest New Mexico Arts Council A

P.O. Box 2777, 87499
325-1264

This is a facilitating agency providing information and technical assistance to regional visual and performing artists and sponsoring a summer showcase of these artists and their work.

Riverfest Arts & Crafts Fair V

326-7602

Held each Memorial Day weekend.

San Juan College Apple Blossom Festival E

San Juan College
326-7602

This San Juan College sponsored celebration includes an Indian Powwow, dance, parade, barbecue and 10-K run. Held in April or early May.

San Juan College Library L

4601 College Blvd., 87401
326-3311

San Juan County Fair E

San Juan County Fairgrounds, McGee Park
326-7602

The largest county fair in New Mexico, this week-long event features a parade, rodeo, fiddlers' contest and exhibits. Held in late August.

San Juan Stage Co., Inc. P

P.O. Box 3226, 87401
632-3668

This community theater group presents six different productions in a season running late August through mid-June. The non-profit organization is composed entirely of volunteers.

San Juan Symphony Orchestra P

4000 Sierra Vista Dr.
P.O. Box 5381, 87401
325-3865

Presents four concerts October through April at the San Juan Community College Theatre at the Farmington Civic Center.

Totah Festival V E

Farmington Civic Center
326-7602

This community event features a juried Native American fine arts and crafts show, an Indian rug auction and a Frontier Days Celebration. Held in early September.

Folsom

Folsom Hotel H

southwest corner of Grand Ave. and Wall Street

Nineteenth century rock building, built in the early 1890s. It was used as the first mercantile store in Folsom. The building is on both the State and National Registers.

Folsom July Jam E

278-2102

Sponsored by the Emergency Medical Technicians from Folsom, Capulin and Des Moines, this event features entertainment by area bands as well as special activities for children and a variety of booths.

Folsom Museum M H

Main Street, 88419
278-2155

This small museum is dedicated to exhibiting the pioneer spirit of this section of New Mexico. Additional exhibits feature the Folsom Man Discovery. The museum is housed in the Doherty Mercantile Building, built circa 1896. The building is on the State Register of Cultural Properties.

Fort Stanton H

Hwy 214
354-2211

The Fort, established in 1855 as a frontier outpost, was an active military installation until 1896. At the turn of the century, it became a U.S. Merchant Marine hospital for tuberculosis patients. The Merchant Marine Cemetery remains as a memorial to those seamen who died from TB. Today, Fort Stanton is a residential facility for the developmentally disabled adults of New Mexico. Fort Stanton is on both the State and National Historic Registers.

Camp Sierra Blanca Library   Ⓛ

P.O. Box 68, 88323
354-2250

Fort Sumner   Ⓗ

Named for the fort built in 1862 to guard the Bosque Redondo Indian Reservation, the town of Fort Sumner grew out of settlements clustered around the fort. It moved to its present site with the construction of the Belen Cutoff of the Santa Fe Railroad around 1907.

Old Fort Days Celebration   Ⓔ

355-7705

Held each year in early June.

Billy the Kid Museum   Ⓜ

1601 East Sumner Ave.
Rt. 1, Box 36, 88119
355-2380

This small history museum offers cowboy memorabilia exhibits from the late 1800s. Featured is Billy the Kid who was shot and killed by Sheriff Pat Garrett in Fort Sumner.

Billy the Kid-
Pat Garrett Historical Days   Ⓔ

Old Fort Sumner
P.O. Box 1881, Taiban, 88134
355-9935

Sponsored by New Mexico Billy the Kid/Pat Garrett Historical Society and held annually in mid-July.

Billy the Kid Outlaw Gang, Inc.
Historical Society   Ⓞ

P.O. Box 1881
Taiban, 88134
355-2555

This organization is dedicated to the protection, preservation and promotion of Billy the Kid/Pat Garrett history in New Mexico.

De Baca County Fair   Ⓔ

County Fairgrounds
355-2381

Held in late August.

Fort Sumner Public Library   Ⓛ

North 7th Street
Drawer D, 88119
355-2832

Fort Sumner State Monument   ⓂⒽ

Billy the Kid Road
Rt. 1, Box 356, 88119
355-2573

This is the site of the Bosque Redondo Reservation where the U.S. government interred nearly 10,000 Navajos and Apaches from 1863-1868. It is also the place where Pat Garrett killed Billy the Kid in 1881, after the military had abandoned the fort. The Kid is buried in the nearby cemetery. A visitor center features history exhibits, and a weekend living history program includes demonstrations of the arms and equipage of frontier soldiers. Fort Sumner is a State Monument, a part of the Museum of New Mexico system. The site is on both the State and National Registers.

Goodnight-Loving Trail   Ⓗ

This famous old cattle trail, running 2000 miles from Texas to Wyoming, was blazed in 1866 by Charles Goodnight and Oliver Loving. In New Mexico the trail followed the Pecos River north to Fort Sumner, where the government needed beef to feed the Navajos at the Bosque Redondo Reservation.

Llano Estacado   Ⓗ

Hwy 60, between Fort Sumner and Clovis

Nomadic Indians and countless buffalo herds dominated this vast plain when the Vasquez de Coronado expedition explored it in 1541. Later it was the focus of Comanchero activity, and in the 19th century it became a center for cattle ranching. The name Llano Estacado, or stockaded plains, refers to the fortress-like appearance of its escarpments.

Readers' Suggestions

This edition of *Cultural Treasures—New Mexico Cultural Resources Directory* is an important step toward the development of a comprehensive inventory of our state's cultural riches.

Your comments and suggestions about this directory are both vital and welcome. Specifically, we seek your help in building upon this foundation with the necessary additions, corrections and deletions.

Please take the time to tell us about those cultural, artistic and historic sites, events and organizations which we have overlooked. Just fill out the form below—or ones like it—and mail it (them) to us. Your assistance is appreciated.

Office of Cultural Affairs
P.O. Box 2087
Santa Fe, New Mexico 87504-2087
(505) 827-8233, or 827-6364

- -

Cultural Treasures—New Mexico Cultural Resources Directory

Name of Resource _____

Contact/Person or Group _____

Address/Location _____

Town _____ Zip Code _____ Telephone _____

Dates of Events _____

Open Hours _____ Admission/Fees _____

Please give a brief description:

_____

_____

_____

_____

_____

_____

_____

_____

Old Fort Sumner Museum   Ⓜ

7 miles southeast of Fort Sumner
Billy the Kid Road
355-2942, 2555

This museum has the distinction of being the authentic grave site of Billy the Kid as well as the original museum of De Baca County. Established in the 1930s, this museum exhibits official historical documents, including handwritten letters by Billy the Kid and Pat Garrett and coroner's reports. Also featured are oil paintings by Howard Suttle depicting the story of Billy the Kid, cowboy memorabilia circa 1860, and antiques and artifacts from the era. The grave site of Billy the Kid and his colleagues Tom O'Folliard and Charlie Bowdre, encased in iron, is located behind the museum.

Fort Wingate   Ⓗ

south of Gallup on Hwy 400

Fort Wingate was a military fort used to contain the Navajo until 1925, when it was turned over to the Bureau of Indian Affairs (BIA). This was a site of treaty meetings, and was established as a fort in 1860 when Anglo warfare with the Navajo intensified. The site was named Fort Wingate when it was moved to another location during the Civil War. It was re-established at Bear Spring in 1868, and was the main peace-keeping force in the area for the next several decades. The BIA used the Fort as a vocational boarding school, one of eight in the area, until 1968. Because of strong support found within the Navajo Tribe for the BIA boarding schools, Fort Wingate became the showcase boarding school for the Navajo during the 1930s, when the existence of the boarding schools was threatened by a new governmental policy of day schools. The district is on both the State and National Registers.

Four Corners

Four Corners National Monument

Corner of New Mexico, Arizona, Utah and Colorado

The only place in the United States where you can stand in four states at once. State seals of Colorado, Utah, Arizona and New Mexico.

Fruitland

Fruitland Trading Post   Ⓗ

Hwy 550

Established in 1886 by the Fruitland Trading Company, this trading post provided necessities for Navajo Indians living on the reservation. It also served as an outlet for locally produced rugs, jewelry and baskets.

Galisteo   Ⓗ

Hwy 41, 30 minutes southeast of Santa Fe

Galisteo was the location of seven Tanoan pueblos dating to 1540. Remnants of their civilizations can be found in the form of numerous petroglyphs in the area. Spanish families settled the town in the late 1700s. Today, the village features a beautiful restored Spanish hacienda, an old church and other adobe structures. Galisteo is on the State Register of Cultural Properties.

Galisteo Pueblo   Ⓗ

junction Hwys 14 and 41, south of Santa Fe

Spanish explorers found several Tano-speaking pueblos in the Galisteo Basin in 1540. They were among the chief leaders of the Pueblo Revolt of 1680. 150 Tano families were eventually resettled in Galisteo Pueblo in 1706. Droughts, famine, Comanche raids and disease led to its abandonment by 1788, with most of the survivors moving to Santo Domingo Pueblo. The pueblo is on the State Register of Cultural Properties.

Gallup   Ⓗ

863-3841

Long a major trading center for the Navajo and Zuni Indians living in communities north and south of the town. Gallup emerged in 1881 from a railroad construction camp. It is named for David Gallup, who in 1880 was paymaster for the Atlantic & Pacific (now the Santa Fe) Railroad.

Atchison, Topeka & Santa Fe Rwy. Depot in Gallup H
201 East 66 Avenue

The depot is a reminder of the railroad's importance in the settlement of this area. Built in 1923, it blends Mission Style with Spanish Pueblo Revival into a unique structure. It was meant to be a tribute to the Native Americans, as it blends ancient and modern architecture. Designed by Mary Colter, chief designer for the Fred Harvey Co., who was responsible for designing important railway structures throughout the Southwest. The depot is on the State Register of Cultural Properties.

El Morro Theater H
205-209 West Coal Avenue

Built in 1928, the theater is the only example of Spanish Colonial architecture in Gallup. The facility is a mainstay of Gallup's entertainment life, historically and today. It enjoys a place on the State Register of Cultural Properties.

El Rancho Hotel H
1000 East 66 Avenue

Built in 1936, the hotel is an excellent example of the Rustic Style, typified by a "picturesque western" look. The hotel was the center of the movie industry in Gallup because it was built and owned by "Griff" Griffith. There is a photo "museum" on the balcony of the lobby. The building is on the State Register.

Gallup Area Arts Council A
105 W. Hill, 87301
722-4209

Gallup Arts and Crafts Fair V
863-4563

This is a multicultural festival with arts/crafts demonstrations, food and entertainment. Held annually in early July.

Gallup Book Fair V
Red Rock State Park
722-3839

Held late October.

Gallup Gallery Concert Series P
108 West Coal, 87306
863-4563

Gallup Historical Society O
P.O. Box 502, 87301
863-5663

The Society owns several historic properties including the Southwestern Mine Office, Gamerco Mine Hoist House, Gamerco Smoke Stack, AT&SF caboose and boxcar, as well as mine memorabilia from a wide variety of area coal mines. Periodic tours of the properties and surrounding area are given in the community. Group tours can be arranged. The Society also conducts the Downtown Walking Tour during New Mexico Heritage Preservation Week, held each year in May. The yearly program includes on-site visits to regional interest areas, speakers, audio and visual presentations, and an annual picnic.

Gallup Summer Indian Dance Program V P
Red Rock State Park
4 miles east of Gallup
P.O. Box 1
Church Rock, 87311
863-3896

Every day of summer, Memorial Day through Labor Day, one of seven dance groups from three tribes (Navajo, Zuni and Acoma) are spotlighted in an evening display of traditional Indian dances. Highlighted by discussions on tribal and regional histories and traditions, arts and crafts and native foods.

Grand Hotel (Ricca's Mercantile) H
306 West Coal Avenue

Built circa 1925, it was originally a dry goods store and bus depot downstairs, and a hotel upstairs. The building is an example of very plainly built Decorative Brick Commercial Style. The exterior of Ricca's Mercantile is so completely unaltered that it stands as a good reminder of how this area looked in the 1920s and 1930s. The building is on the State Register.

Harvey Hotel in Gallup H
408 West Coal Avenue

Built in 1928 (not a Fred Harvey Hotel) in Decorative Brick Commercial Style using locally available building materials (sandstone). The hotel competed with the nearby Grand Hotel for business. It enjoys a place on the State Register of Cultural Properties.

Inter-Tribal Indian Ceremonial Ⓥ Ⓟ

Red Rock State Park
4 miles east of Gallup
P.O. Box 1
Church Rock, 87311
863-3896

Held each year in early August, this is New Mexico's oldest all-Indian exhibition, featuring three major activities: 1) More than $10 million worth of handmade Indian arts and crafts in three separate sales areas, representing more than 1000 Indian artists competing for purse in juried show. 2) Ceremonial Indian dances performed by 15 tribes. Dances are traditional and costuming is authentic. Each tribe dances once each day—total dance program is about two hours daily. 3) All-Indian professional rodeos daily. In addition, there is a powwow featuring hundreds of Indian dancers; a Miss Indian Ceremonial contest; Indian performing arts; and Indian foods from all over New Mexico. The event is sponsored by the Inter-Tribal Indian Ceremonial Association, a state agency charged with promoting and preserving American Indian Culture.

Inter-Tribal Indian Ceremonial Association Ⓐ Ⓥ Ⓟ

P.O. Box 1
Church Rock, 87311
863-3896

This group sponsors the annual Inter-Tribal Indian Ceremonial, the Gallup Summer Indian Dance Program, and the Indian Country Guide Service. Indian Artist referral service is also available. The Association is an agency of the state, charged with preserving and promoting New Mexico's Indian heritage.

McKinley County Court House Ⓗ

201 W. Hill Avenue

Designed by the architectural firm of Trost and Trost of El Paso, Texas, and built in 1938, the building is in the "picturesque" Spanish Pueblo Revival Style. Details include a bell tower with battered walls and vigas; wood beams and corbels; and Indian motif reliefs. The court room has murals painted by Lloyd Moylan which depict the history of McKinley County.

North American Championship Fiddler Contest Ⓟ

City Recreation Center
700 Montoya Blvd.
722-5477

Held in October.

Octavia Fellin Public Library Ⓛ

115 W. Hill Ave., 87301
863-3692

Palace Hotel Ⓗ

236 West 66 Avenue

Built in 1912, the hotel is a hipped-roof, two-story building in modified Richardsonian Romanesque Style. Built on a prominent corner, it is a grand structure of locally quarried sandstone. It is on the State Register of Cultural Properties.

Plateau Sciences Society Ⓞ

P.O. Box 2433, 87301
722-6694

Red Mesa Art Center Ⓥ

105 W. Hill Avenue, 87301
722-4209

The Center, a subsidiary of the volunteer run, non-profit Gallup Area Arts Council, serves the cultural needs and interests of the entire McKinley County area. The Center's monthly exhibits of member artists' work provide a base for contact with other artists, for combining of resources, and a source for arts related information. The Center participates in grant and fundraising projects that involve the diversities of area artists.

Red Rock Museum Ⓜ

Red Rock State Park
P.O. Box 328, 87311
722-6196

This museum, located in a State Park, focuses on Indian arts and crafts, specifically from the Zuni, Hopi and Navajo tribes. The museum is open daily during the summer, weekdays during spring, fall and winter.

Rex Hotel Ⓗ

300 West 66 Avenue

Built in 1910 of locally quarried sandstone in the Stone Commercial Style, it is associated with the second economic coal boom in Gallup. It has a "rustic" appearance and enjoys a place on the State Register of Cultural Properties.

Square Dance Fest-i-gal   E

Red Rock State Park
722-6023

Held in late April

Vasquez de Coronado's Route   H

West of Gallup, I-40

In July 1540, Francisco Vasquez de Coronado, leader of an army of Spaniards and Indians, entered New Mexico from Arizona to the south. He was searching for the mythical Seven Cities of Cibola, which proved to be the six Zuni villages then located near the present pueblo. Vasquez de Coronado was nearly killed during his attack on Hawikuh.

Glenwood

Glenwood Community Center Library   L

P.O. Box 144, 88039

Glorieta

Glorieta Battlefield   H

I-25, east of Santa Fe

The decisive battle of the Civil War in New Mexico was fought at the summit of Glorieta Pass on March 28, 1862. Union troops won the battle when a party of Colorado volunteers burned the Confederate supply wagons, thus destroying Southern hopes for taking over New Mexico. The battlefield is on both the State and National Registers.

Glorieta Pass   H

I-25, east of Santa Fe

This pass served as a gateway through the mountains for Francisco Vasquez de Coronado in 1541 enroute to explore the plains, for Spanish friars attempting to convert Plains Indian tribes in the 1600s, for Apaches and Comanches entering the Pueblo area from the east, and for the Santa Fe Trail from the 1820s to 1880s.

Pigeon Ranch   H

12 miles southeast of Santa Fe

This ranch is a part of the Glorieta pass Civil War Battlefield, and is the only roofed structure still standing from the time of the battle. It was also a stagecoach stop on the Santa Fe Trail. The ranch is on the State Register of Cultural Properties.

Golden   H

Hwy 14, between Santa Fe and Albuquerque

Ruins of old mining buildings and equipment surround an old trading store. The Mission Church of San Francisco, dated to 1839, has a cemetery with names of miners who worked the area and of Hispanic residents of the old town. Long a trading post, Golden is still a popular stop on Hwy 14. A garden of colored glass can be visited across the arroyo.

Grants   H

287-4802

Located just north of the great lava bed known as the Malpais, Grants began as a coaling station for the Santa Fe Railroad. Around 1880 it was known as Grant's Camp, after the Canadian bridge contractor Angus A. Grant. In 1950, the area's vast uranium deposits were discovered.

Bi-County Fair   E

Prewitt Fairgrounds, 19 miles west of Grants
287-9266

Held in early September.

Cibola Arts Council   A

P.O. Box 1540, 87020
285-5082

Cinco de Mayo Fiesta   E

285-4677

Held in early May.

Grants Arts and Crafts Fair   V

St. Teresa Community Center
287-7927

Held in early December.

Mother Whiteside Memorial Library   L

525 West High
P.O. Box 96, 87020
287-7927

New Mexico Museum of Mining ⓜ

100 Iron Street, 87020
287-4802

Visitors walk through the history of the area where Paddy Martinez, an Indian laborer and prospector, discovered, in 1950, a mother lode of uranium. Museum also includes a guided tour into a simulated uranium mine. Indian artifacts, geology exhibits.

Octoberfest ⓔ

City Hall Park
287-4802

Event features music, entertainment, food and street dances. Held the first weekend in October.

Pueblo Revolt Site ⓗ

I-40 east of Grants

The western pueblos of Acoma and Zuni took part in the revolt against Spanish rule which broke out on August 10, 1680. During the 1690s refugees from the Rio Grande pueblos, escaping from reconquest of their lands, joined with local Keresans to form the Pueblo of Laguna.

Wild West Days ⓥⓔ

287-4802

Event features rodeos, chili cookoff, street dances and an arts and crafts fair. Held the 4th of July weekend.

Guadalupe ⓗ

Located about 75 miles west of Albuquerque on the Rio Puerco, Guadalupe is virtually a ghost town. It bustled with activity until World War II, but today it is an interesting skeleton, symbolizing a settlement that has gone full circle—life, growth, prosperity, death. The area has a cultural history of some 10,000 years, from Indian to Spanish occupation. The district is on the State Register of Cultural Properties.

Hagerman

Hagerman Community Library ⓛ

209 E. Argyle
P.O. Box 247, 88232
752-3204

Hatch ⓗ

Originally established as Santa Barbara in 1851, Apache raids drove the settlers away until 1853 when nearby Fort Thorn was established. Abandoned again in 1860 after the fort closed, it was re-occupied in 1875 and re-named for General Edward Hatch, then Commander of the New Mexico Military District.

Hatch Chile Festival ⓥⓔ

267-4847

Arts and crafts, food booths, sidewalk sale, carnival, dancing and music. Held annually Labor Day weekend.

Hatch Public Library ⓛ

P.O. Box 289, 87937
267-5132

Hernandez ⓗ

6 miles north of Espanola on Hwy 84

This is the small town that Ansel Adams immortalized in his photograph of a full moon rising.

High Rolls

Apple Festival ⓔ

High Rolls-Mt. Park
682-2403

This annual event, held sometime during October, features the harvesting and picking of apples, as well as the selling of homemade apple cider, apple pies, etc.

Cherry Festival ⓥⓔ

High Rolls-Mt. Park
437-6120

Celebration of the ripening of cherry orchards. Arts and crafts booths. Cherry picking and sales. Held in mid-June.

Hillsboro ⓗ

32 miles south of Reserve via Hwys 12 and 180

Hillsboro is an old gold mining town which is on the State Register of Cultural Properties.

Black Range Museum M H

Hwy 152
P.O. Box 454, 88042
895-5233

This is a history museum with artifacts of mining and early settlement, circa 1875-1900. The building itself has a colorful history, first as the Ocean Grove Hotel, owned by Sadie Orchard, the madam of area gold and silver mining towns, and later as the Chinaman's Cafe.

Hillsboro Apple Festival E

894-3536

Held annually the first week in September.

Hobbs H

Named for the family of James Hobbs which homesteaded here in 1907. Hobbs became first a trading village for ranchers and then a major oil town after the discovery of oil by the Midwest Oil Company in 1928.

Cinco de Mayo Celebration V E

City Park
397-3202

Parade starts at 10 a.m.; festivities at the Park start at 1 p.m. and continue until 6 p.m. Activities include booths (traditional Mexican food, games, arts and crafts), and live entertainment by local musicians. Annual event held the first week in May.

Confederate Air Force Museum M

Lea County Airport
P.O. Box 1260, 88240
392-5342

This unique museum features aircraft and memorabilia from World War II.

Hobbs Community Players P

397-3202

Hobbs Cultural Council A

200 E. Park, 88240
397-9292

This is a non-profit organization whose purpose is to promote, encourage, direct and sponsor cultural and educational activities.

Hobbs Hoedown Days V E

397-3202

This event, held in late-September, features a dance, parade, contests, and an arts and crafts fair.

Hobbs Public Library L

509 N. Shipp, 88240
397-9328

June Teenth Celebration V E

Washington Park
393-9301

Black awareness and educationally based celebration. Arts and crafts show and plays. Held in mid-June.

Kids Fair V E

397-9292

This event, held in April, features games, contests as well as arts and crafts activities for elementary school age children.

Lea County Cowboy Hall of Fame & Western Heritage Center M

New Mexico Junior College
5317 Lovington Highway, 88240
392-4510

Lea County history museum: Indians, buffalo hunters, soldiers, open range, homesteaders, settlers. Focus is on outstanding Lea County ranchers and rodeo performers.

Lea County Fair V E

397-3202

Held in August, this fair features juried arts & crafts.

Linam Ranch Museum M

Carlsbad Highway, west of Hobbs, 88240
393-4784

Early ranching history museum. Visits by appointment.

Llano Estacado Art Association A

P.O. Box 1455, 88241
397-3202

A nonprofit corporation promoting creative fine art in Hobbs and surrounding areas by means of exhibitions and lectures. Sponsors an annual regional art show, workshops and sidewalk sales. Also awards a scholarship to a fine arts student at the New Mexico Junior College in Hobbs.

Llano Estacado Party/ Cowboy Hall of Fame Induction 🄴

New Mexico Junior College
392-4510

This annual event—held on the third Saturday in November—features a Western Art Show in addition to the Cowboy Hall of Fame induction ceremonies.

May Festival 🆅🄴

Hobbs City Park
300 N. Turner, 88240
397-9292

Arts and crafts fair combined with music festival and class car show held the third week in May.

Nelson Tydings Auditorium 🄿

397-3202

Facility for community performing arts events.

New Mexico Symphony Committee 🄿

P.O. Box 860, 88241
397-4556

Pannell Library 🄻

New Mexico Junior College, 88240
392-4510

Scarborough Memorial Library 🄻

College of the Southwest
Lovington Highway, 88240
392-6561

Southwest Symphony Orchestra 🄿

P.O. Box 101, 88240
392-6478

The purpose of this non-profit group is the encouragement of concert music for school age children, adults and senior citizens. The Symphony is a chamber size orchestra of about 35 musicians, presenting an average of two or three concerts per season. In addition to Symphony performances, the organization sponsors the Southwest Symphony Band which consists of nonprofessional as well as professional musicians.

Isleta Pueblo 🄷

near junction I-25 & Hwy 137,
13 miles south of Albuquerque
869-3111

Isleta Pueblo has an area of 211,002 acres and a population of 3,401. Isleta has had a troubled history. When the Pueblo Revolt began, many members of the community fled to Hopi settlements in Arizona, while others accompanied the Spanish in their retreat to El Paso del Norte. After the rebellion, the Isleta people returned, some bringing Hopi mates and half-Hopi children. In the 1900s the community was split over religious matters as a result of members of Laguna and Acoma Pueblos having joined the community. The solution to this conflict was the creation of the satellite communities, Oraibi and Chicale, and the main pueblo, Isleta. The language is generally Tiwa, with most people speaking English as well. Isleta Pueblo performs several dances open to the public, during July and August, as well as a September Feast and Christmas festivals. Permits for camping, picnicking and fishing can be purchased at Isleta Lakes.

Dances to Commemorate the Christmas Season 🄴

Traditional dances during Christmas week.

Isleta Pueblo Feast Day 🄴

San Agustin Feast Day on September 4th. Morning Mass, procession, afternoon Harvest Dance.

Isleta Pueblo Library Resource Center 🄻

P.O. Box 317, 87022

San Agustin Celebration 🆅🄴

Indian dances—foods, arts and crafts, on August 28.

Jal   H

southeast corner of New Mexico

In the late 1880s the Cowden Cattle Company of Midland, Texas decided to expand into the New Mexico Territory, where stirrup-high gramma grass waved invitingly. They established their New Mexico headquarters at a watering place near the present townsite of Jal, only a couple of miles from the Texas border. To stock this virgin ranchland, the company bought a whole herd from John A. Lynch, an early Texas cattleman. As was common in those days, this herd carried the initials of their owner as a brand. The JAL also became the name of the nearby New Mexico town.

Woolworth Community Library   L

3rd and Utah
P.O. Box 1249, 88252
395-3268

Jemez Pueblo   H

south of Jemez Springs on Hwy 4
834-7359

In 1838, after years of illness and raids by Plains Indians, the dwindling population of Pecos, several miles to the east, was accepted into Jemez Pueblo. The present site of Jemez Pueblo has been occupied since the 16th Century. Most of the buildings date back to the period following the Pueblo Revolt in 1680. Jemez speaks the Tanoan language with the Towa dialect. The Indians of Jemez are widely known as excellent dancers, and their fairs and festivals draw large crowds. One feast is in August, for Our Lady of the Angels, and another in November for St. James. Some Jemez women still make pottery and baskets of plaited yucca leaves. The site is on both the State and National Registers.

Dances to Commemorate the Christmas Season   E

Buffalo Dance.

Jemez Pueblo Feast Day   E

San Diego Feast Day on November 12. Midmorning mass, procession, Harvest Dance.

New Year's Day Celebration   E

Jemez does the Matachinas, the Pumpkin moiety with native drums and the Turquoise moiety with violin and guitar.

Old Pecos Bull Dance   E

Our Lady of the Angels Feast Day on August 2. Bull and Corn Dances.

Our Lady of Guadalupe Feast Day   E

Midmorning mass and procession on December 12, with Matachinas Dance.

Three Kings Day   E

New tribal officers honored and transfer of the Canes of Authority on January 6. There is a huge Buffalo dance also called herd dance which includes deer, mountain sheep, antelope, elk, eagles and hawks.

Jemez Springs

Jemez Springs Community Library   L

P.O. Box 597, 87025
829-3540

Jemez State Monument   M H L

north of Jemez Springs on Hwy 4
P.O. Box 143, 87025
829-3530

The village of Giusewa was occupied by ancestors of the Jemez Indians before the arrival of the Spanish in 1541. Its ruins lie close to those of the great stone mission church of San Jose de Giusewa, which was built by the Franciscans around 1622. The monument features permanent and temporary history/artifacts exhibits as well as a library. This is a State Monument, administered by the Museum of New Mexico, Office of Cultural Affairs.

Jicarilla Apache Reservation   H

P.O. Box 507, Dulce, 87528
759-3242

Gojiiya Feast Day E

Stone Lake
south of Dulce
759-3242

This Jicarilla celebration at Stone Lake is like a Mardi Gras in the country. A blend of religion and revelry, Gojiiya celebrates a variety of important events, from young men's puberty rites to thanksgiving for a bountiful harvest. Gojiiya also commemorates the Jicarilla people's transference of homeland to northern New Mexico from their ancestral home in the plains and mountains of southeastern Colorado, northeastern New Mexico and west Texas, Oklahoma and Kansas. Events during the mid-September observance include ceremonial dances and rituals, footraces of the Ollero (white) and Llanero (red) clans, a powwow and trading bazaar.

Jicarilla Library L

P.O. Box 306, Dulce, 87528
759-3616

Jicarilla Museum M

759-3362

This is an arts and crafts center featuring basketry, beadwork, paintings and other works, located on the Jicarilla Apache Reservation.

Little Beaver Roundup V E

Dulce
759-3242

Rodeo, dances, as well as arts and crafts in mid-July.

Kelly H

29 miles west of Socorro via Hwy 60

Ghost town.

Kingston H

41 miles southwest of T or C via I-25 and Hwy 152

Ghost town.

Percha Valley Bank Museum M

Mining artifacts and antiques in the ghost town of Kingston.

Knowles

Knowles Frontier Days V E

north of Hobbs
397-3202

Arts and crafts booths, food and game booths, barbecue, drawings and raffles, stagecoach rides, as well as live bands playing all day. Held in mid-July.

La Cienega

Harvest Festival at El Rancho de las Golondrinas V E

15 miles southwest of Santa Fe in La Cienega
471-2261

Costumed villagers portray life at harvest time on the Spanish Colonial El Rancho de las Golondrinas (The Ranch of the Swallows), which dates from the early 1700s. Events include Spanish singing, dancing and plays, food, arts and crafts. Held the first weekend in October.

El Rancho de las Golondrinas (Old Cienega Village Museum) M H

15 miles southwest of Santa Fe
Rt. 14, Box 214, 87505
471-2261

This is a true "living history" museum, featuring the original ranch site complex of El Rancho de las Golondrinas (The Ranch of the Swallows). One of the Southwest's most historic Spanish Colonial ranches, Las Golondrinas dates from the early 1700s. The Ranch has been painstakingly restored with refurbished and accurate replicas of structures rebuilt on ancient foundations. In addition to the original ranch site, there is an old mountain village, working water mills, wheelwright and blacksmith shops, a schoolhouse, threshing grounds, and a Penitente meeting house. On special days, the site is populated with costumed docents answering questions about the ranch and local craftsmen demonstrating their skills. Museum is open April through October. Office and gift shop are open year-round. Special festivals take place in early June and early October.

Spring Festival at El Rancho de las Golondrinas   V E

15 miles southwest of Santa Fe
471-2261

Costumed villagers portray life at spring planting time on the Spanish Colonial El Rancho de las Golondrinas (The Ranch of the Swallows), which dates from the early 1700s. Events include Spanish singing, dancing and plays, food, arts and crafts. Held the first weekend in June.

La Cueva   H

State Roads 3 and 21

La Cueva was the commercial center for the Mora Land Grant, first settled in the 1850s. The historic district consists of a grist mill, mercantile store and storage buildings, ranch house and out buildings, and the San Rafael Church. The ranch house was built in 1851 by Vicente Romero, the founder of La Cueva. The district is on both the State and National Registers.

La Luz   H

Located just north of Alamogordo, La Luz is a lush, verdant agricultural community founded by Spanish settlers in the 1860s. The village reflects the old flat-roofed adobes of those times as well as Anglo style houses built 1880-1900. The district is on both the State and National Registers.

D.M. Sutherland House   H

Built in 1863, the Coronado Lodge in La Luz Canyon was the home of Roland Hazard in the 1880s. He was a wealthy Rhode Islander who developed the La Luz Pottery Works. The old inn is a two-story adobe now called Mi Casa. In the early days this lodge was a bar and hotel, a stopping place for stockmen and cowboys. Property is on both the State and National Registers.

Laguna Pueblo   H

45 miles west of Albuquerque on I-40
552-6654

Laguna has witnessed a host of challenges to its way of life. The coming of the railroad in the late 1800s brought problems to the traditional way of life as members of this pueblo were employed in railroad towns from Albuquerque to California. There was a degree of inter-marriage among the Indians and railroad engineers and surveyors, with the effect of splitting the tribe into progressive and conservative factions. Laguna Pueblo comprises six major villages scattered over many acres, with the political center at Old Laguna. This is the largest Keresan-speaking pueblo, with about 8000 members and a heritage of Shoshone, Tanoan, Keresan and Zuni cultures as well as various Plains tribes. The crafts of pottery-making, painting and jewelry-making have enjoyed a resurgence at Laguna. The feast of St. Joseph, celebrated in September, with its arts/crafts exhibits, spirited carnival and sporting events is the pueblo's largest public event. Baseball is big at Laguna, with eight semi-pro teams, and an All-Indian Tournament held at Laguna in September. Also noteworthy—San Jose de La Laguna Mission Church on the State and National Registers.

Feast Day at Encinal, Laguna Pueblo   E

The event includes a Mass, procession and ceremonial dances held at the settlement of Encinal at Laguna Pueblo. Held September 8, celebrating the Nativity of the Blessed Mother.

Feast Day at Mesita, Laguna Pueblo   E

Mass, procession and dances at the settlement of Mesita in Laguna Pueblo. Celebrating the feast day of San Antonio on August 15.

Feast Day at Paguate, Laguna Pueblo   E

This event includes a Mass, procession and dances held at the settlement of Paguate at Laguna Pueblo. Celebrating Santa Elisabet on September 25.

Feast Day at Paraje, Laguna Pueblo   E

This October 17 event is a celebration of the Feast Day of Santa Margarita-Maria at Paraje. There is a Mass, procession and ceremonial dances.

Laguna Pueblo Library   L

P.O. Box 194, 87026
552-6280

New Year's Day Celebration   🄴

Mass, procession and traditional dances.

San Jose Feast Day   🅅🄴

Mass, procession, Harvest Dance, arts and crafts. Brings many visitors, including those from other tribes. Carnival and sporting events, the most important of which is baseball. Laguna Pueblo has eight semi-pro baseball teams and plays against Isleta, Cochiti, and other teams in the area. This special celebration is held on September 19, although the traditional San Jose Feast Day is still celebrated on March 19.

San Jose de La Laguna Mission Church and Convent   🄷

Laguna Pueblo owns the mission, which was built by Pueblo workers, although it is in the charge of Franciscan missionaries. The San Jose de la Laguna Mission is one of the best preserved buildings of its type in the United States. It retains most of the structures and artifacts that were placed in the mission almost 300 years ago. The church and convent are on both the State and National Registers.

San Juan Feast Day   🄴

Grab Day on June 24.

San Lorenzo Feast Day   🄴

Grab Day on August 10.

San Pedro and San Pablo Feast Days   🄴

Grab Day on June 29.

Santa Ana Feast Day   🄴

Mass, procession and dances at the settlement of Seama in Laguna Pueblo. Held July 26.

Santiago Feast Day   🄴

Grab Day on July 25.

Three Kings Day   🄴

New tribal officers honored through the transfer of the Canes of Authority on January 6.

Lamy

Lamy Kite Festival   🄴

Hwy 285 south of Santa Fe
982-1598

This is a unique annual event celebrating the art and sport of kite flying. Contests, prizes and food in Lamy during mid-May.

Las Cruces   🄷

In 1849, following the Mexican War, fields were first broken in Las Cruces. The town became a flourishing stop on the Camino Real, deriving its name, "The Crosses," from the marking of graves of victims of an Apache attack. Since 1881 Las Cruces has been the county seat of Dona Ana County.

Alameda Depot Historic District   🄷

The Alameda area of Las Cruces was a showpiece of the latest fashions in architecture brought into town by the coming of the railroad circa 1881. Today, the district retains its historical character as well as its gardens, trees and broad grassy lawns. The district is on both the State and National Registers.

Amador Hotel   🄷

Amador & Water St.

Built in 1850 by Don Martin Amador, this old hotel played a major role in the history of Las Cruces. Benito Juarez, Pat Garrett and Billy the Kid spent a few nights here. Now home to the Dona Ana County manager's complex, several rooms of the old hotel have been restored with period furniture and artifacts. The building is on the State Register.

American Southwest Theater Company at NMSU   🄿

New Mexico State University campus
P.O. Box 3072, 88003
646-4517

This is a non-profit, semi-professional theater initiated by Tony Award winner Mark Medoff.

Arts in the Park   🅅

P.O. Box 1721, 88004
523-6403

Arts & crafts fair held in late April.

Ballet Folklorico de La Tierra del Encanto   P

Branigan Cultural Center
106 W. Hadley, 88001
382-7198

Branigan Cultural Center   VP

106 West Hadley
P.O. Drawer CLC, 88004
524-1422

This is a city-run facility for the performing and visual arts.

Brazito Battlefield   H

I-10, south of Las Cruces

One of the few battles of the Mexican War to be fought in New Mexico occurred near here on Christmas Day, 1846. U.S. troops under Colonel Alexander W. Doniphan defeated a Mexican army commanded by General Antonio Ponce de Leon. Two days later, Doniphan entered El Paso without opposition.

Chamber Players de Las Cruces   P

New Mexico State University
P.O. Box 3F, 88003
646-3709

Dona Ana Arts Council, Inc.   A

132 W. Las Cruces Street
P.O. Box 1721, 88004
523-6403

The Council serves the Las Cruces area with children's programs, the annual Renaissance Craftfaire, seminars or workshops for artists, concerts for the community, and two outreach programs: El Consejo de los Artes Hispanas for Hispanic artists, and workshops and other events for developmentally disabled adults. The Council also provides technical and board development assistance to non-profit groups as well as advocacy information to arts-related organizations.

El Camino Real (The King's Highway)   H

south of Las Cruces

An important historical road in the United States, running more than 2000 miles from Mexico City to Taos. Parts of the Camino Real were used by Spanish explorers in the 1580s, but it was formally established in 1598 by Juan de Onate, New Mexico's first colonizer and governor. It was later referred to as the Chihuahua Trail.

Jornada del Muerto on the Camino Real   H

I-25, north of Las Cruces

This stretch of the Camino Real leaves the Rio Grande and cuts across 90 miles of desert with little water or shelter. Despite its difficulty, the dreaded "Journey of the Deadman" was heavily used by Spanish, Mexican, and Anglo travelers between El Paso and the northern New Mexico settlements.

Las Cruces Classical Ballet Company   P

1404 E. Idaho, 88001
522-6273

Nutcracker each Christmas season, and other performances throughout the year.

Las Cruces Community Band   P

725 Solano Dr., 88001
524-7176

Las Cruces Community Concerts   P

522-4552

Subscription series.

Las Cruces Community Theater   P

Downtown Mall
523-1200

Las Cruces Natural History Museum   M

Mesilla Valley Mall
P.O. Drawer CLC, 88004
522-3120

Located in the city's Mesilla Valley Mall, this museum is dedicated to increasing public awareness about the environment as well as providing creative scientific educational activities.

Las Cruces Symphony   P

New Mexico State University
P.O. Box 3F, 88003
646-3709

Log Cabin Museum   MH

Main & Lucero
P.O. Drawer CLC, 88004

Local history exhibits housed in a relocated 1850 log cabin from Grafton, New Mexico.

Mesilla Valley Chorale   P

2713 Claude Dove Drive, 88001
522-4362

This is a community choir that presents a concert of classical and light classical music in late November and a "dessert concert" featuring broadway show music each spring.

Mesquite Street Original Townsite Historic District   H

Mesquite Street area

This district represents Las Cruces' original townsite, with typical Spanish/Mexican/American architecture—low, flat-roofed adobes built 1870-1930. It is the largest surviving group of historic structures in Las Cruces. Area is on both the State and National Registers.

Mormon Battalion   H

I-25, north of Las Cruces

The Mormon Battalion, composed of 500 volunteers, left Council Bluffs, Iowa in June of 1846 as part of the expeditionary force of Brigadier General Kearny. The battalion followed the Santa Fe Trail to Santa Fe and down the Rio Grande near here, where it turned west. The 2000-mile march ended in San Diego, California in January of 1847.

NMSU Jazz Festival   P

Music Center, NMSU campus
646-2421

Held in mid-April.

Nestor Armijo House   H

Lohman Ave. & Church St.

This is a wonderful pitched-roof adobe with rich Victorian trimmings. The house was built by an affluent 19th Century rancher and merchant, Nestor Armijo. It was the first two-story home in Las Cruces. The building remains virtually unchanged —a significant example of Victorian/adobe architecture and the home of a "rico" of the period. House is on both the State and National Registers.

New Mexico State Chorale   P

New Mexico State University campus
646-2421

New Mexico State University Art Gallery   M

NMSU campus
University Avenue east of Solano
P.O. Box 30001, 88003
646-2545

The gallery features changing exhibitions of contemporary art, folk art and the permanent collection of Mexican retablos, contemporary prints, and photography. Programs include visiting artists and critics, films, and workshops.

New Mexico State University Library   L

NMSU campus
P.O. Box 3475, 88003
646-1508

New Mexico State University Museum   M

NMSU campus
P.O. Box 3564, 88003
646-3739

General museum—prehistoric and historic Native American artifacts (pottery, basketry, beadwork, rugs, chipped and ground stone) primarily from the Southwest; artifacts of university and local historical interest. Museum is housed in Kent Hall. Programs include guided tours, field trips, lecture series, workshops as well as educational outreach in schools.

New Mexico State University Music Center   P

NMSU campus
646-3709

Pan American Center   P

New Mexico State University campus
P.O. Box 30001
Dept. 3SE, 88003
646-4413

Old Armijo Gallagher House   H

Lohman Ave.

Restored home which is more than 120 years old. Many of the original furnishings are on view on the second floor. The building houses a local savings & loan, but is open to the public during the bank's business hours. Property is on both the State and National Registers.

Onate's Route - on the Camino Real   H

I-10, south of Las Cruces

Juan de Onate, first governor of New Mexico, passed near here with his colonizing expedition in May 1598. Traveling north, he designated official campsites (called parajes) on the Camino Real, used by expeditions that followed. In Onate's caravan were 129 men, many with their families and servants.

Our Lady at the Foot of the Cross Shrine   H

Water & Lohman Ave.

Reproduction of Michelangelo's Pieta dedicated to the Sisters of Loretto who established Loretto Academy in 1875.

Renaissance Craftfaire   V

Young Park
523-6403

Held the first weekend in November.

San Agustin Springs   H

Hwy 70/82, east of Las Cruces

Here in July of 1861, less than 300 Confederate troops intercepted 500 Union soldiers retreating from Fort Fillmore to Fort Stanton. Exhausted from the heat and famished for water, the Union troops struggled across the desert in a five-mile evacuation train. Unable to fight, Major Isaac Lynde surrendered his command without firing a single shot.

Southern New Mexico State Fair   E

Fairgrounds, 13 miles west of Las Cruces
524-1968

Fair is held in late September. Livestock and agricultural displays, rodeo, food booths, contests.

Thomas Branigan Memorial Library   L

200 E. Picacho Ave., 88001
526-1047

Vos Vaqueros/ The Singing Men of Las Cruces   P

730 College Place
524-1658

Long-running choral group focusing on Christmas performances.

Whole Enchilada Fiesta   V E

Downtown Mall
524-1968

World's largest enchilada, parade, arts and crafts, food, dances, entertainment. Fiesta is held the first weekend in October.

Las Trampas   H

Hwy 76

One of the finest examples of Spanish-American agricultural communities in the United States, the village of Las Trampas is closer to the 18th Century than to the 20th. Las Trampas is isolated in a secluded valley, with tradition guiding the way of life. The area is on both the State and National Registers.

San Jose de Gracia Church and Collections   H

Las Trampas Plaza

This church, constructed between 1760 and 1776 on the northside of the Las Trampas Plaza, is probably the best preserved and least altered of the Spanish Colonial pueblo churches in New Mexico. It is considered to be one of the most significant 18th Century Spanish Colonial churches in the United States. The church is on both the State and National Registers.

Las Vegas   H

425-8631

Las Vegas served as an important—and very prosperous—stop on the Santa Fe Trail and later on the Atchison, Topeka and Santa Fe Railway. It was in booming Las Vegas that General Kearny announced the annexation of New Mexico by the United States in 1846. In 1862, during the Confederate occupation of Santa Fe, Las Vegas served as a Territorial capital.

Adele Ilfeld Auditorium   H

New Mexico Highlands University

The most architecturally significant structure on campus. Construction began in 1919, and the auditorium was finally completed in 1931. The front facade is Romanesque Revival. The building has arches and Doric Columns and is constructed of brown brick with a brownstone front facade. It was funded by the New Mexico State Legislature and by the Ilfeld family, in memory of Adele Ilfeld. The auditorium enjoys a place on both the State and National Registers.

Antonio Sanchez Cultural Center   M

166 Bridge Street, 87701
425-8829

This small museum offers traveling exhibits, photographs, paintings and historical artifacts. The Center also showcases the various works of area artists.

Armand Hammer United World College of the American West

5 miles north of Las Vegas
P.O. Box 248, 87731
454-1461

Located on the historic grounds of Montezuma, it is home to 200 students from around the world. The College offers a two-year International Baccalaureate degree for students aged 16-19.

Bridge Street Historic District   H

Bridge Street and vicinity
425-8631

Most of the buildings along this 800-foot long section of Bridge Street were erected between 1880 and 1910, during or just after the period of Las Vegas' economic predominance in the region. The District is significant as an example of the development of a business district in a 19th century New Mexico town, having made the transition from wagon road to a commercially developed area. The district is on both the State and National Registers. A brochure is available upon request by calling the above phone number.

Camp Maximiliano Luna   H

3 miles north of Las Vegas, off Hwy 85

This site was used for encampments of the New Mexico National Guard, 1904-1913 and 1924-1940. King Stadium, built in 1935, was used for spectacular horse shows of the 111th Cavalry, and in 1940 was used for the Cuarto Centennial Pageant. It was also the training ground of the 200th Artillery (formerly the 111th Cavalry) which won nationwide recognition for distinguished service in the Philippines in 1942. It was converted during 1942-1945 into an army camp for the training of thousands of recruits. Currently, the area is home to Luna Vocational Technical Institute. It is on the State Register of Cultural Properties.

Carnegie Park Historic District   H

north of Douglas Ave., around Library Park
425-8631

One of the finest examples of 19th Century landscape architecture in New Mexico (Lincoln Park being the other) exemplifying the principles of the French Beaux-Arts School; namely, symmetry and long vistas of greenspace terminating in a monument or a building. The centerpiece is the Carnegie Library.

Carnegie Public Library   L

500 National Ave., 87701
454-1403

Carnegie is one of the many libraries through the United States built by famed tycoon and philanthropist Andrew Carnegie. The Library was built in 1903 and modelled after Thomas Jefferson's home, Monticello. It is an example of Neo-Classical Revival architecture and has served the City of Las Vegas as a public library since it was constructed.

Castaneda Hotel   H

524 Railroad Avenue, 87701
425-9985

Built in 1898-99 as one of the luxury hotels in the remarkable Fred Harvey system, the Castaneda had the functions unique to such hostelries and served as a significant community center. Today, it, and the Montezuma Hotel near Las Vegas, as well as the Clovis Hotel, are the only Fred Harvey hotels still standing in New Mexico. Its noted guests included Theodore Roosevelt and William Jennings Bryan. The building is on the State Register of Cultural Properties.

Donnelly Library/ New Mexico Highlands University   L

National Ave., 87701
425-7511

Douglas/Sixth Street & Railroad Ave. Historic Districts   H

Douglas St., Sixth St., Railroad Ave.
454-1401

A walking tour of Railroad Ave., which in the 19th Century was comprised of mercantile houses, hotels, saloons and dance halls; and of the Douglas and Sixth Street District, on which some of the finest Victorian commercial buildings in New Mexico are to be found, as well as the city's banks, the Masonic Temple, the Duncan Opera House, the Y.M.C.A., and City Hall. District is on both the State and National Registers.

Hermit's Peak   H

west of Las Vegas, off I-25

From 1863 to 1867 this mountain was the home of Juan Maria Agostini, an Italian penitent who lived there as a hermit, carving crucifixes and religious emblems which he traded for food. Leaving this area, he moved to the Organ Mountains, in southern New Mexico, where he was found murdered in 1869.

July Fiestas   VE

Plaza Park
454-1401

Entertainment, parade, art show, fishing derby, fireworks and food.

Las Vegas Arts Council   A

P.O. Box 2603, 87701
425-1085

The Council sponsors performing artists as well as visual art shows. The organization also administers a six-week children's summer classes project involving more than 250 local children and culminating in a Missoula Children's Theatre production. In addition, the group sponsors the Las Vegas People's Faire, an arts and crafts event held each year on the last Saturday in August.

Las Vegas Plaza Historic District   H

Plaza and vicinity
425-8631

The Plaza was the central business square for the town's founders—34 families that moved to Las Vegas from San Miguel del Bado. Most buildings were erected during period 1880 to 1900. The plaza is on both the State and National Registers.

Las Vegas Railroad and Power Company Building   H

North 12th Street, between San Francisco and Baca Streets

The building, completed in 1907, served as a center of service and production important in community development in the era when electricity was generated locally and mass transportation was provided by the operation of electric trolley cars. The building is on both the State and National Registers.

Las Vegas Rails 'N Trails Days   VE

Historic Roundhouse
425-8631

Commemorating the historic Santa Fe Trail and the arrival of the Atchison, Topeka & Santa Fe Railroad, this return-to-the-Old West event takes place on three days each Memorial Day weekend. Featured are historic tours, parade, crafts show, antique show, Western Art Show, fiddler's contest, barbecue, rodeo, Country & Western dance.

Library Park Historic District   H

Library Park and vicinity
425-8631

Library Park has a central square park with a dominating Neo-Classical Revival structure and surrounding structures of frame and brick. The Midwestern character was imported on the Santa Fe Railroad, which originated in Chicago and arrived in Las Vegas in 1879. The Midwestern influence is also shown in that the library is a Carnegie Public Library, one of the few in the state. The styles of construction in the area create a significant grouping of late 19th and early 20th century structures. A Walking Tour Brochure is available from the Chamber of Commerce. The area is on the State and National Registers.

Lincoln Park Historic District H

southside of New Town
425-8631

Brochure for a walking tour is available through the Chamber of Commerce for this turn-of-the-century park and vicinity, which features charming Victorian-era architecture and tree-lined streets. The district is on both the State and National Registers.

Mission de San Miguel del Bado H

421-2780

Built by the area's early pioneers in 1806, the church and surrounding area are on both the State and National Registers.

Montezuma Hotel H

5 miles north of Las Vegas
P.O. Box 248, 87731
454-1461

Located near the site of a natural hot springs, just a few miles from Las Vegas, this grand hotel was the brainchild of the Atchison, Topeka and Santa Fe Railroad—an attempt to lure wealthy tourists. The Montezuma was designed in the popular Queen Anne style, standing four stories high and costing more than $200,000 to construct in the 1880s. It was considered the most elegant hotel in the far West. Less than two years after its opening, the hotel burned to the ground. It was rebuilt, but the hotel would experience more fires and financial troubles. In 1903, the Montezuma closed never to reopen as a hotel. During a 77-year span, the Montezuma was held by the YMCA, the Baptist Church and a Catholic seminary. In 1982, the Armand Hammer World College of the American West opened on the property. The structure is on both the State and National Registers.

Old Town Residential District H

Perez St. to Mills Ave.; Gonzales Street
425-8631

This district, which includes 34 houses, two churches and some commercial buildings, along with the "Distrito de las Escuelas," represents the bulk of the historic residential architecture of West Las Vegas, a key Santa Fe Trail and New Mexican Territorial city. These residences offer a notably intact record of the transition from a Spanish/Mexican adobe tradition to an Anglo-American, industrial-age, eclectic architecture, characteristic of New Mexico architecture from 1850-1915. The district is on both the State and National Registers.

People's Faire of Northern New Mexico V E

425-1085

Various booths featuring arts and crafts, food, as well as live entertainment. Held on the last Saturday in August at the historic Carnegie Park.

Plaza Hotel H

230 North Plaza
425-8631

Built in 1880, this was the leading hotel in Las Vegas for the reception of numerous visiting businessmen and ranchers, and the principal community center for meetings, banquets and dances until it was superceded by the more luxurious Castaneda Hotel in 1899. It enjoys a place on the State Register of Cultural Properties.

Plaza/Bridge Street Historic District H

The Plaza, and adjacent Bridge Street
425-8631

The Plaza area began to be built-up both before and during the period of Las Vegas' prosperity, after the arrival of the railroad in 1879. This walking tour is comprised of fourteen buildings of historic interest. A brochure is available by calling the above phone number.

Residences of Las Vegas H

425-8631

A driving tour of 24 residences through the city. Examples of nearly every architectural residential style found in America between 1840 and 1940 can be seen among these various residences. A brochure describing these homes is available upon request by calling the above number.

Rough Riders Memorial and City Museum M

727 Grand Avenue
P.O. Box 179, 87701
425-8726

This history museum focuses on Teddy Roosevelt's Rough Riders and offers artifacts of local history.

San Miguel County Fair V E

County Fairgrounds
425-8527

Held in mid-August, the fair offers arts & crafts, food displays, various animal shows and displays.

Southwest Culture Festival   Ⓥ Ⓔ

New Mexico Highlands University, Student Center
425-3745

In addition to art shows, the festival features a series of lectures, dance, music and other demonstrations. Held in mid-July.

Stone Architecture of Las Vegas   Ⓗ

425-8631

A unique feature of Las Vegas' architectural heritage is a remarkable group of stone residences and commercial buildings (also churches and schools) still intact after nearly a century of use. Built between 1880 and 1898, the buildings represent the eclecticism and variety favored by the Victorian era.

W.C.T.U. Fountain in Fountain Park   Ⓗ

Lincoln, Grand and Manzanares Avenues
425-8631

This small, triangular park contains a large stone fountain erected in 1896 by the local Women's Christian Temperance Union. That fountain, now inoperative, still stands as a symbol of the past interplay of two facets of local culture in the boom era before 1900—the excessive imbibing of alcoholic beverages in a host of local saloons by the frontiersmen, and the campaign of dedicated women in their effort to create a wholesome environment in Las Vegas. The park/fountain are on both the State and National Registers.

Lincoln   Ⓗ

This historic town was settled in 1849. It is the site of the Lincoln County War of 1878. The town features sites nearly unchanged from those days, including the Tunstall Store and the Lincoln County Courthouse where Billy the Kid escaped from the law in 1881. The intimate Wortley Hotel, open during summer months, offers rooms furnished with Victorian antiques. Historic sites in town are operated by the Museum of New Mexico (Lincoln is a State Monument), the Lincoln County Heritage Trust, and the Lincoln County Historical Society. Lincoln is on both the State and National Registers.

La Paloma Museum   Ⓜ

P.O. Box 43, 88338
653-4828

This museum features more than 5,000 antiques and other artifacts from the time period 1860-1920.

Lincoln County Fair   Ⓥ Ⓔ

County Fairgrounds
354-2234

The celebration includes livestock judging, a rodeo, as well as a sizeable arts and crafts fair. Held in mid-August.

Lincoln County Heritage Trust   Ⓜ Ⓗ Ⓞ

Hwy 380
P.O. Box 98, 88338
653-4025

This is a local preservation group which operates and maintains historic houses, a historical center, and the restored Wortley Hotel. The Historical Center, Museum Store, Dr. Woods' House, and Wortley Hotel are open to the public. Exhibits within the Historical Center include the Apache Indians, Buffalo Soldiers, Lincoln County War, Billy the Kid, and the ongoing Billy the kid Photographic Research Project. Slide show, seasonal guided tours, and special events.

Lincoln State Monument   Ⓜ Ⓗ

Hwy 380
P.O. Box 98, 88338
653-4372

History museum; historic houses and sites, Old Lincoln County Courthouse; Tunstall Store; Wortley Hotel; San Juan Church; Convento, Fresquez, Brent and Watson houses; Torreon (1850). This is a New Mexico State Monument administered by the Museum of New Mexico, a division of the Office of Cultural Affairs.

Old Lincoln Days   Ⓥ Ⓔ

653-4372

Held the first full weekend in August, "Old Lincoln Days" are celebrated with a Billy the Kid Pageant, parade, living history demonstrations, arts and crafts, and food booths. There is also an old-fashioned fiddler's contest.

Torreon in Lincoln   Ⓗ

653-4372

The Torreon, or rock fort tower, where settlers hid during Indian raids, still stands in the center of Lincoln.

Wortley Hotel   Ⓗ

653-4500

The Wortley Hotel was also once known as the Lincoln Hotel. One of the owners was Patrick F. Garrett, sheriff of Lincoln County. Reconstructed in 1960, the Wortley offers old-fashioned lace comfort and brass beds on a seasonal basis.

Logan

McFarland Brothers Bank   H

This one-story bank building was built in 1904 of native sandstone at a cost of $1000 on Logan's Main Street. It is considered a good example of stone masonry using red stone found in the area and used extensively in construction in the early 20th Century. The building is on the State Register.

Shollenberger Mercantile Company Building   H

Main Street

This is a one-story building of native sandstone fronting on Logan's Main Street. Stone is from a quarry on the Canadian River about two miles south of town. The structure is on the State Register of Cultural Properties.

Lordsburg   H

This town was founded in 1880 on the route of the Southern Pacific Railroad, near that used by the Butterfield Overland Mail Co., 1858-1861. It eventually absorbed most of the population of Shakespeare, a now-deserted mining town three miles south.

Clanton Hideout   H

Hwy 338, west of Lordsburg and south of I-10

The infamous Clanton Gang had two crude dugouts here in the 1880s that served as hideouts and a base for wide-ranging outlaw activities, particularly in connection with the Curly Bill Gang's depredations along the Smugglers' Trail that passed by here. Old Man Clanton was ambushed below the border in revenge for a Skeleton Canyon massacre.

Hidalgo County Fair   E

County Fairgrounds
542-9291

Held in late August.

Lordsburg Arts and Crafts Fair   V

James H. Baxter Memorial Civic Center
542-3734

Held annually in early November.

Lordsburg Coaling Tower   H

This thick-walled concrete coaling tower is one of only a few remaining railroad coaling facilities in the West. It served the Southern Pacific Railway 1926-1951. The tower is on the State Register of Cultural Properties.

Lordsburg-Hidalgo Library   L

208 E. Third St., 88045
542-9646

Lordsburg Railroad Days   E

542-3734

Held on Memorial Day weekend.

McComas Incident   H

Hwy 90, north of Lordsburg

In March 1883, Judge and Mrs. H.C. McComas were killed in this vicinity by a group of Chiricahua Apaches led by Chatto. An extensive manhunt failed to rescue their six year-old son, who had been taken captive. The incident was part of a violent outbreak toward the end of the Apache Wars.

Smugglers Trail   H

Hwy 338, west of Lordsburg and south of I-10

Smugglers once crossed this area with mule trains of contraband from Mexico, to be traded for merchandise in Arizona. In the summer of 1881, a group of Mexican smugglers was killed in Skeleton Canyon by members of the Clanton gang, including Old Man Clanton, Ike and Billy Clanton, and Curly Bill Brocius.

Los Alamos

Bandelier National Monument   M H L

14 miles southwest of Los Alamos on Hwy 4, 87544
672-3861

This spectacular canyon, cut deep into the slopes of the Jemez Volcano, is the site of 12th Century Indian cliff dwellings and surface villages. Area also offers back country hiking, beautiful waterfalls. Monument offers an extensive visitor center with explanatory exhibits, artifacts and a library. It is on both the State and National Registers.

Bradbury Science Museum   M

Los Alamos National Laboratory
P.O. Box 1663, 87545
667-4444

The Museum interprets World War II's historic Project Y—the development of the atom bomb—and displays the Los Alamos National Laboratory's defense, energy, and basic science research through self-guiding, interactive exhibits, computer programs, and films.

Early Christmas Arts and Crafts Fair   V

Los Alamos Middle School
662-9331

One of two annual arts and crafts fairs sponsored by the Fuller Lodge Art Center, held the last Saturday in October.

Fuller Lodge Art Center and Gallery   V

2132 Central Avenue
P.O. Box 790, 87544
662-9331

This art center and gallery features invitational and juried exhibits of artists from New Mexico and the region as well as other parts of the nation and world. The Center sponsors two annual arts and crafts fairs, one held the second Saturday in August on the Fuller Lodge Lawn, the other the last Saturday in October (at the Middle School). Gallery exhibits change monthly.

Los Alamos Arts Council   A

P.O. Box 284, 87544
662-7532

Los Alamos Arts and Crafts Fair   V

Fuller Lodge Lawn
2132 Central Avenue
662-8105

Two events, one held annually in mid-May, another in mid-November.

Los Alamos Concert Association   P

P.O. Box 572, 87544
662-2936

Founded in 1946, this association presents five concert series from September-April, internationally celebrated ensembles and solo musicians.

Los Alamos County Fair   E

662-8105

Fair features a parade and rodeo, food and entertainment. Held each year in August.

Los Alamos County Historical Museum   M H

1921 Juniper Street
P.O. Box 43, 87544
662-6272

History museum—collection of Laura Gilpin and T. Harmon Parkhurst photographs of Los Alamos Ranch School; memorabilia from Ranch School and Manhattan Project; slides, photo archives, oral history tapes, collection of Indian pottery and 1940s pottery, and prehistoric Indian artifacts. Housed in historic Ranch School Guest House (1922); prehistoric Indian ruins on museum grounds; relocated and restored Hispanic Homesteader's Cabin on museum grounds. The Museum Book Shop stocks more than 600 titles of Southwestern literature. The Historical Society sponsors a year-round lecture series and has published 10 award-winning books on the history and natural history of the area. The Museum and its archives are on the State Register of Cultural Properties.

Los Alamos Light Opera   P

667-5876

Los Alamos Little Theater Melodrama   P

1670 Nectar, 87544
662-5493

Melodrama on weekends in January.

Los Alamos/National Laboratory and Ranch School   H

Located near the ancient Indian sites of the Pajarito Plateau, Los Alamos is one of New Mexico's newest towns. In 1942 a boys' ranch school became the headquarters of the Manhattan Project, which led to the development of the atomic bomb. Los Alamos National Laboratories continues to be a center for nuclear and other scientific research. LANL is on both the State and National Registers, and the Los Alamos Ranch School is on the State Register.

Mesa Public Library   L

1742 Central Ave., 87544
662-8240

New Mexico Alliance for Arts Education 🄰

P.O. Box 870, 87544

Affiliated with the John F. Kennedy Center's Education Department, the organization is an advocacy organization dedicated to the promotion of instruction in the arts to New Mexico's students. The group's objective is to strengthen the position of the arts as a discipline in the schools, affecting positively the role of the arts in New Mexico's cultures.

Something Completely Different 🄿

301 El Viento, 87544
662-4513

This presentation, held each year in early March, celebrates women composers of all nationalities and periods. Performers are in appropriate costumes and are accompanied by narrations which provide historical background about the joys and problems encountered by female musicians.

The Coffeehouse 🄿

301 El Viento, 87544
662-4513

The Coffeehouse presents classical chamber music in a night club setting three times a year. Leading New Mexico musicians perform.

Theater New Mexico 🄰🄿

167 Andanada, 87544
662-7472

This is a non-profit corporation whose membership is composed of supporters and participants in all phases of theater activity. The group holds statewide conventions in the spring, and biennial statewide community theater competitions as part of the national organization, the American Association of Community Theatres.

Los Brazos 🄷

Hwy 84

Los Brazos is a village of 25 houses, 11 farm buildings and a schoolhouse, many structures of which date to the late 19th Century. It serves as an excellent display of regional folk architecture in the Spanish tradition. Los Brazos is on both the State and National Registers.

Los Lunas

Atchison, Topeka & Santa Fe Rwy Depot - Los Lunas 🄷

Hwy 85

This is one of the earliest remaining depots in the state, constructed in 1879 when the railway reached Los Lunas from Albuquerque. It remains today as a symbol of the important social and economic impact that the railroad had on Los Lunas. The depot is on both the State and National Registers.

Huning Mercantile and House 🄷

Main Street & Los Lentes

This square adobe building complete with an interior courtyard was constructed in the 1840s. It has been remodeled several times, but still shows its original character. The building has been placed on the State Register of Cultural Properties.

Los Lunas Community Library 🄻

460 Main Street
P.O. Box 1209, 87031
865-6779

Luna-Otero, Tranquilino House 🄷

Hwy 85 & State Road 6

Constructed in the 1880s, this house has retained most of its original design and charm—14-room Victorian, built of adobe. This is the best example of an adobe Victorian in New Mexico. It is now a restaurant. The building is on both the State and National Registers.

Valencia County Arts Council 🄰

P.O. Box 794, 87031
865-2103

In addition to its work in arts education, the Council sponsors the annual All Arts Festival in late October, and the New Mexico Symphony Orchestra Annual Holiday Concert in mid-December.

Los Ojos 🄷

Hwy 84, between Tierra Amarilla and Chama

Historic district where villagers raise nearly extinct churro sheep and weave wool using the old Rio Grande traditions. The district is on both the State and National Registers.

Burns, T.D. Store H

Old State Road 95

The store is a large adobe building with a pitched roof built @ 1875 by Thomas D. Burns, a local merchant and politician. It was the first major community building constructed in Los Ojos. In addition to serving as an important community center, the store was the site for political, social and cultural activities. It housed "El Nuevo Mundo," a newspaper published in the Tierra Amarilla area circa 1907-1908. The store is on both the State and National Registers.

Fiesta De Santiago E

558-7231

Religious procession and community celebration usually held a weekend at the end of July.

La Gruta, Shrine of Our Lady of Lourdes H

Shrine was built in 1919. Location offers a splendid view of the entire Rio Chama Valley. The site is on both the State and National Registers.

Los Ojos Fish Hatchery & Burns Lake Bungalow H

Hatchery Road

The fish hatchery complex was constructed in 1932-1933 as a WPA project in the southern part of the Chama River Valley. It serves as the most prominent reminder of state and federal activity in the area during the 1930s. The complex was designed in the Beaux Arts plan. The complex is on both the State and National Registers.

San Jose Church H

The church was completed in 1936, but it houses a magnificent imported altar which was bought in 1919 to commemorate the area's World War I Veterans.

Los Padillas H

Los Padillas is an extended family settlement, south of Albuquerque, which was resettled in 1718 by Diego de Padilla. His grandparents had lived on the site prior to the 1680 Pueblo Revolt at which time they were forced to abandon it. In the 1790 census the town, referred to as San Andres de los Padillas, had a population of 168. This is the site of the old Los Padillas School, originally built in 1901 and replaced in 1912.

Loving

Espejo's Trail H

Hwy 285, north of the Texas border

Don Antonio de Espejo, leader of the third expedition to explore New Mexico, passed near here on his return to Mexico City in 1583. After learning of the martyrdom of two Franciscan friars from an earlier expedition, he explored the Pueblo country and then followed the Pecos River Valley south.

Loving Community Library L

P.O. Box 1358, 88256
745-3509

Lovington H

Lovington is named after Robert Florence Love, who founded the town on his homestead in 1908. It was a farming and ranching community until the discovery of the Denton pool after World War II turned it into an oil town.

Country Caravan Music Festival P

Lea County Courthouse lawn
396-5311

This is an annual July concert series by the Country and Bluegrass Music Program of South Plains College. Admission is free.

Lea County Fair and Rodeo E

Lea County Fairgrounds, Jake McClure Arena
396-5344

This is one of the largest county fairs in the state with a parade leading to a PRCA-approved rodeo. Held in mid-August.

Lea County Museum M H

103 S. Love
P.O. Box 1, 88260
396-5311

History museum; artifacts of local history; dugout house; Love House; housed in the Commercial Hotel, ca. 1918. Rooms are furnished with old relics collected from Lea County residents and decorated according to function.

Lovington Public Library L

103 N. First, 88260
396-3144

Southeastern New Mexico Arts and Crafts Festival Ⓥ

Lea County Fairgrounds
396-5311

More than 100 exhibitors from New Mexico, Texas, Colorado, Washington State, etc. No commercially manufactured items allowed in the show. Held annually in early November.

Madrid Ⓗ

Hwy 14, south of Santa Fe

Although Madrid still likes to include itself among the ghost towns, it represents a unique example of resurrection. Coal became important in the 1880s and Madrid with it. After World War II, the demand for coal gradually diminished, and long forlorn rows of identical company houses stood empty and decaying. Finally, in 1975, houses were sold to individual buyers and restoration began. It is now being restored as an arts and crafts center. The Old Coal Mine Museum is interesting, and there are enticing shops. Concerts in the summer at the Madrid ballpark. Engine House Theater features live drama in the summers. Madrid is on both the State and National Registers.

Christmas in Madrid Ⓔ

471-3450

Gallery open houses, refreshments, displays of giant nursery rhyme and Christmas figures from famous Christmas displays of Madrid's heyday. Held each year in early December.

Engine House Theater Ⓟ

473-0743

Summer season is Memorial Day through Labor Day, featuring Victorian melodrama with local actors.

Madrid Music in the Open Air Ⓟ

Madrid Park
989-9662

Jazz, bluegrass and chamber music concerts on Sundays during summer in the Madrid park Pavilion.

Mine Shaft Tavern Dinner Theatre Ⓟ

Main Street, 87010
473-0743

Fall season runs first Friday in October through mid-January, featuring original mysteries and popular classic state plays with local actors.

Old Coal Mine Museum ⓂⒽ

Main Street, 87010
473-0743

This small mining museum features a coal mine shaft, railroad and mining artifacts including antique cars and 1900 steam engine 769. The building was formerly a steam engine repair house.

Turquoise Trail Theater Company Ⓟ

983-7317

Plays and melodramas on weekends during the summer.

Magdalena Ⓗ

Hwy 60, west of Socorro

Magdalena is located in a mineral-rich area which became a center of silver mining in the 1860s. In 1885, a railroad was built to the smelter in Socorro, and Magdalena became an important railhead for cattle, sheep and ore. Magdalena is on the State Register of Cultural Properties.

Atchison, Topeka & Santa Fe Railway Depot - Magdalena Ⓗ

Magdalena was the terminus of an Atchison, Topeka and Santa Fe Railway spur constructed in 1884 aimed at tapping the lucrative freight business from western New Mexico's growing mine and livestock interests. The long, narrow, one-story frame depot now houses municipal offices and a community library. The depot is on both the State and National Registers.

Magdalena Mountain Mail Ⓞ

P.O. Box 86, 87825

This organization publishes a monthly historical newspaper, with issues including items from old papers, articles written by or about old timers in the area.

Magdalena Old-Timers' Reunion ⓋⒺ

835-0424

This annual event, usually held on the weekend following the 4th of July, features music and a parade as well as an arts and crafts fair.

Magdalena Village Library Ⓛ

200 N. Main
P.O. Box 145, 87825
854-2261

Manuelito ☐

west of Gallup, near Arizona border

This area contained many Indian pueblos dating from about 500 A.D. to 1325, when it was abandoned. Navajos settled here by 1800. This was the home of Manuelito, one of the last of the chiefs to surrender for confinement at the Bosque Redondo Reservation near Fort Sumner. The Navajos returned here in 1868.

Melrose

Easter Pageant ☐

Roger Parks Ranch south of Melrose
253-4530

This pageant features a Passion Play and Easter breakfast. The play is enacted in nearby caves once used by Billy the Kid.

Melrose Old Timers' Days ☐

253-4530

Parade, rodeo and community barbecue in mid-August.

Mescalero Apache Reservation ☐

P.O. Box 176, 88340
671-4494

The Indians who live today on the Mescalero Apache Reservation are descendants of bands known earlier as Mescalero, Chiricahuas and Lipans. The Mescaleros took their name from the "Mescal cactus," which once supplied the Apaches with food, beverage and fiber. Its stalks were used in making the ceremonial tepee. After the Apaches were confined to this reservation, in mountain rather than desert country, evergreens were used as tepee poles. The tribe owns and manages four recreational areas, including the resort complex, Inn of the Mountain Gods.

Mescalero Apache Ceremonial Coming of Age ☐

671-4494

Held every year during the first week of July, near the 4th of July. Indian dances and rodeo are held each of the four days in addition to the traditional Puberty Ritual Ceremony, Dance of the Apache Maidens and Dance of the Mountain Gods. No cameras are allowed at the ceremonies.

Mescalero Apache Cultural Center Ⓜ

P.O. Box 176, 88340
671-4494

The center features clothing displays of the three subtribes: Mescalero, Chiricahua and Lipan; photographs of Indian leaders, Chatto, Cochise, Noiche, Chihuahua, etc.; historical and descriptive video presentation; and Indian language dictionaries. The center is open weekdays, 8-4:30 p.m.

Mescalero Community Center Library Ⓛ

P.O. Box 176, 88340
671-4494

Mesilla ☐

south of Las Cruces
524-8521

New Mexico village dating to the 1500s and site of San Albino Mission Church. Mesilla was the crossroads of the El Camino Real and the Butterfield Overland Stagecoach route. Billy the Kid was once convicted of murder here and broke out of jail before the sentence was carried out. The Gadsden Purchase was signed on the Mesilla plaza in 1854 which made this New Mexico territory a part of the United States. In 1861 the small town was the western headquarters of the Confederacy. The village retains the charm and ambiance of a slower time in New Mexico's past. Today, Mesilla is known for its restaurants, museums and art galleries. The village is on both the State and National Registers.

Butterfield Trail ☐

south of Las Cruces

Stagecoaches of the Butterfield Overland Mail Co. began carrying passengers and mail from St. Louis to San Francisco, across southern New Mexico, in 1858. The 2,795-mile journey took 21-22 days. In 1861, the service was re-routed through Salt Lake City. Here the trail followed the Rio Grande northward to La Mesilla.

Desert Playwrights Theatre   P

P.O. Box 328, 88046
522-2649

This is a non-profit theatre producing new plays by writers from the Southwest.

Fountain Theater   P

Built in 1905 by the Fountain family as a vaudeville house, legend has it that the old theater is haunted by the ghost of a frustrated actress.

Gadsden Museum   M

P.O. Box 147, 88046
526-6293

This is a history museum, focusing on local Indian and Spanish/Mexican artifacts.

Mesilla Valley Film Society   A

P.O. Box 406, 88046
523-6678

Presents a film series in the old Fountain Theater in Mesilla.

San Albino Church   H

Mesilla Plaza

One of the oldest missions in the Mesilla Valley. Established by order of the Mexican Government in 1851. In 1906 the present building was constructed on the foundation of the original adobe church. The bells of San Albino date to the early 1870s.

Mimbres

Mimbres Fall Roundup   V E

Hwy 35, east of Silver City
538-5679

Food, entertainment, arts and crafts. Held in mid-September.

Mogollon   H

75 miles northwest of Silver City
via Hwys 180 & 159

Mogollon had a reputation in the late 1800s as one of the most wide-open towns in the West. Butch Cassidy and his crowd once headquartered there, and gunmen, claim jumpers and gamblers kept things stepping lively. Not even the great Apache fighters, Victorio and Geronimo, nor troops sent in by the governor, could tame Mogollon. An estimated $19.5 million in gold, silver and copper came from the mines. Mogollon is on both the State and National Registers.

Mogollon Museum   M

Local history exhibit with mining artifacts in the ghost town of Mogollon.

Mora

Palo Flechado Pass   H

near junction Hwys 3 and 38

Palo Flechado (tree pierce with arrows) was a pass much used by Indians, Spaniards and Anglos traveling from the plains by way of the Cimarron River (called La Flecha—the arrow—in 1719). The Flecha de Palo Indians (Apache band) in 1706 inhabited the plains east of the mountains.

St. Vrain's Mill   H

State Road 38

This grinding mill was constructed in 1864 and owned and operated by Ceran St. Vrain. The mill was a large and significant supply mercantile center in the 1800s. It is on both the State and National Registers.

Moriarty

Gregg's Trail   H

east of Moriarty on I-40

Josiah Gregg, merchant and pioneer historian of the Santa Fe Trail, made four expeditions to Santa Fe. On his last, in 1839-40, he blazed a new route from Van Buren, Arkansas, which followed the Canadian River north of here. The new trail became popular with California-bound gold-seekers in 1849.

Moriarty Community Library 🄻

P.O. Box 67, 87035
832-6310

Moriarty Historical Society Museum 🄼🄷🄾

777 Central Avenue SW
P.O. Box 133, 87035
832-4764

This is a history museum, specializing in local artifacts and housed in Moriarty's first fire station.

National Pinto Bean Fiesta 🅅🄴

281-3755

Parade, pinto bean cook-off, contests, crafts, dance. Held in early August.

Old-Fashioned Independence Day 🄴

832-6446

Barbecue, parade, fireworks, rodeo, dance.

Mosquero

Goodnight-Loving Trail 🄷

Hwy 39, near Mosquero

After leaving Fort Sumner, the Goodnight-Loving Trail forked in two directions. This branch, developed by Oliver Loving in 1866, followed the Pecos River to Las Vegas, and the Santa Fe Trail to Raton Pass. The great Texas cattle drives followed this and other routes to Colorado and Wyoming until 1880.

Mountainair 🄷

Founded in 1902, Mountainair developed as a major center for pinto bean farming in the early 20th century until the drought of the 1940s. The region had been occupied earlier by Tompiro and eastern Tiwa pueblo Indians from prehistoric times through the mid-17th century, when it served as a major center for Spanish Franciscan missionaries.

Atchison, Topeka & Santa Fe Rwy Depot - Mountainair 🄷

This depot is California Mission style, with stucco and red-tiled roof, built in 1907. The depot has been placed on the State Register of Cultural Properties.

Mountainair Civic Library 🄻

110 N. Roosevelt
P.O. Box H, 87036
847-2235

Shaffer Hotel 🄷

Broadway

This is an historic hotel finely decorated with unusual wood animal and geometric carvings by the builder, Clem "Pop" Shaffer, a folk artist and environmentalist. The building is on both the State and National Registers.

Mule Creek

Mule Creek Community Library 🄻

P.O. Box 37, 88051
535-2789

Nambe

Nambe Community Library 🄻

Rt. 1, Box 123, 87501
455-7711

Nambe Pueblo 🄷

3 miles east on Hwy 503
from junction with U.S. 84-285
455-2036

In the Tewa language, spoken by the people of the Nambe Pueblo, the word Nambe means "People of the Round Earth." Perhaps this is a reference to the landscape which encircles the pueblo, with its spectacular beauty and the breath-taking view of the Sangre de Cristo mountains in the near distance. The Pueblo is almost completely surrounded by non-Indian residents, and most Pueblo residents are tri-lingual. There has been a recent resurgence and revitalization of interest in the traditional rituals and crafts. Two special and popular festivals are held each year. On July 4th, the Nambe Falls July 4th celebration is held at the recreation park area at the foot of the falls. On October 4th, the annual feast day commemorating St. Francis de Assisi is held at the Pueblo proper.

This feast is preceded by vespers on the evening of October 3rd, with processions and bonfires lighting the entire village. Activities are concluded by a "throw-away" when tribal residents throw food, candy and other commodities unto the performing dancers. There is mad dash amongst the youngsters, who try to gather as many goodies as their hands can hold. Feast day activities attract large crowds both for the dances and the scenery. The Pueblo is on both the State and National Historic Registers. There are excellent facilities for picnicking, fishing and camping at the Nambe Falls Dam, and recreational park area. Advance calls for group gatherings are recommended.

Dances to Commemorate the Christmas Season   E

Traditional dances during Christmas week.

Easter Celebration   E

Mass, procession and dances, including Corn Dance, or other spring dances.

Nambe Pueblo Feast Day   E

In honor of its patron saint, St. Francis de Assisi, on October 4th, a morning Mass and procession is followed by traditional Indian dances.

Nambe Pueblo Waterfall Ceremony   E

Dance teams present the Buffalo, Corn, Deer, Comanche, and Spear dances on July 4th, at the scenic Nambe Falls Recreation Area.

Three Kings Day   E

Transfer of Canes of Authority, honoring new tribal officials on January 6.

Nara Visa

Nara Visa School   H

Hwy 54

Complex is a 1936 WPA project which includes an adobe gymnasium, shower house, storage building, original generator building, pumphouse, old windmill and original playground equipment (merry-go-round, slide, swings and see-saw). The complex is on both the State and National Registers.

Ojo Caliente   H

Hwy 285, north of Espanola

Ojo Caliente ("hot spring") was a strategic point for the defense of the Chama and upper Rio Grande Valleys. Colonization began in the early 18th century, but pressure from the Utes and Comanches delayed permanent settlement until 1793. In 1807, Lt. Zebulon Pike reported a population of 500.

Pecos   H

The upper Pecos River Valley was on the frontier of Pueblo Indian civilization from at least the 13th to the 19th centuries, when the nearby Pueblo of Pecos was abandoned. Despite raids by various Plains Indian groups, Spanish-speaking settlers around 1825 founded what is today the village of Pecos.

Pecos National Monument   M H

south of Pecos, via Hwy 63
P.O. Drawer 11, 87552
757-6414

Pecos was perhaps the greatest of the pueblos when Europeans arrived—it was a major trading center with the Plains Indians. The monument represents a 14th Century pueblo with 17 Century mission ruins. Excavations in the early 1900s and during the 1940s provided much information on the history of the pueblo. Monument includes a visitors center with interpretive exhibits. The sites and ruins are on both the State and National Registers.

Pena Blanca

Cochiti Lake Community Library   L

P.O. Box 132, 87041
465-2213

Peralta   H

south of Albuquerque

One of the last skirmishes of the Civil War in New Mexico took place here on April 15, 1862. The Sibley Brigade, retreating to Texas, camped at the hacienda of Governor Henry Connelly, a few miles from Peralta. Here the Confederates were routed by Union forces under Col. Edward R.S. Canby.

Our Lady of Guadalupe Catholic Church H

This is a well-maintained beautiful adobe church in Peralta. The church is on the State Register of Cultural Properties.

SPAIC A

Society for the Preservation of American Indian Culture
P.O. Box 854, 87042

Picuris Pueblo H

20 miles south of Taos
Hwys 68 to 75
587-2519

Picuris Pueblo is the home of a tribe of Tiwa speaking Indians still governing themselves by a traditional form of government. In the 1960s, archaeologists uncovered a large village near Talpa, now known as Pot Creek Ruin. Excavations revealed that the ancestors of the Picuris people established themselves there around 1250 A.D. The excavation artifacts, as well as contemporary exhibits, are now housed at the Pueblo museum. Micaceous clay cooking pots are still produced by Picuris women. Some other crafts have been revived and are available at the museum. The pueblo is on both the State and National Registers.

Candlemas Day E

Traditional observances on February 2.

Dances to Commemorate the Christmas Season E

Sundown torchlight procession of the Virgin, vespers and Matachinas Dance.

Easter Celebration E

Mass, procession and dances, including Corn Dance.

High Country Arts and Crafts Festival VE

This event, held in early July, is a benefit for the San Lorenzo Mission. The festival features a large tricultural arts and crafts exhibit, dances and a fishing contest.

New Year's Day Celebration E

Mass, procession and traditional dances, including Turtle and Matachinas.

Picuris Pueblo Museum Center MH

P.O. Box 228
Penasco, 87533
587-2519

This history museum features local prehistoric archeological artifacts; photos and text of local historical interest; the artworks of local contemporary artists. The museum also maintains historic pueblo ruins, a church/mission, scalp house, and several inactive kivas.

San Lorenzo Feast Day VE

This two-day commemoration—August 9 & 10—gets underway with sunset dances and includes a morning Mass, procession and followed by afternoon Buffalo, Comanche or Corn Dances; ceremonial footraces; pole climb; and an arts and crafts fair.

Three Kings Day E

New tribal officers are honored on January 6 with the transfer of the Canes of Authority.

Pie Town H

Hwy 60, east of Socorro

Named for its famous pies, this town was built during the 1930s by refugees from the dust bowls of Kansas and Oklahoma.

Pilar H

Hwy 68, between Espanola and Taos

In 1795, 25 families were granted land along the Rio Grande at Pilar, then known as Cieneguilla. The Battle of Cieneguilla was fought at Embudo Mountain near here in March 1854. A large force of Utes and Jicarilla Apaches inflicted heavy losses on 60 dragoons from Cantonment Burgwin near Taos.

Pinos Altos ▣

7 miles northeast of Silver City on Hwy 15

Ghost town. Once inhabited by the Apache Indians, until the white man decided to mine gold — very cautiously in the 1860s. The town never boomed because the Apaches made the enterprise so hazardous. After the Indian threat finally diminished, silver, copper, lead and zinc also figured in this town's mining history until the 1920s. Today, shops occupy the old stores and some of the mine superstructures can be seen in the nearby mountains—a very pleasant spot on the edge of the Gila National Forest. This area is on both the State and National Registers.

Grant County Art Guild/Hearst Church ▣

The adobe Methodist-Episcopal church was built with Hearst money in 1898 and now houses the Grant County Art Guild. Funeral hearse of Pat Garrett (who killed Billy the Kid) and other horse drawn vehicles are displayed here.

Judge Roy Bean Store Site ▣

Probable site of the store operated by Roy Bean and his brother Samuel in the 1860s before the Civil War.

McDonald Cabin ▣

John McDonald, an old Indian fighter, was reportedly in this area as early as 1851, before the discovery of gold or founding of the town. His log cabin is probably the oldest in Grant County.

Pinos Altos Museum ▣

388-5921

This museum features local artifacts in its history exhibits.

Pinos Altos Opera House ▣

This opera house, built in 1969, captures the flavor of an old west opera house and includes elements from historic buildings of the area, including the late Hudson Street red-light district of Silver City. Building includes many excellent artifacts and photos.

Santa Rita Del Cobre Fort & Trading Post ▣

This three-quarter scale reproduction was completed in 1980 and is a fort built at Santa Rita copper mine in 1804 to protect the area from Apaches. It was renamed Fort Webster in 1851.

Placitas

The Placitas Artists Series ▣▣▣

P.O. Box 944, 87043
764-9857

This is a non-profit organization sponsoring seven concerts and art exhibitions during the year in the Presbyterian Church in the village of Placitas. The Series also sponsors outdoor concerts in the summer. The Helios Quartet is Placitas' resident string quartet, with guest artists accompanying the Helios in several of the season's performances. The Series has an education purpose—to promote the work of local artists and musicians; to do outreach programs in the schools; to commission work from New Mexican composers; and to make available to the area the music of Latin American composers.

Pojoaque Pueblo ▣

16 miles north of Santa Fe
Intersection Hwys 285 and 4
455-3460

One of the smallest of the Tewa-speaking tribes. The population disappeared for over a decade as a result of the influenza epidemic of 1918; it was reestablished in 1932. There are structures dating back to before the invasion of the Spanish in the site of the original pueblo, although there is no longer a definable village. The first pueblo to elect a woman governor, there are also many women tribal council members. Arts are pottery, embroidery, silversmithing and beadwork. The principal festival is "Our Lady of Guadalupe Day," held annually on December 12th.

Our Lady of Guadalupe Feast Day ▣

Midmorning Mass and procession. Buffalo, Butterfly, Bow and Arrow and Comanche Dances on December 12.

Pojoaque Pueblo Library ▣

Rt. 1 Box 71
Santa Fe, 87501
455-3612

Portales

Anderson Basin (Blackwater Draw)   H

This is an archaeological site where remains of Clovis Man and Folsom Man were discovered. The sites turned up artifacts, campsites, killsites, and well-preserved Pleistocene animal remains, ie. mammoth bison, sloth, dire wolf. The site is on the State and National Registers.

Bank of Portales   H

123 Main Street

Built in 1902-03, this is Portales' least altered commercial building. Therefore, it retains that turn-of-the-century, brick-style, railroad town-look. The building is on the State and National Registers.

Blackwater Draw Museum   M

Hwy 70, 7 miles north of ENMU
P.O. Box 2029, 88130
562-2254

This multifaceted museum focuses on archaeological collections of Paleo-Indian and archaic material from the nearby Blackwater Draw site. It is primarily a study and research facility. However, visitors are welcome.

Buchanan Hall   P

Eastern New Mexico University
562-2376

Campus facility for performing arts events.

Golden Library   L

Eastern New Mexico University, 88130
562-2624

The library also features a visual arts gallery in the Runnels Room.

Heritage Days   V E

City Park
356-8541

This large annual festival celebrates the western heritage in an authentic, "Old West" atmosphere. Festivities include a rodeo, parade, barbecue, dance, an arts and crafts fair, and entertainment on the square in Portales. Late May.

High Plains Guest Artist Series   P

ENMU School of Music
Station 16, 88130

562-2561

Miles Museum   M

Eastern New Mexico University
P.O. Box 2029, 88130
562-2351

Ethnographic collections of Plains and Puebloan material;exhibits from prehistory to Spanish conquest.

Natural History Museum   M

Eastern New Mexico University
P.O. Box 2289, 88130
562-2723

Natural History Museum; 9,000 specimens of mammals; 5,000 specimens of reptiles and amphibians; 600 specimens of birds; 10,000 specimens of fish; aquatic and terrestrial ecology.

Paleo-Indian Institute   M L

Eastern New Mexico University
P.O. Box 2154, 88130
562-2303

Archeology; anthropology; paleontology; collections housed in branch museums; 1,000 volume library, pertaining to Paleo-Indians and paleontology.

Peanut Valley Festival   V E

356-8541

Held during October harvest season of the world famous Valencia Peanuts. Approximately 95 percent of these peanuts are raised in Roosevelt County and are shipped all over the world. The Festival includes arts and crafts, food booths, peanut olympics, health fair, peanut food fair and entertainment.

Portales Public Library   L

218 S. Ave. B, 88130
356-3940

Roosevelt County Fair   E

County Fairgrounds
356-8541

Held in late August.

Roosevelt County Museum

Eastern New Mexico University
Station No.30, 88130
562-2592

A diverse collection of articles from the late 19th
and early 20th centuries including firearms,
kitchen utensils and an 1896 Sears catalog. Art,
early settlers, ethnology, folklore, archives,
costumes, and pioneer photographs.

University Theatre Center P

ENMU campus
562-2711

Many musical and theatrical performances are
scheduled throughout the year.

Radium Springs

Fort Selden State Monument M H

16 miles north of Las Cruces
via I-25 and Hwy 85
526-8911

This fort, now visible in extensive adobe ruins, was
the boyhood home of General Douglas MacArthur
whose father commanded the post from 1884-1886.
Exhibits describe the soldiers' often harsh life at
this frontier fort. On weekends, a living history program is offered as rangers demonstrate the soldiers' arms and equipage from the period 1865-1888.
Leasburg State Park campground adjoins the
monument. Fort Selden is on both the State and
National Registers. As a State Monument, Fort
Selden is a part of the Museum of New Mexico,
administered by the Office of Cultural Affairs.

Ranchos de Taos

Fort Burgwin Research Center M H L

Hwy 518, south of Ranchos de Taos
P.O. Box 300, 87557
758-8322

Reconstructed 19th Century military fort and prehistoric 13th Century pueblo. This is an academic
campus of Southern Methodist University, with
public lectures every Tuesday night in June, July
and August. Archeological excavation tours are
available if arranged well in advance.

Ranchos de Taos Plaza H

Plaza and vicinity

Established in 1779, the plaza is enclosed by about
20 buildings of frame and adobe, surrounding the
historic mission church of San Francisco de Asis,
built in 1803. The church is the most photographed
and painted church in America, and maybe the
world. It features outstanding "reredos" (altar
screens) and "retablos" (painted images of saints).
The plaza is on both the State and National
Registers.

San Francisco de Asis Church H

Plaza
758-2754

Built in 1815 by Franciscans, it is the most painted
and photographed church in the United States. It is
an outstanding example of adobe mission architecture. This church continues to be a place of wor-
ship and an integral part of the community. The
church enjoys a place on both the State and
National Registers.

Taos Hispanic Arts Council A

P.O. Box 366, 87557
758-1213

Raton H

445-3689

Once the Willow Springs freight stop on the Santa
Fe Trail, the town of Raton developed from A.T. &
S.F. repair shops established when the railroad
crossed Raton Pass in 1879. Valuable coal deposits
attracted early settlers. Nearby Clifton House was a
stagecoach stop until the Trail was abandoned after
1879.

Arthur Johnson Memorial Library L

244 Cook Ave., 87740
445-9711

Friends of Raton Anthropology O

P.O. Box 10, 87740
445-8226

Raton Arts and Crafts Show and Fair V

Ripley Park
445-3689

This juried show and arts & crafts fair features the
work of New Mexico and out-of-state artists. Held
in mid-August.

Raton Arts and Humanities Council Ⓐ Ⓥ Ⓟ

P.O. Box 774, 87440
445-9652

The Council sponsors a performing arts season at Raton's historic Shuler Theater—October through May; a Hispanic Arts season; humanities presentations and the "Old Pass Gallery," representing area visual artists.

Raton Downtown Historic District Ⓗ

First Street vicinity

Raton Downtown Historic District includes a five-city-block area containing the town's original business section extending west from the railroad track along First, Second and Third Streets. Most of the other buildings remaining within the district today were put up during the late 19th and early 20th centuries, to house a wide variety of hotels, saloons, stores, warehouses and railroad facilities. The district is on both the State and National Registers.

Raton Museum Ⓜ Ⓗ

216 S. First Street, 87740
445-8979

History and art museum—artifacts of local and regional interest pertaining to ranching, coal mining, railroading, and pioneer life; original art by New Mexico artists; large photo collection; housed in 1906 Coors Building. Programs include lectures, permanent and temporary exhibits and a visiting scholar program.

Raton Pass Ⓗ

north of Raton
445-3689

This important pass on the Mountain Branch of the Santa Fe Trail was used by Brigadier General Stephen Watts Kearny for his 1846 invasion of New Mexico, and by the Colorado Volunteers who defeated the Confederates in 1862. Richens L. "Uncle Dick" Wooten operated a toll road from 1866 to 1879, when the Santa Fe Railroad crossed the pass. The site is on both the State and National Registers.

Santa Fe Trail Rendezvous Ⓔ

445-3689

Events include a mountain man rendezvous, black-powder shoots, tomahawk and knife throwing, and a tepee village. Held in mid-June.

Shuler Auditorium Ⓗ

133 North Second Street

This auditorium theater was considered one of the finest theaters in the Southwest when it was constructed in 1915 during the mayoral term of Dr. J.J. Shuler. It was used extensively for plays, other performing arts, as well as community meetings and events. The facility was restored in the early 1980s and enjoys a place on the State Register of Cultural Properties.

Sugarite Canyon State Park Ⓗ

10 miles northeast of Raton
via Hwys 72 and 526

Historic exhibits, lakes, visitor center, and campsites. The park's visitor center describes early mining activities in the area.

Willow Springs Ⓗ

445-3689

In 1861, the U.S. Army established a government forage station here by a small spring. A well was dug, and the station became a water stop for Barlow and Sanderson stagecoaches. With the arrival of the railroad in 1879 and the founding of Raton, the station was incorporated into the new town and eventually was razed.

Rayado Ⓗ

between Cimarron and Springer

Rayado was the first permanent colony in the area. The settlement was used as a rest stop and trading area along the mountain branch of the Santa Fe Trail. In 1929 it came into the possession of the Tulsa oilman, Waite Phillips, who donated the property to the Boy Scouts of America in 1941, when it became the southeastern corner of Philmont Scout Ranch. Kit Carson Museum is located in the Rayado district, and Rayado village is available for exterior viewing. The village consists of a chapel (1902), Maxwell-Abreu home and outlying buildings (1848), and a chapel east of the highway. The road to Rayado was built in the ruts of the Old Santa Fe Trail. The district is on the State Register.

Red River   ⊞

Red River is an excellent example of a pioneer mining settlement in the Rocky Mountains, with structures dating from the 1880s and 1890s. Of special interest are the Red River Schoolhouse and Miners Hospital buildings, constructed in 1914-15 during the final stage of mining prosperity in Red River City. The district is on both the State and National Registers.

An Old Fashioned Christmas in November   ⊞

754-2366

Tree lighting, square dancing, madrigal singers in late November.

Aspencade Celebration   ⊻⊞

754-2366

Art show, square dance, German wurstfest in early fall.

Gold Rush Days   ⊻⊞

754-2366

Music, arts and crafts, square dancing, chile cook-off on the last weekend in May.

Red River Public Library   ⊔

P.O. Box 1020, 87558
754-2272

Red River Summer Melodrama Season   ⊞

Mine Shaft Theater, Red River Inn
754-2930

Series runs in June—Wed., Sat.; July-September—Wed., Thurs., Sat., Sun.

Tall Pines Museum   ⊞⊞

Tall Pine Resort
P.O. Box 567, 87558
754-2241

Local history, mining exhibits housed in a historical cabin built during the region's early mining days.

Reserve

Reserve Village Library   ⊔

P.O. Box 587, 87830
533-6276

Rio Rancho

Rio Rancho Public Library   ⊔

3900 Southern Blvd., 87174
892-1717

Roswell   ⊞

Roswell was a watering place for the Pecos Valley cattle drives of the 1870s-80s. It was incorporated in 1891 and is the seat of Chaves County, named for Col. J. Francisco Chaves, Civil War soldier and delegate to the U.S. Congress from the Territory of New Mexico. In the 1930s, Dr. Robert Goddard conducted experiments in liquid fuel rocket flights here.

Castano de Sosa's Route   ⊞

Hwy 70, northeast of Roswell

In 1590-91 Gaspar Castano de Sosa, a Portuguese by birth, took an expedition up the Pecos River in an attempt to establish a colony in New Mexico. His venture was a failure, but it led to a permanent settlement under Don Juan de Onate in 1598. Castano de Sosa passed near here in the winter of 1590.

Chaves County Historical Museum   ⊞⊞

200 N. Lea, 88201
622-8333

Located in the 80 year-old former home of J.P. White, this history museum has set about to interpret the history of southeastern New Mexico, with particular emphasis on the Pecos Valley, 1865-1940. The facility houses a library and archives with papers of some 125 local individuals and businesses, as well as an extensive photography collection.

Chaves County Historical Society   ⊡

200 N. Lea, 88201
622-8333

Chisum Trail   ⊞

Hwy 70/380, west of Roswell

Sometimes confused with the Chisholm Trail from Texas to Kansas, the Chisum Trail was used by New Mexico rancher John S. Chisum to supply cattle to the Indian agencies in Arizona. In 1875, Chisum sent 11,000 head over this route, which winds from Roswell to Las Cruces, then roughly follows modern I-10 west to Arizona.

Chisum's South Spring Ranch   H

Hwy 2, south of Roswell

In 1875, John S. Chisum, the "Cattle King of the Pecos," made this the headquarters of a cattle ranching empire which extended for 150 miles along the Pecos River. Ranch buildings are on the State Register of Cultural Properties.

Eastern New Mexico State Fair   E

Southeastern New Mexico State Fairgrounds
623-9411

Livestock and agricultural displays, rodeo, parade, carnival, dances. Week-long event held yearly in late September.

Festival in the Park   V E

Cahoon Park
624-6720

Held in mid-July.

General Douglas L. McBride Museum   M

New Mexico Military Institute
P.O. Box J, 88201
624-8221

Military history museum—dedicated to the historical preservation of the New Mexico Military Institute and US military history, specifically the contributions of NMMI graduates in US military conflicts. The museum's collections include firearms, static displays (M-42 Duster), uniforms, insignia, decorations. There is also a research library, photographic archives. Group tours are available. Exhibition of the Howard Cook Guadalcanal paintings and Peter Hurd paintings.

New Mexico Military Institute Historic District   H

NMMI Campus

The campus of the Military Institute in Roswell—built about 1909 through 1936—shows an amazing quality and coherence of architecture and campus planning. The historic campus features a single, consistent "modified Gothic Revival style," complete with symmetrical quadrangles and formal axes. This campus is on both the State and National Registers.

Spectacular Air Show New Mexico   E

Roswell Industrial Air Center
623-5906

This annual air show attracts nearly 50,000 people, and features such attractions as vintage crafts and the U.S. Army's Golden Knights. Held annually in May.

Roswell Artfaire   V

623-5695

Held each year in late April.

Roswell Community Concerts   P

623-5695

Roswell Community Little Theater   P

1101 N. Virginia
622-1982

This is an amateur company that produces five plays each season, running September through early June. One play is produced every six to seven weeks, with five performances of each production.

Roswell Fine Arts League   A

P.O. Box 2928, 88201
623-9556

Roswell Museum and Art Center   M L

100 West 11th Street, 88201
624-6744

Art and science museum; extensive collection of New Mexican and Southwestern art; Peter Hurd collection of paintings and prints; Robert H. Goddard rocket collection; Witter Bynner Oriental Collection; Rogers Aston Gallery of Indian and Western art; anthropological material from Blue Mound Excavation; archeological and ethnological collection of Southwestern Indian art; 2000 volume library. Group tours, studio classes, outreach to local schools, guest lecture series and films. The Goddard rocket collection is on the State Register.

Roswell Public Library   L

301 N. Pennsylvania Ave., 88201
622-3400

Roswell Symphony Orchestra   P

P.O. Box 2425, 88201
623-5882

Roy

Chicosa Lake State Park   H

Hwy 120, northeast of Roy

Goodnight-Loving cattle trail stop, visitor center, campsites. Fishing for rainbow trout. This natural lake was a favorite watering stop on the Goodnight-Loving cattle trail. Facilities include historic exhibits.

New Goodnight Trail   H

Hwy 120, east of Roy

Charles Goodnight, the great Texas cattleman, used the Trinchera Pass branch of the Goodnight-Loving Trail until 1875. In that year, he blazed this trail northward from Fort Sumner, passing near Tucumcari and Clayton. This was the last trail created by Goodnight, marking the end of his operations in New Mexico.

Ruidoso   H

Originally known as Dowlin's Mill, the town was located on the Chisum Trial which ran from the Pecos River to Arizona. By 1885 it had attracted a store, blacksmith shop and a post office which was named Ruidoso after the local stream. Several incidents of the Lincoln County War occurred here, including the murder of Paul Dowlin in May 1877.

Aspenfestival   V E

257-7395

New Mexico State Marching Band Contest, New Mexico State Open Chili Cook-Off, arts and crafts fair, bicycle race. Held in early October.

Blazer's Mill   H

Hwy 70, south of Ruidoso

An early fight in the Lincoln County War occurred near this sawmill on April 5, 1878, when several men of the McSween faction, including Dick Brewer and Billy the Kid, attempted to arrest Buckshot Roberts. Roberts and Brewer were killed, and two others wounded, in the battle that followed.

Christmas Fair   V

257-7395

Held annually in November.

Hubbard Art Award   V

1-800-622-6023

Juried fine arts award.

Old Mill, Ruidoso   H

Sudderth Drive

An old grist mill built in 1853 and called Dowlin's Mill. It once housed a post office and a roadhouse where visitors included Black Jack Pershing and Billy the Kid.

Ruidoso Art Festival   V

257-7395

In addition to more than two dozen resident artists, some well known national artists are represented. The Festival which includes related workshops is sponsored by the Chamber of Commerce each summer during late July.

Ruidoso Little Theater   P

Ruidoso Financial Center Road
258-3206

Ruidoso Public Library   L

Sudderth and Junction Road
P.O. Box 3539, 88345
257-4335

St. Joseph's Mission   H

Hwy 70, south of Ruidoso

Father Albert Braun, who directed the construction of the remarkable mission church of St. Joseph, served as chaplain in both World Wars. He first came to Mescalero in 1916, and later built this stone church in memory of Americans killed in World War I. It took him almost 20 years to complete, and was dedicated in 1939.

San Antonio   H

I-25, south of Socorro

In the mid-1800s San Antonio was the last outpost on the Camino Real before the Mesilla Valley to the south. Today it is known as the birthplace of Conrad Hilton and the site of the first Hilton Hotel, located in his family's adobe house near the train station.

Carthage-Tokay-Farley   H

Hwy 380, east of San Antonio

Important coal-mining towns from the 1880s to 1925 when the mines closed. Originally developed by the Santa Fe Railroad and later operated by the Carthage Fuel Company mainly to fire the Kinney brick kilns in Albuquerque. Farley was a limestone quarry. The Hilton Mine belonged to the father of Conrad Hilton.

Hilton Bar at the Owl Bar H

The front bar in New Mexico's favorite hamburger joint—the Owl Bar in San Antonio—was originally located in the Hilton Mercantile Store during the early 1900s. Hilton was the father of Conrad Hilton of hotel fame. When the mercantile burned to the ground in 1945, devoted citizens of San Antonio saved the bar and moved it to its present location in the Owl Bar. The bar is on the State Register of Cultural Properties.

San Antonio Fiesta E

835-0470

Held each year in mid-June.

San Cristobal

D.H. Lawrence Ranch and Shrine H

near Taos

Home of the famous writer and sometime painter. Owned by the University of New Mexico in Albuquerque and used for their seminars. Only the shrine, built for Lawrence by his wife, Frieda, is open to the public. The Kiowa Ranch was given to D.H. Lawrence and his wife in 1924-25 by Mabel Dodge Luhan. Frieda continued to live at the ranch after her husband's death. In 1934 she built a shrine for Lawrence's ashes. Aldous Huxley was among the many visitors to the ranch.

San Felipe Pueblo H

30 miles northeast of Albuquerque off I-25
867-3381

San Felipe is one of the most culturally conservative of all the Keresan-speaking people, stubbornly retaining their traditional religion and customs despite relentless pressures from the outside world. Although outsiders generally are not encouraged to visit the pueblo, the pueblo does welcome visitors at certain times of the year. San Pedro's Day festival is a popular event in June, but the Green Corn dances in May are the main attraction to outsiders and other pueblo people. Hundreds of men, women and children, dressed in traditional costume, dance throughout the day, accompanied by a male chorus. The unique feature of the pueblo, and the center of attraction on feast days, is the huge sunken bowl of the plaza, three feet below the level of the surrounding space. Used for centuries for ceremonial occasions, it has been worn away until today it is an ideal stage for the colorful spectacles. The mission church appears much today as it did during the 18th Century. Pueblo is on the State Register of Cultural Properties.

Candlemas Day E

Buffalo Dance on February 2.

Easter Celebration E

Mass, procession and dances.

San Felipe Pueblo Feast Day E

Huge all-day Corn Dance on May 1.

San Felipe Pueblo Library L

P.O. Box A, 87001
867-4693

Three Kings Day E

Ceremony of the transfer of the Canes of Authority, honoring new tribal leaders on January 6.

San Geronimo H

Forest Rd. 18 & Tecolote Creek
2 miles southwest on Hwy 283

Resembling a ghost town, the group of 26 weathered adobe, rock and log buildings that now comprise the village was once a thriving village of several hundred buildings. In the 19th century it was one of the largest and most prosperous trade centers in the eastern Sangre de Cristo Mountains, situated on a branch of the Old Santa Fe Trail. The villagers retain their early agricultural customs, irrigating crops in the creek bottom by means of the acequia madre (mother ditch), and grazing animals in the hills of the valley. As practiced in the Hispanic land grants, the traditional communal land use provoked fierce Spanish-American conflict in New Mexico. San Geronimo played a significant role in political and social history as headquarters of Las Gorras Blancas (The White Caps), one of the most important late 19th century protest movements in the Southwest. The district is on both the State and National Registers.

San Ildefonso Pueblo H

20 miles north of Santa Fe; Hwys 285 to 4
455-2273

San Ildefonso is one of the best-known New Mexico pueblos because of the famous black-on-black pottery which originated there, and which was revived in the 1920s. The potter Maria Martinez has long been known by world-wide collectors, and other potters and watercolor painters have come to the attention of the public as well. The San Ildefonso people have lived in the present site since before 1300 A.D. A particularly important festival is the Buffalo-Deer Dance, performed on San Ildefonso's feast day. Other dances are held in June, July and September. The pueblo is on both the State and National Registers.

Black Mesa H

This 1,000 foot mesa was the site where San Ildefonso warriors held off De Vargas in 1694. Located on San Ildefonso Pueblo land, it is sacred to the people.

Dances to Commemorate the Christmas Season E

Matachinas Dance.

Easter Celebration E

Mass, procession and dances.

Eight Northern Indian Pueblos Artist and Craftsman Show V

Traditional and contemporary Indian arts and crafts. Over 600 North American Indian artists and craftsmen sell their work at 300 booths. Food booths. Traditional Pueblo and Plains dances between 11 a.m. and 4 p.m. Scheduled for the third Saturday and Sunday in July annually.

New Year's Day Celebration E

Mass, procession and traditional dances.

San Antonio Feast Day E

Corn Dance on June 13.

San Ildefonso Pueblo Community Library L

Route 5, Box 315A
Santa Fe, 87501
455-2424

San Ildefonso Pueblo Feast Day E

Firelight Buffalo and Deer dances and church procession in the pueblo plaza. Midmorning Mass, procession; Buffalo, Deer and Comanche dances. January 22-23.

San Ildefonso Pueblo Museum M

Route 5, Box 315-A
Santa Fe, 87501
455-2424

This museum features contemporary and traditional pottery, paintings and other artifacts, emphasizing the rich history of San Ildefonso Pueblo.

Three Kings Day E

Canes of Authority transferred to new tribal officers on January 6.

San Jon

Billy the Kid P

Caprock Amphitheatre
576-2455

Outdoor historical drama produced by New Mexico Outdoor Drama Association. Thursday-Saturday, mid-June through mid-August.

San Juan Pueblo H

One mile north of Espanola on Hwy 68, left onto Hwy 70
852-4400

Twenty-two years before the Pilgrims landed at Plymouth Rock, San Juan Pueblo became the site of the first capital of New Mexico, proclaimed so by the conquistador Juan de Onate. The pueblo has a well-known art center, the O'ke Oweenge Arts & Crafts Co-Operative, where visitors may watch many of the artisans working in a variety of art forms, and where jewelry, pottery, and other work from more than 100 artists may be purchased. Numerous ceremonies take place throughout the year, under the auspices of the two-part social system, the Winter People and the Summer People. The pueblo is on both State and National Registers.

Dances to Commemorate the Christmas Season   E

Sundown torchlight procession of the Virgin, vespers and Matachinas Dance on December 24. Turtle Dance on Dec. 26.

Eight Northern Pueblos Arts Council   A

P.O. Box 969, 87566
455-3144

San Gabriel de Yungue-Qwinge   H

Hwy 285, north of Espanola

This archaeological site represents an early Tewa Pueblo as well as the first European settlement established in New Mexico, founded by Don Juan de Onate. The area was occupied by Spanish colonists from 1598 through 1610. The site is on both the State and National Registers.

San Juan Pueblo Community Library   L

P.O. Box 1099, 87566
852-4400

San Juan Pueblo Feast Day   E

Midmorning mass, procession and Comanche and Buffalo Dances on June 24.

Three Kings Day   E

New tribal leaders are honored on January 6 with the transfer of the Canes of Authority.

San Lorenzo

Pinhole Resource   A

Star Route 15
P.O. Box 1655, 88057
536-9942

San Miguel   H

Southwest of Las Vegas on Hwy 3

Although this small country village was a significant settlement in the late Spanish, the Mexican and the Territorial periods of New Mexico, it is currently off any major highways, and greatly reduced in population. The atmosphere is strongly evocative of its past, and even the casual visitor is impressed with a clear notion of early 19th Century village life, since intrusions are few. The area is on both the State and National Registers.

San Rafael

south of Grants on Hwy 53

San Rafael, formerly known as El Gallo, is located at a spring near the Malpais, the great lava flow to the east. The area was visited by members of Vasquez de Coronado's expedition in 1540. In 1862, it was selected as the original site of Fort Wingate, focus of the campaign against the Navajos.

San Ysidro

Vasquez de Coronado's Route   H

Hwys 4 and 44 in Sandoval County

In the fall of 1540, Francisco Vasquez de Coronado's army traveled from Zuni to his chosen winter headquarters in the Tiguex province on the Rio Grande. Here the advance guard of the army followed the river from the Isleta area to Alcanfor, a pueblo near Bernalillo, where it camped for two winters. The San Ysidro land grant was given to Antonio de Armenta, the chief justice stationed at Jemez Pueblo, and Salvador Sandoval in May 1786. San Ysidro Feast Day is celebrated on May 15.

Sandia Park

Eames Ranch Movie Set   H

west on Hwy 22, left at Rancho Allegra subdivision

Reconstructed western town used as a location for movies. Usually off limits to the public, but the town can be seen from the roadside.

East Mountain Rendezvous   E

281-5765

A community fair begun in 1987 and held the first weekend in August. The return of old mountain men from winter trapping is celebrated with booths, music, food, etc.

Pa-ako Pueblo Ruins   H

2 miles north of San Antonito on Hwy 14

Foundations of a pueblo known to Spanish explorers.

Tinkertown Museum   Ⓜ

Hwy 536 on the way to the Crest, 87047
281-5233

A unique and unusual display of an animated, miniature, wood-carved western town, bottle glass rooms, and potter's studio set at the turn of the century. The current village has more than 6,000 objects on display.

Turquoise Trail Arts Council   Ⓐ

P.O. Box 722, 87047
281-5765

Sandia Pueblo   Ⓗ

Hwy 85, 14 miles north of Albuquerque
867-3317

The Sandia Pueblo, in the Tiwa language, is called Na-Fiat or "sandy place" or "dusty." In ancient times the pueblo people found it necessary to irrigate large areas for agriculture. Today, they are still among the most successful Indian farmers, although the acreage devoted to farming is greatly reduced. Much of their farming land is leased out to non-Indians. During the Pueblo Revolt of 1680, the Sandia people, greatly outnumbered by the Spanish, fled the pueblo and joined the Hopi tribes in Arizona. After 60 years of exile, during which time their two cultures mixed, they returned to their ancestral home: In 1748, the governor granted them their land. The only festival open to the public at the Sandia Pueblo is the San Antonio's day Corn and Buffalo Dances which take place in June. Remains of the early village of Sandia, established about 1300, then known as Nafiat, are still visible near the present church. It was one of the pueblos visited by Coronado in 1540-41.

Sandia Pueblo Feast Day   Ⓔ

San Antonio Feast Day is celebrated on June 13 with a midmorning Mass, procession and afternoon Corn Dance.

Sandia Pueblo Resource Center   Ⓛ

P.O. Box 6008
Bernalillo, 87004
867-2876

Santa Ana Pueblo   Ⓗ

Hwy 44, 8 miles northwest of Bernalillo
867-3301

The location of the original Santa Ana pueblo is unknown, for all the members of the community left or were killed during the Pueblo Revolt of 1680. After the re-conquest of the New Mexican territory by the Spanish in 1692-1694, the place known as Santa Ana pueblo was founded about eight miles northwest of Bernalillo. The people of the pueblo usually maintain two residences, one a farming community along the Rio Grande, the other a traditional home near the Jemez Creek. There is an excellent sales outlet, the Ta Ma Myia Co-Operative Association, which handles their crafts, as well as food. Please check with the governor's office before entering the pueblo area, which is generally closed except on certain ceremonial days. In June and July, the Santa Ana Pueblo conducts several ceremonial dances which are open to the public, notably the Corn Dance. The Santa Ana Pueblo, or Tamaya Pueblo, is a Keresan-speaking pueblo. Traditional arts and crafts include woven belts, pottery and wood crosses inlaid with straw. Santa Ana is on both the State and National Historic Registers.

Dances to Commemorate the Christmas Season   Ⓔ

Variety of traditional dances during Christmas week.

Easter Celebration   Ⓔ

Mass, procession and traditional dances.

New Year's Day Celebration   Ⓔ

Mass, procession and traditional dances in the afternoon.

San Juan Feast Day   Ⓔ

Corn Dance on June 24.

San Pedro and San Pablo Feast Days   Ⓔ

Corn Dance on June 29.

Santa Ana Pueblo Feast Day   Ⓔ

Morning Mass, procession and afternoon Corn Dance, on July 26.

Three Kings Day   Ⓔ

New tribal officers are honored through the transfer of the Canes of Authority on January 6.

Santa Clara Pueblo H

south of Espanola on Hwy 30
753-7330

Santa Clara is perhaps best known for its pre-historic Puye Cliff Dwellings, caves hollowed in the rock. The cliff dwellings have a 740-room pueblo ruin, a ceremonial chamber, a "Great Community House" as well as petroglyphs in parts of the dwellings. Self-guided tours are available, and a guided tour with a pueblo feast is available to visitors during the summer from April-September, Monday-Friday. Tour visitors should call five days in advance for reservations. Dances and festivals open to the public include: in June, Comanche Dances; in August, Harvest, Buffalo and Corn Dances as well as the patron saint feast day of Santa Clara on August 12. Still cameras are allowed with permit, but no movie or video cameras are permitted. The pueblo is on both the State and National Registers.

Holy Innocents Day E

Children's Dances on December 28, with Matachinas and other traditional dances on Christmas Day.

Puye Cliff Dwellings H

1.3 miles west of Santa Clara Pueblo on Hwy 5
753-7326

The prehistoric Puye Cliff Dwellings offer an extraordinary combination of 700-room pueblo ruin, ceremonial chamber, a "Great Community House," and petroglyphs. Self-guided tours are available and a guided tour with a pueblo feast is available during the summer with advance reservations. The cliff dwellings enjoy places on both the State and National Registers.

San Antonio Feast Day E

Corn Dance on June 13.

Santa Clara Pueblo Community Library L

P.O. Box 580
Espanola, 87532
753-7326

Santa Clara Pueblo Feast Day E

Midmorning Mass and procession followed by afternoon Corn and Harvest Dances on August 12.

Three Kings Day E

New tribal leaders are honored on January 6.

Santa Cruz H

Hwy 76, near Espanola

In 1695 Governor Diego de Vargas founded Santa Cruz de la Canada south of the Santa Cruz river. The town was later moved to this site north of the river. The church facing the plaza dates from the 1730s. Santa Cruz was an important stop in the Camino Real between Santa Fe and Taos.

La Iglesia y La Plaza de Santa Cruz de la Canada H

First settled in the mid-17th Century, the village of Santa Cruz is home to an extraordinary church, La Iglesia, built during the 1730s. It features thick adobe walls and a large restored "reredo," painted wooden altarscreen. The church is on both the State and National Registers.

Santa Fe

"Oldest House" H

215 E. De Vargas, off Old Santa Fe Trail

Although the exact origin of this house is unknown, it was labelled the "oldest building in Santa Fe" on the Stoner map of 1882, and a building in its approximate position appears on the Urrutia Map (circa 1760). Tree-ring specimens in some of its vigas date them as being over 200 years old. The Oldest House may be the last remnant of the Pueblo of Analco, circa 1200 A.D. The lower part of the buildings are constructed in pre-Spanish, Pueblo Indian style. This structure is on the State Register.

Acequia Madre H

Garcia and Acequia Madre Streets

Acequias, or ditches, were an important factor in Santa Fe's early history, for by cutting off the water supply from the main ditch (Acequia de la Muralla) which ran along the edge of the fortress and castle, the Indians forced the evacuation of the Spaniards from the Palace of the Governors in 1680, and by a similar strategy 13 years later, De Vargas regained its control. Little if any of that acequia remains, which ran along the north wall of the city, but the Acequia Madre, on the south side of the Rio de Santa Fe, still flows when the irrigation gates are opened, and may be seen today along the street of the same name. The acequia is on the State Register of Cultural Properties.

Archbishop Lamy's Chapel H

Bishop's Lodge Road

This modest structure was built in the foothills north of Santa Fe by the first bishop of New Mexico, John B. Lamy, in the late 1860s to serve as his private retreat. The chapel is now on the grounds of the Bishop's Lodge Resort. Chapel is on the State Register of Cultural Properties.

Architect Society House Tours E

988-8965

Occurs annually on a Sunday in mid-August. Tours of contemporary and historical houses by Santa Fe architects. Designed with the architectural education of the general public in mind and sponsored by the Santa Fe Chapter of the American Institute of Architects.

Arias de Quiros Site H

E. Palace Avenue

Captain Diego Arias de Quiros was a native of Spain who was recruited by De Vargas and campaigned with him during the Reconquest. In 1697 he successfully petitioned De Vargas for a grant of property on "the north side of the Plaza," extending from the "torreon" at the east end of the Palace to what is now the east boundary of Sena Plaza. His own house, built at the west end of the site (the approximate position of the present gas station), was sold in 1746 by his widow to Don Manuel Sanz de Garvisu, Lieut. of the Royal Presidio. Among the present buildings on the site (all of which were built no later than the middle-to-late 1700s or early 1800s) is "Prince Plaza" at 115 E. Palace Avenue, which was bought in 1879 by L. Bradford Prince, who later became Territorial Governor.

Artist Equity A

Rt. 14, Box 740a, 87505
473-5180

Arts New Mexico A

P.O. Box 1966, 87504-1966
982-4491

This is an association of arts organizations, individuals and other interested parties which encourage arts programs in education; increase preservation of the state's cultural heritage; and provide information about the arts in New Mexico.

Atchison, Topeka & Santa Fe Railway Depot - Santa Fe H

Garfield Street

This depot was constructed in 1909 in the California Mission style of architecture. This style was adapted by the Santa Fe Railway for many of its depots and hotels in the West, aimed at introducing passengers to regional architecture. Depot is on the State Register of Cultural Properties.

Banjo and Fiddle Contest P

Santa Fe Rodeo Grounds
Rt. 7, Box 115-BK, 87505
983-8315

The Annual Santa Fe Banjo and Fiddle Contest began as a modest gathering in 1974. It is now the oldest and largest festival of its kind in New Mexico, featuring two days of competition in several bluegrass and old-time music categories. Held each year on Labor Day weekend, Saturdays include contests and/or workshops in bluegrass and old-time fiddle, mandolin, guitar, hammer dulcimer, bass, folksinging, clogging, and contradancing. Saturday nights feature an "everyone's invited" jam session, and folk dance sponsored by the New Mexico Folk Music & Dance Society. On Sundays are competitions in old-time band, bluegrass band, and songwriting. In addition, the winners from Saturday perform between bands. The event is known throughout the state for the parking lot picking that goes on throughout the weekend. The weekend's events are sponsored by the Southwest Traditional & Bluegrass Music Association. It is funded in part by grants from the National Endowment for the Arts and the New Mexico Arts Division.

Barrio de Analco H

Old Santa Fe Trail and De Vargas Street area

This district surrounding the Chapel of San Miguel was occupied in 1620 by Mexican Indians who came with Franciscan missionaries, or in the train of Spanish officials. The original Chapel was built for them shortly after their arrival. In the 1680 Pueblo Revolt, when the Barrio de Analco was razed, the Indians who escaped retreated with the Spanish to El Paso, where the majority chose to remain rather than return to New Mexico after the Reconquest. By 1776, the district was occupied by married enlisted men, servants, Indians, and genizaros (mixed-race). "Analco" is said to be a Nahuatl word meaning "on the other side"—in this case the other side of the Santa Fe River. Area is on both the State and National Registers.

Behind Adobe Walls Garden Tour   ▣

selected residences in Santa Fe
983-6565

This popular showcase tour runs on selected dates in late July and early August.

Borrego House   ▣

724 Canyon Road

Although named for the socially and politically prominent Borrego Family, who owned it from 1839 to 1906, this house was built by Geronimo Lopez before 1769, the year his will was filed. In it he specified that the property consisted of "an orchard of 14 trees and farming land" as well as this house. The rooms at the rear are the most ancient; the large one across the front, with its portal supported by tapered, handmade columns, was added in the 19th century. The historic building is now a restaurant. The building is on the State Register of Cultural Properties.

Camino del Monte Sol Historic District   ▣

Camino del Monte Sol and vicinity

From New Mexico's entrance into the Union in 1912 until World War II, this area of Santa Fe was the center of a nationally known colony of artists. These artists led efforts to recreate the city's historic adobe architecture while preserving and building their own Pueblo Revival adobe homes. The district contains some of the first houses designed by John Gaw Meem, the premier professional architect of the Revival styles. The district is on the State Register of Cultural Properties.

Canyon Road   ▣

In pre-Spanish times, this street was an old Indian trail leading up through Santa Fe Canyon and the mountains to the Pueblo of Pecos. One of the older districts of the city, Canyon Road is about two miles long and is picturesquely narrow. It was the conduit down which the Indians came over the hills during the bloody Pueblo Revolt against the Spanish Colonists in 1680. The many art galleries, shops and restaurants lining Canyon Road make it a popular place for an afternoon's walk.

Center for Contemporary Arts   ▣▣

291 East Barcelona Road
P.O. Box 148, 87504
982-1338

Nationally recognized for its excellent programming, the Center for Contemporary Arts presents the work of international, national, and regionally known contemporary artists in visual arts exhibitions, nightly film screenings, dance concerts, new music concerts, performance art events, poetry readings, and video screenings.

Chefs of Santa Fe   ▣

P.O. Box 8520, 87504
471-8200

Organization focused on the culinary arts.

Christmas at the Palace   ▣

Palace of the Governors, on the Plaza
827-6474

This rich annual event brings traditional New Mexico holiday festivities to the Santa Fe community. Farolitos and luminarias light the historic Palace's portal and courtyard; biscochitos, coffee and cider are served; and storytelling and music fill the rooms of the Palace. The true saint (Claus) will be in the courtyard, with his elves, to chase evil away. Held each year in mid-December.

Cristo Rey Church   ▣

1107 Cristo Rey; upper Canyon Road
983-8528

One of the purposes of this large adobe church was to provide a fitting sanctuary for the large painted stone "reredos" (sculpted religious panel), originally commissioned by Gov. Marin del Valle in 1760 for La Castrense on the Plaza. The magnificent artwork was done by Mexican carvers imported by del Valle. The stone plaque of Our Lady of Light in the lower center portion of the "reredos" was formerly imbedded above the door of La Castrense. The church was built in 1939-40.

Cross of the Martyrs & Commemorative Walkway H

entrance: corner Paseo de Peralta & Otero Streets

A winding brick walkway to a huge white cross, that was dedicated during Fiesta de Santa Fe, September 1920, in commemoration of the Franciscans killed in the Pueblo Revolt of 1680. The cross was erected by the local Knights of Columbus and the Historical Society of New Mexico. An earlier Cross of the Martyrs stood on a hill near the Hayt-Wientge House, a familiar Victorian landmark at the north edge of downtown. The Cross played a role in various religious processions over the years.

Don Gaspar Historic District H

Don Gaspar Avenue

A residential district located south of the State Capitol Building, this area is unique in Santa Fe because of its reflection of the three phases of New Mexico architecture. First, there were traditional adobes, then the eastern American residential styles that came with the railroad, and finally the Revival styles of traditional New Mexico architecture. The bulk of the structures were built 1912-1945. This district is on both the State and National Registers.

Donaciano Vigil House H

518 Alto Street

This house, probably one-half of a larger one, was bequeathed to Donaciano Vigil by his parents in the 1830s. He was prominent in New Mexico affairs both before and after the U.S. occupation in 1846, having served as secretary to Gov. Manuel Armijo during the Mexican regime, and as Secretary of New Mexico (appointed by Gen. Kearny in 1846); as Civil Governor after the assassination of gov. Bent (1847048); and as Secretary of the Territory and Register of Land Titles (1848-50). Visitors are welcome to tour the house when the "Open" sign is displayed.

El Rancho de las Golondrinas MH

please see La Cienega for description

El Zaguan (The Passageway) H

545 Canyon Road

This charming old hacienda, with its garden, was bought in 1849 by James L. Johnson, prominent Santa Fe merchant. At that time it consisted of two rooms, with adobe walls four feet thick, but other rooms were added—a private chapel, a "chocolate room," a "treasure room," and a semi-detached room at the west to house Mr. Johnson's library. At one time the house contained 24 rooms, with servants' quarters across the street. It was renamed El Zaguan because of the long passageway running from the patio to the garden. This garden reportedly was laid out by Adolph Bandelier, and its peony bushes—imported from China over 100 years ago—are still flourishing. Two large horse-chestnut trees, planted by Johnson, are city landmarks. In 1962 the building was again purchased for preservation by El Zaguan, Inc. and one of its apartments is now an office for the Historic Santa Fe Foundation, Old Santa Fe Association, and Spanish Colonial Arts Society. The rest are private apartments. The property is on the State Register.

Ensemble of Santa Fe P

Loretto Chapel, 219 Old Santa Fe Trail
988-4640

A chamber music group with members largely drawn from the Orchestra of Santa Fe, the Ensemble performs music of the 18th through the 20th Centuries, including premieres of contemporary works. The Ensemble performances are held at the exquisite Loretto Chapel.

Estampa Flamenca P

Picacho Plaza Hotel
750 N. St. Francis Dr., 87501
982-1237

Summer performances of the Maria Benitez Spanish Dance Company begin mid-June and continue through mid-September.

Felipe B. Delgado House H

124 W. Palace Avenue

An excellent example of local adobe construction modified by late 19th century architectural detail, this house was built in 1890 by Felipe B. Delgado, socially prominent Santa Fe merchant. He had been one of the principle owners of mule-and-ox-trains operating to and from Independence, Missouri, and Chihuahua. He was a descendant of Capt. Manuel Delgado, who came here in 1778 with the Spanish Royal Army. Building is on the State Register.

Fiestas de Santa Fe   E V P

Plaza and vicinity
P.O. Box 4516, 87501
988-7575

Established in 1712 to commemorate the peaceful reoccupation of Santa Fe by Don Diego De Vargas in 1692, Fiestas de Santa Fe, is the oldest community festival in the nation. Fiestas encompasses three colorful days, blending the old with the new in festivities for all ages. There's pageantry with the Fiesta Queen and her Court, plus Don Diego De Vargas and his 17-member retinue. There are two parades, dancing, singing, arts and crafts, religious processions and regional food. Fiestas begins the Friday after Labor Day with the spectacular burning of Zozobra (Old Man Gloom), the most distinctively Anglo contribution to the 277-year-old Fiesta. At least 50,000 people turn out annually at dusk to see the 40-foot-tall-effigy burn and thus "dispel the sadness of the past year." After the burning, the celebration moves on to the Plaza, where festivities continue through the weekend, with features including a popular children's pet parade and an historical/hysterical parade.

Fogelson Library Center   L

College of Santa Fe campus
St. Michael's Drive, 87501
473-6577

Footsteps Across New Mexico   E

211 Old Santa Fe Trail
Inn at Loretto
982-9297

Historical theater: multi-media presentation on New Mexico and its prolific past. Admission charge. Open daily, year-round.

Governor's Gallery   V

State Capitol, 87503
827-3017

Art gallery. Temporary art exhibits; annual Governor's Award for Achievement in the Arts; public openings.

Greer Garson Theater   P

College of Santa Fe campus
St. Michael's Drive, 87501
473-6511/6439

Some of Santa Fe's most enthusiastic theatrical performances are held at the beautiful Greer Garson Theater facility. The College of Santa Fe's Department of Performing Arts offers at least four productions per year, five performances each.

Guadalupe Feast Day at the Santuario   E

100 Guadalupe
988-2027

Begins at 6 a.m. on December 12.

Guadalupe Historic Foundation   O

Santuario de Guadalupe
100 Guadalupe Street, 87501
988-2027

The Guadalupe Historic Foundation, a non-profit corporation, administers the Santuario de Guadalupe as a "living preservation." Events in music, drama, art, education and religion are held at the Sanctuary.

Historic Preservation Division   O

224 E. Palace Avenue
P.O. Box 2087, 87504
827-8320

This Division identifies, preserves and protects New Mexico's archaeological, architectural and historic resources. It places significant cultural resources on state and national registers and administers federal and state tax incentive programs. It also manages development grants for the preservation of historic structures. The Historic Preservation Division is a part of the State Office of Cultural Affairs.

Historic Santa Fe Foundation   O

El Zaguan
545 Canyon Road
P.O. Box 2535, 87501
983-2567

Formed in 1961 to complement The Old Santa Fe Association; its primary purpose is to help preserve the unique buildings of Santa Fe which still remain standing from the rich and colorful past.

Historical Society of New Mexico   O

P.O. Box 5819, 87502

Encourages a greater appreciation and knowledge of New Mexico's architectural and cultural heritage. Education, publicity and preservation programs. Publishes a newsletter and books, and presents special activities and events. The Society offers advisory services upon request. Founded in 1859.

History Library/ Museum of New Mexico   L

Washington Avenue
P.O. Box 2087, 87504
827-6470

This is a history library associated with the Museum of New Mexico's Palace of the Governors history museum in Santa Fe. The library is noted for its extraordinary collections of Southwest and Spanish Colonial material; New Mexican history; Adolph Bandelier Papers.

IAIA Learning Resource Center/Library   L

IAIA campus
St. Michael's Drive, 87501
988-6670

Institute for Spanish Arts   A

P.O. Box 8418, 87504
983-4234

Institute of American Indian Arts Museum   M

1369 Cerrillos Road, 87501
988-6281

Exhibits the largest collection of contemporary Native American art in the nation. The Museum features alumni exhibitions and special shows drawing on American Indian work from around the country. The 8000-piece collection of paintings, sculptures, prints, photography, jewelry, traditional arts, textiles and costumes includes work of IAIA students since 1962 and works of leading Indian artists from across the country. Museum resources include a large collection of photographs of Indian groups and color slides of Indian art; video library on Indian art and culture; resource files on tribal museums and Indian biographical materials.

James A. Little Theater   P

New Mexico School for the Deaf campus, Cerrillos Road
827-6712

Facility for a variety of performing arts throughout the year.

La Bajada   H

I-25, south of Santa Fe

La Bajada, or "the descent," marks the division between the Rio Arriba, or "upper river," and the Rio Abajo, or "lower river," sections of New Mexico. This steep and dangerous grade was long an obstacle to caravan traffic going from the Rio Grande Valley to Santa Fe.

La Castrense (site)   H

68 E. San Francisco Street

The finest church of 18th century New Mexico, built in 1760, stood on this site—the chapel of "Our Lady of Light," or "La Castrense"—a military chapel under both Spanish and Mexican rule. After U.S. occupation in 1846 it was used as an ammunition storehouse until Donaciano Vigil led opposition of such use of it, and the government turned it over to Bishop Jean Baptiste Lamy in 1851. For seven more years it was used as a chapel, but was sold to Simon Delgado and partially demolished to make room for shops. Its large stone "reredos" is now housed in the Church of El Cristo Rey.

Laboratory of Anthropology   M H

708 Camino Lejo
P.O. Box 2087, 87504
827-8941

The Lab's collection includes more than 50,000 Indian artifacts. This anthropological and archaeological research facility offers a comprehensive book collection on all aspects of the Southwest—as well as a consulting staff with expertise in archaeology and ethnology—to members of the public doing research in these areas. Small exhibits within this gracious example of Spanish Pueblo Revival architecture, designed by Santa Fe architect John Gaw Meem, are periodically displayed. The Lab's prestigious collections are showcased for the public in the nearby Museum of Indian Arts and Culture. The facility is a part of the Museum of New Mexico, administered by the Office of Cultural Affairs. The Lab is on both the State and National Registers.

Las Posadas   E

Plaza/Palace of the Governors
827-6463

Las Posadas is the traditional reenactment of Mary and Joseph's search for shelter before Jesus' birth. The couple, with Mary riding a donkey, will circle the Santa Fe Plaza, singing for entrance at several doors. The devil makes an appearance and all doors remain closed until at last the holy ones are admitted to the Palace of the Governors courtyard. Held in mid-December.

Learning Resource Center   L

Santa Fe Community College campus, 87505
471-8200

Loretto Chapel   H

Old Santa Fe Trail and Water Street
984-7971

The Chapel of Our Lady of Light was built for the Sisters of Loretto, the first nuns to come to New Mexico. Archbishop Lamy had only been in Santa Fe a year when he requested that the Sisters of Loretto establish a school for young ladies here. The Sisters arrived in 1852. Patterned after the famous Parisian church, The Sainte Chappelle, The Loretto Chapel was begun in 1873. A popular but unsubstantiated legend concerns the chapel's extraordinary staircase, which contains two complete 360 degree turns, a double helix with no central or visible support. The chapel was nearly complete when it became apparent the choir loft upstairs would not fit. The Sister's prayers were answered when a master carpenter appeared, built the remarkable staircase, and then left mysteriously before being paid. The chapel is listed on the State Register of Cultural Properties.

Los Caballeros De Vargas   O

460 W San Francisco, 87501
982-8611

A group of men who for more than 30 years have brought historical accuracy and pageantry to many of Santa Fe's community celebrations. For example, each year during the Santa Fe Fiesta, the Caballeros stage a dramatic reenactment of General Don Diego De Vargas' reconquest of Santa Fe for the Spanish in 1692.

Mountain Man Rendezvous   E

Palace of the Governors courtyard
827-6473/6474

As a benefit for Museum of New Mexico's Palace of the Governors, the Palace Mountain Man Rendezvous and Buffalo Roast is held annually late August. During the two days before the Rendezvous, a Mountain Man Trade Fair is held in the central courtyard of the Palace. Upon rows of blankets are displayed old-style beadwork, wearing apparel, guns, knives and many other artifacts, all for sale. On Rendezvous Day, Mountain Man music, black powder shooting, blacksmith forging, knife and tomahawk throwing, lectures on the Old Santa Fe Trail, slide presentations, films and much more are held in the courtyard. The Mountain Man's Dinner caps off the event.

Museum of Fine Arts   M H L

on the Plaza
P.O. Box 2087, 87504
827-4471

The Museum shows works by outstanding artists of the Southwest, including Georgia O'Keeffe, Andrew Dasburg, Laura Gilpin, Ernest Blumenschein, Marsden Hartley, and Eliot Porter. The works of contemporary artists are also exhibited. The museum building itself is an outstanding example of the Pueblo-revival style of architecture that has become synonymous with Santa Fe style. During summer months, the world-famous Santa Fe Chamber Music Festival makes its home in the Museum's St. Francis Auditorium. The Museum is a part of the Museum of New Mexico, which is administered by the State's Office of Cultural Affairs.

Museum of Indian Arts and Culture   M L

710 Camino Lejo
P.O. Box 2087, 87504
827-8941

This newly opened museum houses exhibits and programs focusing on the Pueblo, Navajo and (Apache) Indian peoples of the Southwest. Located near the Laboratory of Anthropology—whose prestigious collections it exhibits—this museum strives to communicate the message that Indian culture in this region is strong, vibrant and growing. A Living Traditions program presents Indian artisans working in traditional and contemporary artforms—basketry, pottery, jewelry, weaving, beadwork and more. The museum is the newest member of the Museum of New Mexico, a state system which is administered by the Office of Cultural Affairs.

Museum of International Folk Art   M L

706 Camino Lejo
P.O. Box 2087, 87504
827-8350

The world's largest collection of international folk art—and the nation's most important collection of Hispanic folk art—all are here. The world-class Girard Collection occupies an entire wing with its unusual exhibition design. The newly-opened Hispanic Heritage Wing now offers a permanent exhibition space for the Museum's outstanding collection of Hispanic folk art from around the world. The museum is a family member of the Museum of New Mexico, a state-run institution administered by the Office of Cultural Affairs.

Museum of New Mexico   M H L

113 Lincoln Ave.
P.O. Box 2087, 87504
827-6460

Established more than 80 years ago, the State-operated Museum of New Mexico is a system of four museums in Santa Fe, five historic site monuments around the state, four research libraries, an artifact conservation laboratory, an archaeological research section, a statewide programs and education unit, an award-winning museum press and an exhibitions design and fabrication workshop. Museums in Santa Fe include the Palace of the Governors, Museum of Fine Arts, Museum of International Folk Art and Museum of Indian Arts and Culture/Laboratory of Anthropology. Historic site monuments include Fort Selden, Fort Sumner, Jemez, Coronado and Lincoln. This large Museum Division is administered by the State Office of Cultural Affairs.

Musica Antigua de Albuquerque   P

Please see Albuquerque for description.

National Park Service
Southwest Regional Office   H

1100 Old Santa Fe Trail, 87501
988-6340

This structure is thought to be the largest adobe office building in the United States (24,000 sq. ft.). It was constructed by the Civilian Conservation Corps in the late 1930s. The Spanish Colonial style building is beautiful, centered around an open courtyard and set in native vegetation of piñon, juniper and chamisa. It is on both the State and National Registers.

Native American Artists Association   A

535 Cordova Rd., Suite 105, 87501

New Mexico Arts Division   A

224 E. Palace Avenue
P.O. Box 2087, 87504
827-6490

The Arts Division supports programs of artistic excellence throughout the state. Matching grants are made to support nonprofit, tax-exempt art organizations through the Grants-in-Aid program. The Division also runs programs including Artists-in-Residence and Art in Public Places. The Division works closely with the National Endowment for the Arts. The Division is administered by the State Office of Cultural Affairs.

New Mexico Community Foundation   O

P.O. Box 149, 87504
982-9521

The Foundation's "Churches: Symbols of Community" program provides technical assistance and money for purchase of materials to communities wishing to preserve their historic churches.

New Mexico Council on Photography   A

P.O. Box 2406, 87504
982-2611

New Mexico Dance Coalition   P

P.O. Box 284, 87504
989-9846

Presents an annual "Choreographers' Showcase" where local choreographers present their work to an audience in a professional production.

New Mexico Music Educators
Association   A

1150 Don Gaspar, 87501
982-1091

The association promotes the advancement of music education through New Mexico's public, private and parochial schools and other educational institutions.

New Mexico Records Center & Archives   L

404 Montezuma, 87501
827-8860

The New Mexico Legislature in 1959 created the Records Center & Archives as the official facility for the receipt, storage and disposition of all inactive and infrequently used records generated by state government. Governed by the Commission of Public Records, the Center is responsible for the custody, care, preservation and disposition of all public records created by state agencies. Materials are open to the public for purposes of research.

New Mexico Repertory Theatre P

P.O. Box 9279, 87504
984-2226

This is a resident professional theater company with a mainstage season of six productions running October to May. The company features an eclectic mix of classical and adventuresome new plays. NMRT consistently presents the world premieres of Tony Award-winning Mark Medoff's new works. New on the agenda is The Millennium Project: a retrospective of 20th Century American theater during the ten seasons of the 1990s. Special programs include The Humanities and the State, the Student Matinee series, and statewide tours. For group rates, contact the Box Office Manager. Performances in Santa Fe are at the Armory for the Arts on Old Pecos Trail. The Rep also maintains an Albuquerque address at P.O. Box 789, 87103, telephone 243-2226.

New Mexico School for the Deaf Library L

1060 Cerrillos Road, 87501
827-6743

New Mexico State Library L

300 Don Gaspar, 87503
827-3800

Founded in 1929, the State Library offers a variety of services to state government agencies, libraries and citizens of the state. Services include circulation and reference, materials for the blind and physically handicapped and several bookmobiles. The State Library assists other libraries by providing consultation, grants-in-aid, training, technical assistance and coordination of inter-library loan service. The State Library is administered by the State Office of Cultural Affairs.

Old Federal Building H

Cathedral Place

This is a large government building in the Pueblo Revival architectural style—built by the U.S. Treasury Department in 1920. The building is on both the State and National Registers.

Orchestra of Santa Fe P

P.O. Box 2091, 87504
988-4640

Founded in 1974, this is Santa Fe's longest-running performance organization comprised of local professional musicians. Under the direction of William Kirschke, the Orchestra features Baroque, Classical and contemporary programs, as well as guest artists. A specific composer is featured during February concerts, and the orchestra's holiday production of Handel's "Messiah" has become a local tradition.

Padre Gallegos House H

227-237 Washington Avenue

Both sections of this house were built soon after 1857 as the residence of Padre Jose Manuel Gallegos—a colorful, controversial priest who was defrocked by Archbishop Lamy in 1852. He was one of the most important political figures in 19th century New Mexico, having served two terms in the Mexican Departmental Assembly while still a priest, and under the Americans, as an elected senator to the First Legislative Assembly in 1851. During and after the U.S. Civil War, the building was used as a rooming house. In 1872 the office of the Secretary of the Territory was located here.

Palace of the Governors M H L

Santa Fe Plaza
P.O. Box 2087, 87504
827-6474

Built in 1610 by the Spanish government, the Palace is the oldest continuously occupied public building in the United States. The adobe fortress and government center has been a home for colonial Spain, Mexico, Pueblo Indians, the U.S. Army and even the Confederacy. Bordering the downtown Plaza, the center of life in Santa Fe, the Palace's exhibits highlight nearly 450 years of European presence in the Southwest, but the star of the show is the adobe building itself. The Palace Press is also here, a living exhibit of historic hand-operated letterpresses. The Palace is a family member of the Museum of New Mexico, administered by the State's Office of Cultural Affairs. The Palace is on both the State and National Registers.

Pueblo Revolt Site H

north of Santa Fe, on Hwy 84-285

The Tewa pueblos of San Juan, San Ildefonso, Santa Clara, Pojoaque, Nambe and Tesuque were responsible for directing the 1680 Pueblo Revolt after the Spaniards captured two Indian runners at Tesuque on August 9. Joined by Taos and Picuris they formed into two divisions and on August 15 laid siege to Santa Fe.

Rainbow Warrior World Music and Arts Festival   VP

Paolo Soleri Amphitheater
989-8898

This is a transcultural environmental celebration of music, dance and storytelling as well as an international bazaar with foods, arts and crafts, children's programs, healing arts and more. Held in late August.

Randall Davey Audubon Center   MH

End of Upper Canyon Road
P.O. Box 9314, 87504
983-4609

The Center is an 135-acre nature sanctuary and historic site. Here in 1847 the U.S. Army Quartermaster built the first sawmill in the New Mexico Territory. The sawmill was later converted into a home and studio by the Santa Fe artist, Randall Davey. It is listed on both the State and National Registers of Historic Buildings. The National Audubon Society now owns and operates the site as a state office and education center. The Center is open to the public.

Recursos de Santa Fe   A

826 Camino del Monte Rey A-3, 87501
982-9301

Recursos is an educational non-profit organization specializing in professional destination management services for museum, academic, professional, and special interest groups. Recursos offers unique tours, seminars and writer's conferences focusing on the traditional and contemporary aspects of art, culture, history, literature, cuisine, and natural history of the multi-cultural Southwest and Americas.

Rio Grande Arts Co-op   A

2518 Calle Delfino, 87505
473-0643

Rio Grande Depot, Santa Fe   H

Guadalupe & Garfield Streets

The Rio Grande Depot was built in 1903 at a cost of $4497 for the Santa Fe Central Railway, a predecessor of the New Mexico Central Railway. The depot was also used by the Denver & Rio Grande and the Atchison, Topeka & Santa Fe until 1941. The building is now a restaurant.

Saint John's College Library   L

Camino Cruz Blanca, 87501
982-3691

San Miguel Chapel   H

401 Old Santa Fe Trail, 87501
983-3974

This mission church, among the oldest built in America, was constructed by the Tlaxcala Indians who came to New Mexico as servants of the Spanish soldiers and missionaries. The original structure predated the 1680 Pueblo Revolt, but the church was so severely damaged in the fighting that, when it was rebuilt in 1710, new foundations had to be laid for walls. Excavations reveal that the area surrounding the oldest church was settled as early as 1100 A.D. Five-hundred years later, part of the abandoned pueblo was rebuilt by the Tlaxcalan Indians into the first chapel. Permanent exhibits and taped tours. The chapel is on the State Register of Cultural Properties.

Sangre De Cristo Chorale   P

P.O. Box 4462, 87502
662-9717

Quality chorale ensemble music is highlighted by this 27-member group directed by Sheldon Kalberg. The group offers a repertoire of Classical, Baroque, Renaissance and Folk/Spiritual music, both a capella and with instrumental accompaniment. Fall and Spring concerts are performed at the Santuario de Guadalupe or St. Francis Auditorium, while the December performance is a Christmas Dinner Concert at St. John's College. All concerts are also offered in Los Alamos.

Santa Fe Actor's Theatre   P

430 W. Manhattan
982-8309

This theatre is dedicated to fostering the growth of the performing arts in Santa Fe. Producing director Nicholas Anthony Ballas leads the theatre with playwrights ranging from Sam Shepard to Euripides, produced year-round in a 100-seat, modular performance space in a historic warehouse in the Guadalupe district. A full spectrum of actor-training for both adults and children is also offered, ranging from improv groups to studio.

Santa Fe Arts Commission [A]

200 Lincoln Avenue
P.O. Box 909, 87504-0909
984-6707

The Commission provides leadership by and for city government in supporting arts and cultural affairs and recommends programs and policies that develop, sustain and promote artistic excellence in the community of Santa Fe. Funding for the Commission comes from three sources: The majority of income comes from a percentage of the Occupancy Tax collection and is used to contract with organizations for promotion of their local events. Proposals are rated on tourism and artistic impact. One percent of Capitol Improvement Project bonds is used to fund an Art in Public Places program. The New Mexico Arts Division and the National Endowment for the Arts provide the final funding in the form of grants for special projects.

Santa Fe Chamber Music Festival [P]

640 Paseo de Peralta
P.O. Box 853, 87504
983-2075

The Festival is a summer event of international renown, drawing on talent from around the world. Organized in 1973, the Festival performs in the beautiful, historic St. Francis Auditorium at the Museum of Fine Arts near the Santa Fe Plaza. Performances are taped by National Public Radio for broadcast nationwide.

Santa Fe Children's Museum [M]

1050 Old Pecos Trail
P.O. Box 15484, 87506-5484
989-8359

This museum offers hands-on, participatory exhibits designed to intrigue, involve, and challenge visitors of all ages. Exhibits are designed especially for children two to 12. Regular hours are Thursday-Saturday 10-5, and Sundays noon-5. Visitors should call for information on special programs.

Santa Fe Community Orchestra [P]

473-2688

Organized in 1982, this is an orchestra of energetic and accomplished amateurs, presenting three to four concerts each year. A variety of orchestral music is featured, highlighting original pieces written by local composers. Concerts are generally free and open to the public, performed at St. Francis Auditorium. Rehearsals are Thursday evenings, September through June.

Santa Fe Community Theatre [P]

142 E. De Vargas St.
P.O. Box 2084, 87504
988-4262

Founded in the 1920s, the Santa Fe Community Theater has the distinction of being the oldest theater group in the state. Approximately 8,000 people attend the regular shows, Fiesta Melodrama and one-act-series produced throughout the year. The productions include an adventurous mix of avant garde, established drama and musical comedy.

Santa Fe Concert Association [P]

P.O. Box 4626, 87502
984-8759

This is the oldest musical organization in Santa Fe. Its September through May season features international soloists and ensembles on its Distinguished Artists Series, performances for young people on its Youth Concerts, the annual Christmas Eve Specials of the Musica de Camara Ensemble as part of its Special Events, and Sponsored Events of local performers. Performances are held at the historic St. Francis Auditorium at the Museum of Fine Arts.

Santa Fe Council for the Arts [A]

1300 Luisa St., Suite 5, 87501
988-1878

The Council sponsors and presents individuals in the performing arts. Its events schedules have always been an eclectic mix of concerts (including Classical, Jazz, Avant Garde, Contemporary and Third World music). Lectures and youth workshops. While for some events admission is charged, many others are free to the public.

Santa Fe Dance Company [P]

983-9456

Performances reflecting new contemporary dance concepts are presented several times each year. A summer series highlights performing guest artists, and the company also conducts spring tours throughout New Mexico.

Santa Fe Dance Foundation   P

1504 Cerrillos Road, 87501
983-5591

This is a professional dance school specializing in classes for ages three through teens and adults. Year round classes are offered in ballet, modern and creative dance with intensive summer workshops presented by guest instructors. Annual recitals, Choreographers' Showcase, lecture-demonstrations, and a full-length original ballet, "Alice in Wonderland," are presented throughout the year.

Santa Fe Desert Chorale   P

219 Shelby
P.O. Box 2813, 87504
988-7505/2282

The Desert Chorale is well-known for its eclectic programming, bringing together music from the 16th and 17th Centuries with the music of today. The Desert Chorale performs at the acoustically-excellent Santuario de Guadalupe, mid-June through the end of August, and at Christmas. The group is comprised of 24 to 30 paid, professional singers selected during a nation-wide recruiting tour.

Santa Fe Festival Foundation   A

628 Paseo De Peralta, 87501
988-3924

This nonprofit community service organization works to enhance Santa Fe as an arts center. The Foundation annually produces the Santa Fe Festival of the Arts, a juried arts show held the third weekend in October, as well as an annual arts and crafts fair, usually held later in the fall.

Santa Fe Fiesta Council   EO

P.O. Box 4516, 87501
988-7575

Among other activities, the Council organizes each year's Santa Fe Fiesta, together with all of its year-round complimentary events, ie. selection of annual Fiesta Queen and her Court; selection of Diego De Vargas and his staff; annual Fiesta Ball, etc.

Santa Fe Gallery Association   A

P.O. Box 9245, 87504
988-4168

Santa Fe Guitar Society   P

P.O. Box 4421, 87502
984-0214

The Santa Fe Guitar Society offers a series of solo guitar performances by artists of local, regional, national and international renown. Performances are held at the Santuario de Guadalupe and other Santa Fe locations. The nonprofit Society conducts informative monthly meetings which are open to the public.

Santa Fe Indian Market   V

Santa Fe Plaza
320 Galisteo Suite 600, 87501
983-5220

Each August, more than 800 premiere Indian artisans participate in Indian Market's spectacular juried competition, the oldest and largest exhibition and sale of Indian art in the world. Held in August since 1922, Indian Market features the display and sale of handmade baskets, pottery, rugs, jewelry, drums, kachinas, sand paintings and much more. All objects presented at the Market must be genuine handcrafted Indian work. Indian Market draws huge crowds of visitors who come to see this finest single presentation of Indian arts in the Southwest. Rows of booths are set up in the streets around the Plaza. Exhibit pieces are judged in advance, and at dawn's early light on the first market day, collectors compete to put dibs on award-winning items.

Santa Fe Institute of Fine Arts   A

P.O. Box 9608, 87504
983-6157

This organization is involved in arts education.

Santa Fe Performing Arts Company and School   P

P.O. Box 579
Tesuque, 87574
473-2240

This organization offers a variety of classes for students aged eight to adult. Classes include acting, jazz, ballet, voice, mime and improvisation. An after school program starts in September and ends in May. A five week intensive summer school is held yearly at the Greer Garson Theatre and culminates with a production. The company also offers educational theatre productions for private and public schools during the academic school year.

Santa Fe Plaza   H

The heart of the city since 1610, the Santa Fe Plaza has been the site of countless historical, cultural and social events. It was in the Plaza that the Pueblo Indians revolted against Spanish rule in 1680; it was here they capitulated to General Don Diego De Vargas in 1693. For many years the Plaza served as the end of the "Old Santa Fe Trail" from Missouri, with freight wagons and laden burros keeping the dirt stirred up continuously, It also served as the end of "El Camino Real" from Chihuahua. Since its initial design, the Plaza had undergone many looks, from a utilitarian meeting place in early days, to a tree-shaded park complete with white picket fence, to an expanse of lawn crowned by a crenelated gazebo, to the lovely, lively, shaded heart of the city it is today. The Plaza enjoys a place on both the State and National Registers.

Santa Fe Powwow   E V P

Downs at Santa Fe
320 Galisteo Suite 600
983-5220

Sponsored by the Southwestern Association on Indian Affairs Inc., this is a traditional powwow (no contests) with social dancing, exhibition dancing, food, and Indian Market artists sale booths. Held in May.

Santa Fe Public Library   L

145 Washington Avenue, 87501
984-6780

Santa Fe School of Contemporary Music   P

982-3719

Student, teacher and student/teacher music ensemble groups offer a variety of jazz-oriented performances. The performance schedule, comprised mainly of exciting new compositions, is year-round at various locations. The school also presents a host of half-day summer workshops, which are open to interested visitors, by internationally known U.S. and European jazz musicians.

Santa Fe Society of Artists   A

P.O. Box 2031, 87504
438-3758

Santa Fe Summer Concert Series   P

Paolo Soleri Outdoor Amphitheater
984-6760

Held at the beautiful Paolo Soleri Outdoor Amphitheater on the Santa Fe Indian School campus, the Santa Fe Summer Concert Series brings big-name acts to Santa Fe in the summertime. More than two dozen concerts and special events.

Santa Fe Summerscene   E P

Plaza, Amelia White Park or Fort Marcy Park Amphitheater
107 Huddleson, 87504
989-8062

Santa Fe Summerscene, co-sponsored by the Santa Fe Chamber of Commerce and the City, offers a wide variety of family-oriented free entertainment for visitors and residents alike. Season consists of four major evening events, plus more than 50 evening programs and lectures, featuring local and regional personalities. The Evening Concert Series, featuring classical to rock, begins in mid-June, Tuesdays and Thursdays at 7 p.m. at either the Plaza, Amelia White Park or Fort Marcy Park Amphitheater. There is also a Noon Concert Series on the Plaza, featuring Jazz, Latin, Cajun, Bluegrass, Folk and Rock music; Tuesdays and Thursdays; June through August.

Santa Fe Symphony Orchestra and Chorus   P

P.O. Box 9692, 87504
983-3530

Founded in 1984, this full symphony orchestra performs under the direction of Stewart Robertson, September through May. Six concerts featuring classical and contemporary works are presented annually at the Sweeney Center. A festival of lectures, chamber music and a symphonic concert is held each year in March; a children's concert in February; and a free choral concert in December.

Santa Fe Trail [H]

Plaza stretching southeast of town

Colonization of New Mexico in 1598 laid the foundation for one of the most dramatic trade routes in the history of Western civilization—The Santa Fe Trail. For more than two centuries after the first colonists arrived, the only communication with the outside world was through Mexico. In 1805 Zebulon Pike began his historic trip; and after his report, pioneers from the States followed in his footsteps. James Purcell rode across the prairies from Missouri in 1805 and in 1821, Captain William Becknell, called the Father of the Santa Fe Trail, blazed the route which was to remain open and in use until the coming of the railroad in 1880. Once Mexico won her independence from Spain in 1822, traders and trappers from the east were welcome in New Mexico. Stagecoaches followed with passengers headed West to make their fortunes, or to find a home, but chiefly the old Trail was a trail of commerce. Santa Fe, where the Santa Fe Trail ended at the Plaza, was called "the City of Desire." The coming of the railroad in 1880 ended the use of the Trail.

Santa Fe Women's Ensemble [P]

982-9385

The Ensemble is comprised of 12 semi-professional singers from the Santa Fe area. They offer spring and fall seasons of classical music from all periods with occasional musical accompaniment. Their spring concerts are held at St. Francis Auditorium, while their four traditional Christmas Concert performances are conducted at the beautiful Loretto Chapel.

Santuario de Guadalupe [M][H]

100 Guadalupe Street, 87501
988-2027

Art and history museum; Archdiocese of Santa Fe collection; mural painted 1783; Italian Renaissance paintings; Mexican baroque paintings; housed in historic Nuestra Senora de Guadalupe Church, 1781. The Sanctuary contains one of the largest and finest oil paintings of the Spanish Southwest, "Our Lady of Guadalupe," dated 1783 and signed by Jose de Alzibar, one of Mexico's most renowned painters. The Guadalupe Historic Foundation, a non-profit corporation, administers the Sanctuary as a "living preservation." Events in music drama, art, education and religion are held at the Sanctuary.

School of American Research [M][O]

P.O. Box 2188, 87504
982-3584

Supports and conducts world-wide anthropological research; Research center, Indian arts collection; 7000 pieces of pottery, jewelry, basketry, paintings, textiles, costumes; ten anthropological publications per year; research archeology. Open only to researchers, members and special group visits; inter-museum loan; Native American scholarship program; Wetherhead Fellowship program; advanced seminars.

Sena Plaza [H]

E. Palace Avenue

Originally part of the Arias de Quiros lands, this property and the small patio to the west came into the hands of the Sena family, through a bequest, in 1844, to the mother of Don Jose D. Sena, a major in the U.S. Civil War, who later inherited it. After 1864, he and his family occupied sections of the house on three sides of the large central patio, with a coach house, stable, chicken house, and servants' quarters on the north. The second story on the east and north portions were added in 1927 when the building was sold and remodeled into business offices and shops. It is on the State Register of Cultural Properties.

Serenata of Santa Fe [P]

989-9662

This chamber music group of professional musicians performs an October through May concert schedule at the Episcopal Church of the Hold Faith, 311 E. Palace Avenue. June through October, they perform outdoor concerts in the little community of Madrid, just southwest of Santa Fe. The group specializes in searching out little known but outstanding works by composers ranging from classical to contemporary.

Seton Village [M][H][L]

I-25, east of Santa Fe

Ernest Thompson Seton (1860-1946), naturalist, artist, writer, authority on Indian lore, and first Chief Scout of the Boy Scouts of America, lived here during the last part of his life. The village includes his home, art collection, library and Indian Museum.

Shakespeare in the Park   P

P.O. Box 2188, 87504
988-3251

This group offers several free productions of
Shakespeare's plays throughout August and
September at an outdoor location in Santa Fe.

Something in the Air   P

P.O. Box 579
Tesuque, 87574
473-2240

This is an annual spring dance concert at the James
A. Little Theater on the campus of the New Mexico
School for the Deaf. Directed and choreographed
by Cathy Roe, the performance features a variety
of jazz and modern dance styles as well as sign
language choreography which integrates sign as an
important element in the dance.

Southwest Children's Theatre   P

1412 4th Street, 87501
984-3055

Southwest Repertory Theatre   P

982-1336

Three plays and one musical Tuesdays-Sunday in
Santa Fe, late July through mid-August.

Southwest Traditional & Bluegrass Music Association   AP

Rt. 7, Box 115-BK, 87505
983-8315

This organization's goal is to educate the public
about traditional forms of acoustic American and
Spanish music. The association sponsors an
annual winter concert and a summer series of concerts featuring local musicians. It also presents the
annual Santa Fe Banjo & Fiddle Contest each Labor
Day weekend, a two-day festival of competition
and workshops.

Southwestern Association on Indian Affairs   A

320 Galisteo, Suite 600, 87501
983-5220

This association organizes each summer's Santa Fe
Indian Market, the oldest, largest and most prestigious of its kind in the world. SWAIA also sponsors an annual Santa Fe Powwow in May.

Spanish Colonial Arts Society   A

P.O. Box 1611, 87504
983-4038

Among other activities, sponsors the annual Spanish Market, held in late July.

Spanish Market   V

Plaza and courtyard of the Palace of the Governors
983-4038

During the last full weekend of July, the Annual
Traditional Spanish Market and the Annual Contemporary Spanish Market are held on the Santa
Fe Plaza and the courtyard of the Palace of the
Governors. Many exhibitors are from the remote
villages of Northern New Mexico, and all applicants to exhibit must be at least one-quarter
Hispanic. Traditional Spanish Market's sponsoring
group, the Spanish Colonial Arts Society, narrows
their applicant list from several hundred to
between 60 and 75 exhibitors annually. The Contemporary Spanish Market, located in the courtyard of the Palace of the Governors, has space for
only 35 exhibitors, although they receive nearly
double that number of applicants. Wares for sale
include "santos," "bultos," "retablos," embroidery,
textiles, weaving, straw appliques, tinwork, filigree
jewelry, metal products and handmade furniture.

St. Francis Auditorium   P

Museum of Fine Arts, on the Plaza
827-6463

This historic theater is a part of the Museum of Fine
Arts facility. During summer months, it is home for
the world-famous Santa Fe Chamber Music
Festival.

St. Francis Cathedral   H

131 Cathedral Place
982-5619

Begun by Santa Fe's first archbishop, Frenchman
Jean Baptiste Lamy, in 1869, the Romanesque St.
Francis Cathedral is architecturally foreign to Santa
Fe's Spanish heritage. The Cathedral and the
archbishop himself were the inspiration for Willa
Cather's famous novel "Death Comes For the Archbishop." The Cathedral houses the oldest representation of the Madonna in the United States. Her
small wooden statue, known as "La Conquistadora" was brought to Santa Fe by De Vargas in 1693.
A Confraternity in her honor exists in Santa Fe,
many of whose oldest families are members. The
Feast of Corpus Christi is celebrated in June with a
noon Mass and a procession around the Plaza. The

following Sunday the statue of La Conquistadora (the Madonna) is carried through the city to the chapel. The return procession during the third week concludes with a High Mass celebrated by the archbishop.

St. Michael's Dormitory H

Old Santa Fe Trail and De Vargas Street area

When this building was erected in 1878, it was three stories high with classrooms and community room on the first two floors and a dormitory on the third. Architecturally it was typical of the 19th Century, with a tower, porticos, galleries, a veranda, and a Mansard roof. Its graceful two-story portal is one of the few remaining in Santa Fe. In 1926 the building was nearly destroyed by fire, but was saved from complete destruction by its students.

Sweeney Convention Center P

201 W. Marcy
984-6760

Many performances and cultural events are held at the Sweeney Convention Center. Call for current events. Performances include those of the New Mexico Symphony Orchestra, Santa Fe Symphony, Santa Fe Concert Association, theatrical groups, and concerts ranging from Rock and Roll to Country Western. The Santa Fe Concert Association holds free concerts for school children at the Sweeney Center when guest artists are in town. Shows include the Antique Indian Art Show, Continental Antique Shows, Antique Quilt Shows and Arts/Crafts Fairs.

The Santa Fe Opera P

U.S. 84-285; north of Santa Fe
982-3851

The internationally famous Santa Fe Opera draws music lovers from this hemisphere and from around the world. It ranks among the finest companies in the United States today. Performances are staged in a spectacular outdoor amphitheater. The building, located on the crest of a wooded hill north of the city, curves with the terrain, its roof partially open to the sky. Founded in 1957, The Opera remains under the guidance of its founder and artistic director, John Crosby, and continues to draw acclaimed singers, directors, conductors— and huge crowds. Each year's offerings are a blend of classics and innovative works by contemporary composers.

Theater at the Nifty P

Old Las Vegas Highway
984-1781

The Nifty Cafe occasionally hosts contemporary dramatic productions, as well as comedy and musical revues.

Theatre of Music P

982-2221

The Theater of Music offers northern New Mexico's most exuberant productions of Broadway musicals. The Theater will kick off its 11th season in 1990. Winter and spring productions.

Western States Arts Federation A

236 Montezuma, 87501
988-1166

A regional consortium of the arts in the West, WESTAF offers programs in the various artistic disciplines: fellowships and exhibition opportunities for visual artists; an awards program for writers and publishers in literature; and a fee support program for presenters of the performing arts. The organization's publications include "National Arts Jobbank" (bi-weekly arts employment bulletin); "Building for the Arts" on facility planning, design and construction; and "Cultural Tourism" on how the arts and tourism can work together.

Wheelwright Museum of the American Indian M L

704 Camino Lejo
P.O. Box 5153, 87502
982-4636

Originally dedicated to Navajo ceremonial art, the Wheelwright, founded in 1937, has a floor plan patterned after a Navajo hogan. The museum has expanded its original focus to include works of all American Indian cultures, including both contemporary crafts created by Native Americans all over the country, and historical pieces. This is a privately-run institution.

Winterfestival E

Santa Fe Ski Basin and in town
983-8200

A community-wide extravaganza for skiers and non-skiers alike. It includes four days of contests, prizes and entertainment ranging from the Great Santa Fe Chile Cook-off to skiing and winter sports competitions. Held in February.

Witter Bynner Foundation for Poetry Ⓐ
P.O. Box 2188, 87504
988-3251

Zona de Teatro Ⓟ
468 W. San Francisco St., 87501
989-8036

Santa Rita

Chino Mines Company Copper Mining Museum Ⓜ
Former Santa Rita townsite
15 miles east of Silver City
P.O. Box 7, Hurley, 88043
537-3381

Mining exhibits with overlook of open-pit mine. Open Memorial Day through Labor Day.

Kneeling Nun Ⓗ
Hwy 90, east of Silver City

Most famous of the many historic landmarks in the Black Range country is the Kneeling Nun. So named for its resemblance to a nun kneeling in prayer before a great altar. Many legends have grown up around the giant monolith which rests near the summit of the Santa Rita Range.

Santa Rita Copper Mines Ⓗ
Hwy 90, east of Silver City

Copper has been mined here since 1804. For five years, development by Francisco Manuel Elguea resulted in some six million pounds of copper being transported annually to Mexico City by mule train. Brief periods of activity were halted by Apache opposition until the coming of the railroad in the 1880s, when the area became a major copper producer. This area is on the State Register of Cultural Properties.

Santa Rosa Ⓗ
472-3763

The Spanish explorer Antonio de Espejo passed through this area in 1583, as did Gaspar Castano de Sosa in 1590. Santa Rosa, the Guadalupe County seat, was laid out on the ranch of Celso Baca y Baca, a politician and rancher in the late 1800s. It was named for his wife, Dona Rosa.

Fiestas de Santa Rosa de Lima Ⓔ
472-3763

Traditional celebration held during the third week in August.

Moise Memorial Library Ⓛ
208 Fifth St., 88435
472-3101

Santa Rosa Days Ⓔ
472-3763

This celebration is the traditional opening of the summer season. Because Santa Rosa has long been known for its lakes and springs, providing summer recreation and relaxation, Santa Rosa Days is a celebration for locals and visitors alike. Softball tournament, youth activities, car show, fishing derby, parade, Pecos River 10-K and 2-mile runs, entertainment, exhibitions. Held Memorial Day weekend.

Trail of the Forty-Niners Ⓗ
I-40, near junction with Hwy 84

To give gold-seekers another route to California, Captain Randolph B. Marcy and Lt. James H. Simpson opened a wagon road from Arkansas to New Mexico in 1849. Marcy's Road, although very popular with the Forty-Niners, still was never as well-traveled as the Santa Fe Trail. Here the route parallels I-40 to Albuquerque.

Santo Domingo Pueblo Ⓗ
off I-25, between Santa Fe & Albuquerque
465-2214

Life at Santo Domingo seems to have remained very traditional, even with the arrival of the white man. Crafts of pottery, jewelry and weaving supplement the income of the essentially farming community. Great emphasis continues to be placed on the religious organization, which is the core of the social structure. One of the most dramatic of pueblo ceremonials is enacted at Santo Domingo on August 4 when the feast day of their patron saint, St. Dominic, is celebrated. Santo Domingo Indians are known for their expertise as traders, and visitors who wish to own the special arts and crafts of this pueblo may be able to trade for a piece of pottery or a rug instead of purchasing it. Santo Domingo is listed on both the State and National Historical Registers.

Dances to Commemorate the Christmas Season E

Traditional dances during Christmas week.

Easter Celebration E

Mass, procession and traditional dances.

New Year's Day Celebration E

Festivities include a morning Mass, followed by a procession and traditional dances, ie. Turtle, Matachinas.

San Juan Feast Day E

Rooster Pull on June 24.

San Pedro and San Pablo Feast Days E

Rooster Pull on June 29.

Santiago Feast Day E

Rooster Pull on July 25.

Santo Domingo Pueblo Feast Day E

More than 500 Indians participate in Corn Dance on the feast day of St. Dominic on August 4.

Santo Domingo Pueblo Indian Arts & Crafts Market V

Held on Labor Day weekend.

Three Kings Day E

Transfer of the Canes of Authority, honoring new tribal leaders on January 6.

Shakespeare H

1.5 miles south of Lordsburg

Ghost town, with guided tours the second Sunday of each month. After a silver strike in 1869, a townsite was laid out at the old stage stop of Mexican Springs. Named Ralston City, a diamond swindle caused its collapse in 1874. The town was revived as Shakespeare in 1879, but the depression of 1893 closed the mines and made it a ghost town. This area is on both the State and National Registers.

Shiprock H

This area has been part of the Navajo homeland for centuries. The town of Shiprock is named for the great peak nearby, which figures importantly in Navajo legend. Early in the 20th century, Shiprock was made headquarters of the Northern Navajo Agency.

Navajo Community College Library L

P.O. Box 580, 87420
368-5291

Navajo Nation H

northwest corner of New Mexico, northeast Arizona
(602) 871-4941

The Navajo Nation is the largest Indian group in the country, with about one-third of the population living in New Mexico, the majority living in Arizona, and a few residing in southern Utah. The center for Navajo business and government is Window Rock, Arizona, near the Arizona-New Mexico border west of Gallup. Major cultural events include: Northern Navajo Fair in Shiprock annually in late September, early October, which includes Yeibichei dances along with other activities. Key ceremonials include—Night Chant, Mountain Chant, Squaw Dance. Navajos are known for their fine blankets and silverwork.

Northern Navajo Fair V E

368-4164

Rodeo, Yeibichei dances, Powwow, traditional singing and dancing, arts and crafts. Held late September, early October.

Shiprock Cultural Media Center L

P.O. Box 6002, 87420
368-5181

Shiprock Pinnacle H

southwest of town of Shiprock

In Navajo, Tse be dahi, meaning "rock with wings." The Navajos hold that it was the great bird that brought them from the North. The monument rises 1700 feet off the desert floor and is visible 100 miles away. (lava formation).

Silver City H

Silver City is located in the midst of rich mineral deposits. The Santa Rita Copper Mines, opened in 1805, were the second such mining operation in what is now the United States. A silver strike in 1870 began the commercial mining for which the area is still known. The Apache chiefs Victorio, Geronimo and Mangas Coloradas figure in the town's history.

Billy the Kid - Cabin Site H

one block north of Broadway bridge

Billy the kid spent part of his childhood here in a cabin with his mother, brother and stepfather William Antrim.

Billy the Kid - Jail Site H

304 N. Hudson

Parking lots are presently on the site of the former jail where in 1875 Billy the Kid was held for stealing from a Chinese laundry. A slender boy of 15, Billy escaped by climbing out the jail's chimney.

Billy the Kid - Mother's Grave H

Memory Lane/Silver City Cemetery

Catherine McCarty, Billy's mother, came to Silver City with her second husband, William Antrim in 1873. She died of tuberculosis in September 1874, and was buried in the town cemetery.

Black's Addition Historic District H

College, Black and Market Streets area

This was the first subdivision of Silver City, and it features a wide variety of architectural styles from Queen Anne to Territorial. Built 1870s-1920s, this is a cohesive and handsome old neighborhood. This area is on the State Register of Cultural Properties.

Blue Grass and Fiddlers' Contest P

Western New Mexico University Campus
538-3785

Held each year in mid-September.

Chihuahua Hill Historic District H

Copper, Spring and Chihuahua Streets area

This was a small Spanish-speaking community of the 1870s, featuring Spanish and Indian building styles. The district shows interesting use of dug-outs, stacking houses into a hillside by terracing. It was the original "Mexican Village" of Silver City. This district is on both the State and National Registers.

Department of Expressive Arts V P

WNMU campus
P.O. Box 680, 88062
538-6614

This department at Western New Mexico University sponsors a number of events throughout the year, including the Madrigal Feast and Program (held in early March), the Jazz Festival (late February or early March), and fall and spring theater productions (November and April).

Festival of Trees E

Church of Latter Day Saints
538-5260

Christmas tree displays in early December.

Francis McCray Gallery V

Western New Mexico University campus, 88062
538-5921

This facility presents contemporary art and varied exhibitions, as well as an annual Christmas Art Sale the second Saturday in December.

Frontier Days V E

Gough Park
538-3785

This annual event features an ice cream social at the Silver City Museum as well as entertainment, food booths, a gem and mineral show, hot air balloons, and arts & crafts. Held on July 4th.

Gila Cliff Dwellings National Monument M H

44 miles north of Silver City via Hwy 15
P.O. Box 100, 88061
534-9461

This National Monument offers a natural history museum, emphasizing the archaeology, botany, ethnology and history of the larger archaeological site which features natural cave houses of the Mogollon cliffdwellers. Site is on both the State and National Registers.

Grant County Fair E

County Fairgrounds
388-1559

Exhibits, livestock, rodeo, entertainment, food. Held each year in late September.

H.B. Ailman House   ⊞

312 West Broadway

The house, constructed in 1881, is a grand old Victorian mansion. Beginning in the 1930s, the Ailman House served as the firehouse for the Silver City Volunteer Fire Department. The bell in front of the house sounded fire alarms as well as tolled curfew for the city's youngsters. The building now houses the Silver City Museum. This structure is on both the State and National Registers.

Miller Library   🅛

Western New Mexico University campus, 88061
538-6350

Mining Days   🆅🅔

Gough Park
538-3785

Old-time storefronts, contests, food, entertainment, auction as well as arts & crafts. Held annually on Labor Day weekend.

Silver City Arts Council   🅐

P.O. Box 1830, 88062
538-2505

Silver City Historic District   ⊞

This is the original townsite of Silver City, a major mining town founded in 1870. The district features early prestigious homes, many in the Victorian style, as well as buildings in a business section characterized by locally made red brick. This area is on both the State and National Registers.

Silver City Museum   🅜⊞

312 West Broadway, 88061
538-5921

History museum—frontier Victoriana; collection of articles from early 20th century model mining town of Tyrone; Southwest Indian artifacts; historical documents and photographs. This museum is housed in the 1881 H.B. Ailman House which contains a large new gallery for changing exhibitions. Programs include workshops, lecture series, school tours and special events.

Silver City North Addition Historic District   ⊞

College Ave. area

This affluent area in Silver City contains outstanding architecture from the early 1880s when local mining was booming. Featured are beautiful mansions on wide, tree-lined streets. This district is on both the State and National Registers.

Silver City Public Library   🅛

515 W. College Ave., 88061
538-3672

Star Hotel Site   ⊞

corner of Hudson and Broadway

Billy the Kid waited tables here and lived with owners following his mother's death.

Spring Square Dance Festival   🅔🅟

Western New Mexico University
388-1773

Western New Mexico University Fine Arts Auditorium   🅟

WNMU campus
538-3785

Western New Mexico University Historic District   ⊞

WNMU campus

WNMU was developed in the early 1900s, one of the first Territorial institutions of high education and one that played a major role in the history of New Mexico education. The campus features the work of prominent regional architects—John Gaw Meem, Trost & Trost, and Charles Whittlesey, Chief Architect of the Santa Fe Railway Co. The campus is on the State Register.

Western New Mexico University Light Hall Auditorium   🅟

WNMU campus
538-3785

Located on campus in historic Light Hall, this facility is the site for chamber music, light drama programs and public meetings.

Western New Mexico University Museum [M]

Fleming Hall, WNMU campus, 88062
538-6386

This is a history museum featuring the Eisele Collection of Mimbres and Southwest Artifacts; Hinman and Harlan Photographic Collections (1870-1940); WNMU Campus Collection, photos, mementos, yearbooks (1894-present); Upton Collection of household items; White legal office collection; mining and ranching history collections; Ruben Gonzalez sculptural/collage exhibit; Mimbres storage ollas from Imhoff Cave (1000 A.D.); Gateway Station for the Gila Wilderness Area.

Socorro [H]

First seen by the Spanish in 1581 and visited by Juan de Onate in 1598. Piro-speaking Pueblo Indians reportedly supplied much-needed corn, hence the name Socorro (help in Spanish). The Church of Nuestra Senora de Pilabo del Socorro was built about 1629. Abandoned in the Pueblo Revolt of 1680, the present town was founded in 1816.

Atchison, Topeka & Santa Fe Railway Depot - Socorro [H]

706 Manzanares Ave.

This depot was built in 1880 upon the arrival of the railroad which had broad and deep impact on Socorro's development. The last passenger run through Socorro was made in 1968. The depot is on the State Register of Cultural Properties.

Bosque del Apache Fall Festival [V][E]

Bosque del Apache
National Wildlife Refuge
835-1828

Events including arts & crafts at the bosque in late November.

Chihuahua Historic District [H]

The district features structures built in the 1880s—adobe with mud plaster walls and pitched roofs. The district is on the State Register of Cultural Properties.

East Abeytia Avenue Historic District [H]

Constructed in the late 19th Century the district is a great example of New Mexico Bungalow houses. The area is on the State Register of Cultural Properties.

Espejo's Expedition on the Camino Real [H]

I-25, south of Socorro

In 1582-83, Antonio de Espejo and his party paralleled the Rio Grande north to the Bernalillo area. He was trying to learn the fate of two Franciscan friars who had stayed with the Pueblo Indians after the Rodriguez-Sanchez Chamuscado expedition returned to Mexico in 1581.

Fort Craig [H]

I-25, south of Socorro

This was the largest Civil War fort in the West. It was built in 1854 to protect travelers between El Paso and Albuquerque. It guarded the Jornada del Muerto Trail and the Rio Grande Valley. The largest Civil War battle in New Mexico took place a few miles north of the fort at Valverde on Feb. 21, 1862. Here the Confederate army of New Mexico under Henry Hopkins Sibley clashed with troops loyal to the union under Edward Canby. This battle, and the one at Glorieta which followed, decisively ended Confederate aspirations in the Southwest.

Hispanic Heritage Celebration [E]

835-4080

Held in October around Columbus Day.

Juan Nepomuceno Garcia Opera House [H]

Abeyta Ave. & California

The Garcia Opera House in Socorro is an excellent example of the Neo-Greek architecture that had flourished in Midwest towns before finding its way to the frontier. The long adobe, pitched roof building was constructed in 1886 to provide facilities for traveling operatic troupes—popular in many boom towns across the West. The opera house is on both the State and National Registers.

Macey Center [P]

New Mexico Tech campus
835-5342

Martin Speare Memorial Library Ⓛ

New Mexico Tech campus, 87801
835-5614

Mesa del Contadero Ⓗ

I-25, south of Socorro

The Chihuahua Trail passed by the large volcanic mesa on the east bank of the Rio Grande, marking the northern end of the Jornada del Muerto (Journey of the Dead Man). "Contadero" means "the counting place," or a narrow place where people and animals must pass through one-by-one.

Mineralogical Museum Ⓜ

New Mexico Tech campus, 87801
835-5420

This is an Earth sciences and mining museum with emphasis on minerals, fossils and mining artifacts. The museum features more than 1,300 specimens on display.

Old San Miguel Mission Ⓗ

303 Bernard
835-1620

This is a beautiful restored mission church (active 1615-28) with five-foot walls, carved beams and corbels. The south wall of the structure was part of the original 1598 mission. Artifacts from the mission are on display in the nearby church office, with Monday-Friday business hours. The church is on the State Register of Cultural Properties.

San Miguel Fiesta ⓋⒺ

835-0424

Arts and crafts, food booths, outdoor dances. Fiesta mass and procession on Sunday. Held in early August.

Socorro Arts Council Ⓐ

Rt. 1, Box 40, 87801
835-5525

Socorro County Fair Ⓔ

County Fairgrounds
835-0424

Parade, exhibits and a rodeo—yearly in early September.

Socorro County Historical Society Ⓞ

P.O. Box 923, 87801

Socorro Plaza (Kittrel Park) Ⓗ

Socorro Plaza—now Kittrel Park—is the center of the old town of Socorro dating from 1816. It was an important stopping place on the Chihuahua Trail as well as a significant outpost of the Spanish and Mexican authorities during the Civil War. The Socorro Plaza is on the State Register of Cultural Properties.

Socorro Public Library Ⓛ

401 Park Street, 87801
835-1114

Socorro Spring Fest ⓋⒺ

Plaza
835-0424

This annual event, usually held in mid-May, features a parade, Western street dance, and an arts and crafts fair.

State Science Fair Ⓔ

New Mexico Tech campus
835-5608

Held annually in early April.

Val Verde Hotel Ⓗ

203 Manzanares Street

This outstanding building is one of the last Spanish Mission style structures still standing designed by Henry Trost, a student of Frank Lloyd Wright. When it was built in 1919, the Albuquerque Morning Journal wrote, ". . . from the standpoint of beauty and convenience, it stands without a peer." The Val Verde is now a restaurant. The building is on both the State and National Registers.

Valverde Battlefield Ⓗ

I-25, south of Socorro

The first major battle of the Civil War on New Mexico soil occurred at Valverde in February of 1862 when a Confederate force of Texas Volunteers under General H.H. Sibley defeated Union forces commanded by Col. E.R.S. Canby stationed at Fort Craig. From here, Sibley marched north and was defeated in Glorieta Pass near Santa Fe.

Vasquez de Coronado's Route Ⓗ

I-25, south of Socorro

In 1541 an expedition from the army of Francisco Vasquez de Coronado, New Mexico's first explorer, marched south 80 leagues to investigate the pueblos along the lower Rio Grande. The group reached that part of the infamous Jornada del Muerto, now covered by Elephant Butte Lake, where the river disappeared underground.

Springer H

Located in the old Maxwell Land Grant and near the Cimarron Cutoff of the Santa Fe Trail, Springer served as Colfax County seat from 1882 to 1897. Several men were killed here in one of the late flare-ups of the Colfax County War, a dispute between land grant owners and settlers.

Colfax County Fair E

445-5381

Parades, exhibits, livestock sale, rodeo, barbecue and dances.

Dorsey Mansion H

30 miles northeast of Springer off Hwy 56

Two-story log and stone mansion built by 1800s cattleman. The structure is on both the State and National Registers.

Fred Macaron Library L

6th and Colbert
P.O. Box 726, 87747
483-2848

Point of Rocks H

Hwy 56, east of Springer

Point of Rocks was a major landmark on the Santa Fe Trail. Located in Jicarilla Apache country, it was near here that the party of Santa Fe merchant J.W. White was attacked in 1849. Kit Carson was a member of the military party organized to rescue White's wife and daughter.

Santa Fe Trail Museum and Historical Society M H O

Maxwell Street
P.O. Box 323, 87747
483-2394

This history museum features artifacts of the Santa Fe Trail and early pioneer life. The facility also offers art exhibits. It is located in a former county courthouse built in 1881.

Steins H

I-10, west of Lordsburg

This was once a bustling railroad station town supporting 1000 residents during its peak of prosperity, 1905-45. The first station at Steins was built in 1858 by the Butterfield Overland Mail Co. Steins Peak Station got its name from a mountain named for Major Enoch Stein, a member of the U.S. Dragoons who camped there. Steins pass served East and West bound wagon trains in the 1800s. The ghost town lies near Doubtful Canyon, known for its Indian massacres.

Sunspot

Sunspot Solar Observatory M

18 miles south of Cloudcroft
Forest Road 64, 88349

Telescope and other equipment to monitor the sun. Exhibits.

Taiban

Billy the Kid Outlaw Gang Headquarters Museum M O

Hwy 60-84, east of Taiban
P.O. Box 1881, 88134
355-9935

Operated by the Billy the Kid Outlaw Gang, Inc. Historical Society, this museum offers memorabilia, exhibits and 1880s paraphernalia. The Society itself is a non-profit corporation committed to the preservation, protection and promotion of "America's Most Enduring Legend;" to mark the Billy the Kid-Pat Garrett Trail throughout the heart of New Mexico; and to combat the Brushy Bill prevarications and defend New Mexico history.

Shootout at Stinking Springs E

2 miles east of Taiban
355-9925

This is a reenactment of Billy the Kid and his gang's surrender. Held in mid-December.

Talpa H

South of Taos on Hwy 518

This small community was the site of prehistoric pit houses and includes the settlement of Llano Quemado, site of excavations carried out by the Smithsonian Institution. Talpa was settled in the late 18th Century by the Spanish.

Taos H

The Spanish community of Taos developed two miles southwest of Taos Pueblo. It later served as a supply base for the "Mountain Men," and was the home of Kit Carson, who is buried here. Governor Charles Bent was killed here in the anti-United States insurrection of 1847. In the early 1900s, Taos developed as a colony for artists and writers.

Cantonment Burgwin—1852-1860 H

South of Taos on Hwy 518

Never officially designated a fort, this post was built to protect the Taos Valley from Utes and Jicarilla Apaches. It is named for Capt. John H.K. Burgwin, who was killed in the Taos uprising of 1847. It was abandoned in 1860 and is now the site of the Fort Burgwin Research Center.

Ernest Blumenschein Memorial Home and Art Museum M H

2 blocks west of plaza
Ledoux Street, 87571
758-0505

Blumenschein was the cofounder of the Taos Society of Artists. His paintings, as well as those of his talented wife Mary Green Blumenschein and their daughter Helen and works of the other Taos Artists are exhibited in the home. The house is furnished with traditional Taos furniture, as well as European antiques and artwork from around the world. It is restored to its original adobe plaster inside and out. The house is on both the State and National Registers.

Governor Bent Museum M H

117 Bent Street
P.O. Box 153, 87571
758-2376

This is a history museum housed in the Governor Bent House, built circa 1830. It is the site of Charles Bent's death during an uprising in 1847. A gallery in the home features both early Taos art and contemporary works. The house enjoys a place on the State and National Historic Registers.

Harwood Foundation of the University of New Mexico M H L

Ledoux Street, 87571
758-3063

Research library, art museum; Taos art, 1898-present; Patrocinio Barela sculptures; santos; historic photographs; Persian miniatures; Rio Grande tinwork; Spanish Colonial furniture.

Intermountain Weavers Conference A

P.O. Box 1749, 87571
758-9650

This organization conducts a biennial fiber arts conference in odd-numbered years in the nine state intermountain West. Registration is open to any person interested in taking workshops and seminars and attending other programs on the fiber arts.

Kit Carson Foundation M H O

P.O. Drawer CCC, 87571
758-0505

Historical organization celebrates Taos' rich past through the operation of three historic sites—Kit Carson Home, Martinez Hacienda and Blumenschein Home.

Kit Carson Home and Historical Museum M H

Old Kit Carson Road
P.O. Drawer B, 87571
758-0505

Kit Carson, the famous mountain man and scout, purchased this 12 room adobe home in 1843 as a wedding gift for his bride, Josefa Jaramillo. Three of the rooms are furnished as they might have been when Carson and his family lived there for 25 years. He is buried in nearby Kit Carson Park. There are fascinating exhibits on all periods of Taos' prolific history. The exhibits include gun and mountain man displays, as well as an Indian room, Spanish room and Taos room. Collections feature Spanish and early American furniture; arms and equipment; fur trapping equipment; costumes and textiles; Indian and archeological artifacts; religious articles; tools and farm equipment; photographs. The house is on both the State and National Registers.

Kit Carson Park and Cemetery H

In 1868, Christopher "Kit" Carson, the legendary guide, scout, soldier, and trapper, died in Fort Lyons, Colorado. The next year, his body and that of his wife Josefa were brought home to Taos. Others buried here include soldiers killed in the 1847 rebellion protesting the U.S. annexation of New Mexico, and art patron Mabel Dodge Luhan.

Martinez Hacienda   ᴹᴴ

2 miles west of Taos Plaza
State Road 240, 87571
758-0505

Situated on the banks of the Rio Pueblo, this fortress-like building with massive adobe walls and no exterior windows is the only remaining Spanish Colonial Hacienda open year-round to the public. The hacienda has 21 rooms and two large placitas, or courtyards; Spanish Colonial furniture and furnishings; tools and equipment. This is a fine representation of life in Spanish Colonial New Mexico.

La Loma Plaza Historic District   ᴴ

west edge of Taos

The plaza represents a small residential area settled circa 1795. This is considered one of two well-preserved defensive plazas in New Mexico (the other being Chimayo). A highlight of the district is the beautiful San Antonio Chapel. The plaza area is on both the State and National Registers.

La Morada de Taos   ᴹᴸ

Las Cruces Road, 87571
758-9898

Historical research library; archives; research and conservation center.

Mabel Dodge Luhan's Taos Estate   ᴴ

P.O. Box 3400, 87571
758-9456

Former estate of a wealthy Bostonian, active in art and literary circles, who came to live in Taos in the 1920s and married a Native American in Taos. The estate is now owned by a non-profit organization, Las Palomas de Taos, a learning center offering workshops, institutes and special programs. Bed and Breakfast when no workshops are in progress. The house is on State and National Historic Registers.

Meet the Artist Series   ᴱ

Taos Inn
125 Paseo del Norte
758-2233

In this innovative program visitors have an opportunity to meet with nationally known Taos artists every Tuesday and Thursday evening, as they share via discussions, studio tours, on-the-spot demonstrations, slide shows and performances, the inspiration and process behind the finished work of art. The program runs May 15-June 21, and then again October 15-December 15.

Nicolai Fechin Institute and Home   ᴹᴴᴼ

Main Street
P.O. Box 832, 87571
758-1710

Master artist and craftsman Nicolai Fechin spent his early life in his homeland of Russia, later moving to America where he was greatly influenced by Taos. Built in 1928, the Fechin House is a traditional southwestern adobe house with handcarved doors, windows, gates, posts, fireplaces, and other features of a Russian country home. The renovated, historic home contains the furnishings and art objects of Fechin. It is on both the State and National Registers. The Fechin Institute uses the house and studio as a center for its activities. The Institute is a cultural-educational nonprofit organization aimed at presenting and developing Fechin's unique approach to learning, teaching, and creating. Among its many activities, the Institute features yearly Fechin exhibits as well as a series of posters, cards and books.

Old Taos Trade Fair   ⱽᴱ

Martinez Hacienda
758-7505

A reenactment of Spanish Colonial living in the 1820s, featuring authentic music; weaving, baking and carving demonstrations; and native foods and crafts. Held each year in early fall.

Pueblo Revolt Site   ᴴ

Hwy 68, south of Taos

The 1680 Pueblo Revolt began at the Pueblo of Taos when Pope, a religious leader driven from San Juan by Spanish authorities, sent runners carrying a knotted cord to other pueblos designating the number of days until the uprising. Tiwa warriors from Taos and Picuris moved south on August 10 to beseige Santa Fe.

Society of the Muse of the Southwest   ᴬᴾ

117 E. Plaza, Suite H, 87571
758-0081

This group sponsors literary and performing arts events throughout the year, such as Master Writers Theatre, Summer Writers Series, and the Taos Poetry Circus.

Stables Art Center of the Taos Art Association   V P

P.O. Box 198, 87571
758-2036

Art gallery; works of local artists; located in historical 1898 Manby-Thorne House; sculpture garden; auditorium. Nine thematic fine arts exhibits annually; guided tours; films; lectures; gallery talks; concerts; dance recitals; arts festivals; drama; workshops; temporary and traveling exhibitions.

Taos Art Association   A

133 Paseo del Pueblo Norte, 87571
758-2052

Taos Arts Celebrations   V P

120-J Bent St., 87571
758-0516

This is a non-profit organization sponsoring Taos Spring Arts Celebration, a three-week open door on the visual, literary and performing arts. Events include gallery opening, art shows, concerts, arts & crafts fair. Held each May and June. The group also sponsors Yuletide in Taos, an early holiday excursion into the traditions, culture and arts of New Mexico. Held each December.

Taos Balloon Rally   V E

758-8100

Hot-air balloons, parades, dances, entertainment, arts and crafts. Held in October.

Taos Canyon   H

north of Taos

In 1692, after having been driven from New Mexico by the Pueblo Revolt of 1680, the Spanish began to re-establish their rule. In one of the last battles of the reconquest, in September 1696, Governor Diego de Vargas defeated the Indians of Taos Pueblo at nearby Taos Canyon.

Taos Fall Arts Festival   V E

various locations
758-3873

A number of events including the Old Taos Trade Fair, the Wool Festival, arts and crafts fair, culminating in San Geronimo Feast Day at Taos Pueblo on September 29 and 30. The Old Taos Trade Fair is a reenactment of Spanish Colonial living in the 1820s. Authentic music, weaving, baking and carving demonstrations, native foods and crafts, held at the Martinez Hacienda. The Wool Festival is held at Kit Carson State Park and includes demonstrations of shearing, spinning and weaving. Lamb delicacies and beautiful handmade items are for sale. The arts and crafts fair is held the last weekend of the Festival. Late September, early October.

Taos Plaza   H

Established in the 18th Century, the Taos Plaza has a long history as a trading and political center in New Mexico. It became well known in the 18th Century for its annual trade fair held jointly by the Spaniards, Taos Pueblo Indians and roving Comanches. It was also a focal point for the 19th Century trappers and has seen an influx of artists during the 20th Century. It is on both the State and National Registers.

Taos Pueblo Children's Theatre   P

117 E. Plaza, Suite H, 87571
758-0081

Group offers performances of dramatized traditional "coyote tales" and original dramas, created and performed by members of Taos Pueblo. Ages of troupe members range from 10 to 40 years-old.

Taos School of Music Chamber Music Festival   P

P.O. Box 1879, 87571
776-2388

Classical and contemporary chamber music concerts performed by the American String Quartet, pianist Robert McDonald, and gifted international students. Mid-June through mid-August, at the Taos Community Auditorium and Hotel St. Bernard.

Vasquez de Coronado's Route   H

Hwy 68, south of Taos

Under orders from Francisco Vasquez de Coronado in 1540, Captain Hernando de Alvarado explored among the pueblos and followed this route from Espanola to the Pueblo of Taos. Captain Francisco de Barrionuevo also passed this way the following year on his way to the same pueblo.

Wool Festival   V E

Kit Carson State Park
758-3873

An arts and crafts fair is offered along with feature demonstrations of shearing, spinning and weaving. Lamb delicacies and beautiful handmade items are available. Held in early fall.

Yuletide in Taos Ⓥ Ⓔ

various locations
758-0516

This is an early holiday excursion into the tradition, culture and arts of Northern New Mexico. It features romantic farolito tours, candlelight dinners, special dance performances, ski area festivities, arts events, holiday food and craft fairs. Held in early December.

Taos Pueblo Ⓗ

Two miles north of Taos
758-8626

The Pueblo at Taos is one of New Mexico's authentic examples of the survival of Pueblo Indian life, literally unchanged since 1540 when Coronado saw buildings and customs closely resembling those which can be seen today. It has survived nearly 1000 years of volatile history—from invasions by the Spaniards in the 1540s, to the Pueblo Revolt of 1680, to the Taos rebellion against the United States government in 1847 that left 150 Taos Indians dead. In addition to shops and scenery, Taos Pueblo offers several dances throughout the year to which all are welcome. The San Geronimo Feast Day, for example, is held annually on September 30. It features dances, races, pole-climbing and an arts and crafts fair. The pueblo is on both the State and National Registers.

Dances to Commemorate the Christmas Season Ⓔ

Procession of the Virgin ceremony with dances and bonfires on December 24. Deer or Matachinas Dances on Christmas Day.

New Year's Day Celebration Ⓔ

Mass, procession and dances.

San Antonio Feast Day Ⓔ

Corn Dance on June 13.

San Juan Feast Day Ⓔ

Corn Dance on June 24.

Santa Ana Feast Day Ⓔ

Corn Dance on July 26.

Santa Cruz Feast Day Ⓔ

This commemoration features a Blessing of the Fields followed by a Corn Dance and footraces on May 3.

Santiago Feast Day Ⓔ

Corn Dance on July 25.

Taos Pueblo Feast Day Ⓥ Ⓔ

Vespers at San Jerome Chapel, San Geronimo Eve (Thursday). Also sundown dance. Fiesta of San Geronimo (Friday): midmorning Mass, procession, trade fair (arts and crafts), relay races, pole-climbing by Koshares (clowns). September 29, 30.

Taos Pueblo Powwow Ⓥ Ⓔ

north of Taos in El Prado
758-8626

Competition in traditional and fancy Indian dances. This event also features an arts and crafts fair. Held in July.

Three Kings Day Ⓔ

New tribal officers are honored the Transfer of the Canes of Authority ceremony on January 6.

Tatum

Tatum Arts and Crafts Spring Festival Ⓥ

Tatum Community Building
398-5011/5325

Held each year in early April.

Tatum Community Library Ⓛ

400 E. Ash
P.O. Box 156, 88267
398-4822

Tesuque Pueblo H

10 miles north of Santa Fe on U.S. 84-285
983-2667

Tesuque is noted for having very early contact with Europeans because of its closeness to Santa Fe. Tesuque is considered by many to be one of the most traditional of the Tewa-speaking Pueblos. The Tesuque people played an important role in the Pueblo Revolt of 1680. While many of the people of Tesuque today work in Santa Fe, Los Alamos, or at tribal offices, they continue to strive to maintain the traditional way of life. Many Tesuque men are actively involved in farming, while Tesuque women work to create brightly colored pottery using traditional designs. The pottery is usually sold from the artists' homes. Tesuque Pueblo has dances in late May or early June, November, and around Christmas. The annual Feast Day is November 12, and the public is welcome to attend. The pueblo is on both the State and National Registers.

Blessing of the Fields E

Corn Dance held in late May or early June.

Dances to Commemorate the Christmas Season E

Traditional dances during Christmas week.

Tesuque Pueblo Feast Day E

Midmorning Mass, procession; Buffalo, Comanche, Corn, Deer and Flag Dances. San Diego Feast Day on November 12.

Three Kings Day E

Ceremony focusing on the installation of new tribal officers on January 6. Transfer of the Canes of Authority.

Texico

Atchison, Topeka & Santa Fe Railway Depot - Texico H

Hwy 70

This red-tile roofed, Spanish style depot retains its authentic charm, looking just as it did in 1908 when it was built. It stands as one of the few visible reminders of the Belen Cutoff. The depot is on the State Register of Cultural Properties.

Border Town Days VE

769-0425

Three-night rodeo, parade, barbecue, arts and crafts, water polo. Held in late July.

Thoreau

Blessed Kateri Tekawitha Academy & Community Library L

P.O. Box 909, 87323
862-7465

Three Rivers H

Hwy 54, north of Tularosa

Located in the Tularosa Basin east of the great lava flows known as the malpais, Three Rivers was once prominent in the cattle empires of Albert Bacon Fall, John S. Chisum and Susie McSween Barber, "the cattle queen of New Mexico." Charles B. Eddy's El Paso & Northeastern Railroad reached here in 1899.

Three Rivers Petroglyphs H

Hwy 54, 3 miles east of Three Rivers

Three miles to the east of Three Rivers is mile-long array of pictures pecked into the solid rock walls of a volcanic ridge. They include both geometric and animal forms. They were likely made by prehistoric Mogollon Indians between ca. A.D. 1000 and 1400. Site is on the State Register of Cultural Properties.

Tierra Amarilla H

Hwy 84, south of Chama

In 1832 the Mexican government made a large community land grant to Manuel Martinez and other settlers, but settlement was delayed by raids by Utes, Jicarilla Apaches and Navajos. Tierra Amarilla, first called Nutritas, became the Rio Arriba County seat in 1880. In 1967 it was the focus of conflicts between National Guardsmen and land rights activist Reies Lopez Tijerina.

El Vado Dam   H

Located on the Rio Chama, this dam was completed in 1935 and is a rare example of the extensive use of steel in reservoir construction. The dam is on the State Register of Cultural Properties.

Fiesta de Santo Nino   E

Observed every Labor Day weekend. Religious procession, parade and village celebration.

Fort Lowell   H

North of Tierra Amarilla

Fort Lowell was established in the 1860s to protect the area around Tierra Amarilla from the southern Utes. The Army abandoned the post in 1869, but it was used as agency headquarters for the Utes from 1872 until 1881. It was built mostly of adobe and today has eroded into the earth with little remaining.

Tierra Amarilla Historic District   H

The village and isolated farmhouses of La Tierra Amarilla are among the best preserved examples of late 19th Century Hispanic New Mexico settlement patterns, folk architecture and building techniques. Structures date from about 1860. The district is on the State and National Registers.

Tijeras

Old Church of Santo Nino Museum   M H

This museum features local history exhibits in a former church, built in 1929.

Tijeras Canyon   H

East of Albuquerque along I-40

This pass between the Sandia and Manzano mountains has been a natural route for travel between eastern New Mexico and the Rio Grande Valley since prehistoric times. Known as Canon de Carnue in the Spanish colonial period, it takes its present name from the village of Tijeras, Spanish for "scissors."

Timberon

Smith Memorial Library   L

P.O. Box 101, 88350
987-2223

Tome

Tome Parish Museum   M

9 miles north of Belen via Hwy 304
P.O. Box 397, 87060
865-7497

This is a local religious history museum featuring relics and artifacts, paintings, statues and santos.

Torreon

Torreon Community Center Library   L

P.O. Box 70, 87061

Tortugas

Our Lady of Guadalupe Festival   E

Near Las Cruces
526-8171

This celebration—held each year on December 12—features a pilgrimage to Tortugas Mountain, with a torchlight descent. There is also a Mass and a Matachinas Dance.

Truchas   H

Hwy 76, between Espanola and Taos

In 1754, Governor Tomas Velez Cachupin granted land on the Rio Truchas to families from Santa Cruz and Chimayo. Because Nuestra Senora del Rosario de Truchas was on the northern frontier, and subject to attack by Plains Indians, the governor stipulated that the houses should form a square with only one entrance. This small village on the "high road" to Taos was also the set for the film "The Milagro Beanfield War," based on John Nichols popular novel.

Truchas Community Center Library   L

P.O. Box 7, 87578
689-2323

Truth or Consequences H

In 1581, Captain Francisco Sanchez Chamuscado took possession of this region for the King of Spain, naming it the Province of San Felipe. Significant European settlement of the area, however, did not occur until the mid-1800s. Once called Hot Springs because of its curative natural hot springs, "T or C" in 1950 took its present name from Ralph Edwards' radio program.

Fort McRae H

East of T or C, near Engle on Hwy 52

Named for Captain McRae who died at the Battle of Valverde, this fort was built in 1863 near the midpoint of the Jornada del Muerto. One of its missions was to deny Navajo and Apache raiding parties the use of a popular east-west trail. The fort was closed in 1876 but continued to be used by travelers for a few years thereafter.

Geronimo Days Peace Gathering VE

P.O. Box 1029, 87901
894-6600

This annual event, held Columbus day weekend, features music and storytellers, games and rides, Apache Spirit Dancers, arts and crafts, living history and films, food and a street dance.

Geronimo Springs Museum M

325 Main Street
P.O. Box 1029, 87901
894-6600

History museum—artifacts of city and county cultural heritage; Indian artifacts; mineral and rock collection; art exhibits.

Geronimo's Spring H

The Indians knew of the great curative powers of the mineral waters of this spring long before the white man came. According to legend, Geronimo, famous Apache war chief, often stopped here to bathe and relax.

Lake Valley H

49 miles southwest of T or C
via I-25 and Hwys 152 & 27

Ghost town.

Old Time Fiddlers' State Championship P

Convention Center
894-3536

Held annually in mid-October.

Sierra County Fair E

Fairgrounds
894-2375

Held in mid-September.

Sierra County Historical Society O

325 Main, 87901
894-6600

Sierra County Powwow VE

Elephant Butte Community Center
894-3238

This annual event—held in mid-January—features a gem and mineral show, arts and crafts fair, and a country jamboree.

Truth or Consequences Fiesta VE

894-3536

Parade, stage show, gem and mineral show, fiddlers as well as an arts & crafts fair. Held in early May.

Truth or Consequences Public Library L

1 Library Lane
P.O. Box 311, 87901-0311
894-3027

Tucumcari H

461-1694

This area was troubled by both Comanches and Comancheros, New Mexicans who traded illegally with the Indians, until the military campaigns of 1874. With the coming of the railroad in 1898, the small community of Liberty, eight miles to the north, moved here to form the nucleus of Tucumcari, which was incorporated in 1908.

Comanche Country H

I-40, west of Tucumcari

By 1700 the Comanches had acquired the horse and began moving into this area. They drove out the Jicarilla Apaches, and their raids on New Mexico's eastern frontier posed a threat to Indian, Spanish and Anglo settlements for more than a century. The Comanches were finally defeated by the U.S. Army in 1874.

Fort Bascom   H

Hwy 104, north of Tucumcari

Fort Bascom (1863-1870) was built to protect this area from Comanches. In 1864, Kit Carson led a campaign against the Comanches, as did General Philip Sheridan in 1868. The fort was also established to control the Comancheros, New Mexicans involved in illegal trade with the Comanches. Fort Bascom was abandoned in 1870.

Mesa Redondo Cowboy Camp Meeting   E

Hwy 18, 12 miles south of Tucumcari
769-0425

Old time Gospel singing and camp preaching fellowship. Held in late July.

Pinata Festival   E

461-1694

Held in late June.

Quay County Fair   E

461-1694

Held in mid-August.

Tucumcari Arts and Crafts Fair   V

461-1694

This annual fair featuring New Mexico artists is held annually during the first week in June.

Tucumcari Arts and Humanities Council   A

461-0260

Tucumcari Craft Fair   V

461-1694

Held in early December.

Tucumcari Historical Institute Museum   M H O

416 S. Adams, 88401
461-4201

History and folk-art museum housed in 1904 courthouse, operated by the Tucumcari Historical Institute. Collection items range from 12,000 B.C. Indian artifacts to a 1926 fire truck.

Tucumcari Mountain   H

vicinity of Tucumcari

Tucumcari Mountain has long been a landmark for travelers along the Canadian River. Pedro Vial mentioned it in 1793, while opening a trail between Santa Fe and St. Louis. In order to find the best route from Arkansas to California, Captain Randolph B. Marcy led an expedition past here in 1849.

Tucumcari Public Library   L

602 S. Second St., 88401-2899
461-0295

Tularosa   H

Hwy 54, north of Alamogordo

The first successful European settlement in the Tularosa Basin dates from 1862, when 50 or 60 Hispanic farmers moved from the Rio Grande Valley. Heavy Anglo settlement began in the 1880s as settlers and cattlemen from farther east began moving into New Mexico. Tularosa appears as "Oasis" in the novels of western writer Eugene Manlove Rhodes.

Round Mountain   H

Hwy 70, 10 miles east of Tularosa

This cone-shaped landmark about 10 miles from Tularosa was once known as Dead Man's Hill, and has been the backdrop for several military encounters. In April 1868 a small group of soldiers and Tularosa settlers engaged in battle with about 200 Mescalero Apaches.

St. Francis de Paula Fiesta   E

585-2855

Celebration of historic battle with the Indians over land possession. Festivities include crowning of the Queen, traditional street dancing, games, food and entertainment. Held in mid-May.

Tularosa Original Townsite Historic District   H

The village of Tularosa was settled in 1862 in the lush, green Tularosa basin. The village has come full circle from peaceful farming town, to the last of the frontier towns, back to quiet rural town. Tularosa's early homes were small, simple, flat-roofed adobes, many with a unique feature—fortified having only small "rifle holes" for openings. The townsite is on both the State and National Registers.

Tularosa Rose Festival E
585-2855

Annual celebration of the blooming of the roses at Tularosa. Parade, concessions, crowning of the Rose Queen, barbecue. Held in early May.

Tularosa Village Museum M
301 Central Avenue, 88352
585-2057

Local pioneer exhibits, artifacts.

Vadito

February Fest E
Sipapu Lodge and Ski Area
587-2240

This winter carnival—held annually in late February—features ski races, music concerts and a snow art sculpture contest.

Lauriano Cordova Memorial Museum M
P.O. Box 14, 87579
587-2443

This is an old mill museum, featuring a miller's cabin, tool room, medicinal herb and vegetable gardens, ovens, corrals and a chicken run. The museum offers guided tours and two scheduled festivals per year—4th of July and Labor Day.

Mountains of Talent Art Series V
Sipapu Lodge Ski Area
587-2240

Art series runs Jan. 1-March 26 and April 1-June 21.

Vaughn H
Hwy 60, west of Fort Sumner

Vaughn, a division point in the transcontinental railway system, is located along the route of the Stinson cattle trail. In 1882, Jim Stinson, manager of the New Mexico Land and Livestock Co., drove cattle along this important trail from Texas to New Mexico's Estancia Valley.

Huntsinger Public Library L
P.O. Box 68, 88353

Velarde H
Hwy 68, between Espanola and Taos

Founded in 1875, this small farming community was first named La Jolla. It was once famous for finely woven blankets. Here the Camino Real left the Rio Grande and followed a canyon northeast to Embudo Creek where it began a climb over the mountains to Taos.

Wagon Mound H
This last great landmark on the Santa Fe Trail was named for its resemblance to the top of a covered wagon. At Wagon Mound, travelers could cross from the Cimarron Cutoff to Fort Union, which is located on the Mountain Branch of the Trail. The two branches joined south of here at Watrous.

Waterflow

Hogback Trading Post H
Hwy 550

Established in 1871, this trading post provided necessities for Indians living on the reservation. It also served as an outlet for locally produced rugs, jewelry and baskets.

Watrous H
The Mountain Branch and the Cimarron Cutoff of the Santa Fe Trail meet at Watrous. This important spot on the Trail was first known as La Junta, "junction" in Spanish. In 1879, with the coming of the railroad, it was named for Samuel B. Watrous, a prominent local rancher.

Fort Union National Monument M H
425-8025

This was an 1800s fort guarding the Santa Fe Trail. A military museum on the grounds features exhibits/artifacts. The fort is on both the State and National Registers.

Living History Portrayal of Frontier Garrison Life   E

Fort Union National Monument
425-8025

This program features lectures, demonstrations about muskets, women on the frontier, the infantry, cavalry, Fort Union and the Civil War, and the Santa Fe Trail. Runs Memorial Day to Labor Day, annually.

Loma Parda   H

6 miles northwest of Watrous of Hwy 161

Ghost town.

Santa Fe Trail   H

East of Watrous on I-25, near Hwy 477

Opened by William Becknell in 1821, the Santa Fe Trail became the major trade route to Santa Fe from Missouri River towns. The two main branches, the Cimarron Cutoff and the Mountain Branch, joined at Watrous. Travel over the Trail ceased with the coming of the railroad in 1879.

White Oaks   H

Northeast of Carrizozo

Now a ghost town, once a booming mining camp. Two large old homes are still occupied. A museum has relics of White Oaks' past. White Oaks is on both the State and National Registers.

White's City

Million Dollar Museum   M

Main Street, 88268
785-2294

More than 50 collections, including the doll and doll house collection, 6,000-year-old mummified Indians, the Whittling Cowboys ranch guns, chinaware, old vehicles, music boxes and thousands of items of the old West.

Winston   H

38 miles northwest of T or C via I-25 and Hwy 52

Ghost town.

Winston Fiesta   E

894-3536

Held annually in mid-April, this is an old-fashioned style country festival with games, food and entertainment.

Zia Pueblo   H

35 miles northwest of Albuquerque on Hwy 44
867-3304

The location of Zia Pueblo was chosen by the Indians in about 1250 A.D. when they moved down the Jemez River to another site. The Pueblo site is so harmonious with its surroundings that only sharp eyes usually notice the settlement unless the road sign calls attention to it. Although the Pueblo itself is inconspicuous, its Sun Symbol, the Zia symbol of perfect friendship among united cultures, is familiar to all New Mexicans, for it is the official state insignia appearing on the flag. Zia Pueblo suffered disastrous losses during the Pueblo Revolt. Six hundred people were killed and additional conflicts lasting for years reduced the population still further. They are still a small community of agricultural workers and livestock raisers, but they have a strong sense of identity and have produced beautiful traditional works of art. Prominent among Zia crafts is pottery. The principal festival is the Corn Dance on the feast day of our lady of the Assumption in August. The pueblo is on both the State and National Registers.

Dances to Commemorate the Christmas Season   E

Traditional dances during Christmas week.

Easter Celebration   E

Mass, procession and traditional dances.

Three Kings Day   E

Ceremony honoring new tribal leaders on January 6.

Zia Enrichment Library/ Cultural Center   L

San Ysidro, 87053
867-3304

Zia Pueblo Feast Day   E

Our Lady of Assumption Feast Day on August 15. Corn Dance.

Zuni Pueblo   ⊞

Hwy 53, 30 miles south of Gallup
782-4481

Old and modern pueblo dwellings of Zuni Indians
known for their fine silver and turquoise jewelry.
Beautiful Mission Church of Nuestra Senora de
Guadalupe in the pueblo plaza. Colorful Shalako
Kachina dance every December draws visitors from
around the world. Other dances—Rain Dance in
June, many in August during McKinley County
Fair. The pueblo is on both the State and National
Registers.

McKinley County Fair   ⊟

Held annually in August.

Shalako Ceremony and Dance   ⊟

One of the most famous of the Kachina dances,
Shalako is held early December to celebrate
the end of the old and the beginning of the new
year, and to bless all the new houses of the pueblo
erected during the year. The costumes of the
dancers are unsurpassed in color and design. This
ceremony, which begins with a ritual crossing of
the small river which runs through the pueblo,
takes most of the night. People come from all over
the nation and world to see this dance and colorful
ceremony.

Zuni Cibola Complex   ⊞

Consists of four separate archeological sites that
illustrate the development of Zuni culture: Village
of the Great Kivas, Yellow House, Kechipbowa,
and Hawikuh. Village of the Great Kivas is most
commonly visited, with its impressive and beautiful petroglyphs and historic pictographs.

Zuni Fair   ⊟

Held at Zuni Pueblo fairgrounds annually in early
September.

Zuni Public Library   ⊡

P.O. Box 339, 87327
782-5630

Zuni Rain Dance   ⊟

Held in June.

Public Art in New Mexico

Albuquerque

Anderson, David
"Almond Blossom/Astronomy"
Sculpture 1986
Median on Osuna west of I-25

Armijo, Federico
"Del Pasado al Futuro" 1986
NM Museum of Natural History

Busstop Sculpture 1983
Lomas & Entrada NW

"Formas al Cielo" Sculpture 1989
University of New Mexico

Blankley, Rod
"Images" Sculpture 1988
Emerson School, Carrillo Park
620 Georgia SE

Boydstun, Jeanette
"Presto" Wall-work 1984
Parking Structure Entrance
5th & Copper NW

Clancy, Patrick
Photo Mural 1986
NM Youth Diagnostic &
Development Center
4000 Edith NE

Drexel, William & Harris, O.K.
"Solar Arc" Sculpture 1985
UNM / Central and Girard NE

Eck, C Anthony
"Interweave" Sculpture 1984
East Central Multi-Service Center
7525 Zuni SE

Egri, Ted
"Hand of Friendship" Sculpture 1962
Civic Plaza, 3rd & Tijeras NW

Findley, Tommie
"Las Vegas" Wall Sculpture 1983
Busstop
Lomas & Rancho Seco Road NW

**Fitzgerald, Ed, Mark Prouse
and David Jones**
"Center for Theatre Costume Exhibit"
Mixed Media 1990
Public Library/Wool Warehouse

Foster, Gus
"Cimarron Palisades"
Panoramic Photography 1986
NM Youth Diagnostic &
Development Center
4000 Edith NE

Fox, Lincoln
"The Sheepherder" Sculpture 1990
The Albuquerque Museum

Goodman, William
"Zia" Sculpture c.1967
Civic Plaza

Green, Maera
"Picture Fountain" Sculpture 1990
Los Volcanes Senior Center

Guzman, Gilberto
"The Harvest" Mural 1984
Parking Structure Entrance
4th & Copper NW

Haddaway, Ed
"A Tree of Mixed Metaphors"
Sculpture 1988
The Albuquerque Museum

Hamilton, Susan & Bruce
"Ice Palace" Sculpture 1986
Carrie Tingley Hospital
1127 University NE

Hanbury, Una
"Phoenix Rising from the Ashes"
Sculpture 1985
Rio Grande Zoological Park
903 10th SW

"Lioness and Cub" Sculpture 1984
Rio Grande Zoological Park
903 10th SW

Hyde, Doug
"Walk in Beauty" Sculpture 1983
The Albuquerque Museum

Jimenez, Luis
"Southwest Pieta" Sculpture 1987
Martineztown Park
Roma & Edith NE

Keller, Reed
Ceramic Tile Mural 1982
Animal Control Center
8920 Lomas NE

McCain, Buck
"Don Francisco Cuervo y Valdes,
Founder of Alburquerque" 1988
Rio Grande & Romero NW

Kimball, Celia
"Heritage" Mural 1985
Taylor Ranch Fire Station
6100 Taylor Ranch Road NW

Magennis, Beverly
"Full Circle" Sandbox 1990
Zia School Park
440 Jefferson NE

Mason, Molly
Blue Tile Walls 1983
Busstop at 11th & Lomas NW

Mattox, Charles
Laser Light Sculpture Project
Portable Projector 1987

Meine, Carol & Wasilewski, Richard
Playground Mural 1982
Jackson Elementary School
4720 Cairo NE

Moore, Paul
"George Maloof" Sculpture 1990
NM Motor Vehicles Department
3401 Pan American Freeway NE

Moroles, Jesus Bautista
"Floating Mesa"
Fountain Sculpture 1984
The Albuquerque Museum

Oppenheim, David
"Dreams and Nightmares:
Journey of a Broken Weave"
Sculpture 1987
UNM / Stanford NE

**Pearson, J./Stetson, Diana/Bull, C.
Abdalla, N./Culver, D./Johansen, C.
Loving, R./McCulloch, F./Peterson, R.
St. Aubyn, J./Wenger, J./White, R.L.**
Don Quijote Portfolio 1982
Old Main Library
423 Central Avenue NE

Peart, Jerry
"CrossRoads" Sculpture 1984
Pedestrianway, 4th & Central

Perry, Sarah
"Gorilla Route #66" Sculpture 1990
Tramway Library Center
for Public Art

Red Sun Lyon, Elizabeth
"The Shield" Wall-Relief 1986
West Side Policy Comm. Substation
Coors & Los Volcanes NW

Rivera, Reynaldo "Sonny"
"Los Cibolos del Rio Grande"
Fountain 1990
Rio Grande Zoo

Roderick, Judy & Bilan, Peter
Entry Hall Sculpture 1982
Palo Duro Senior Center
5221 Palo Duro NE

Rose, Ramsay
"Gridlock" Banners 1984/
Parking Structure Facade
5th & Copper NW

Saville, Ken
"Big Hearted Joy Beasts"
Animal Control Center
8920 Lomas NE

Schroeder, Willard
"Brave Men" Sculpture 1984
Ernie Pyle Library
900 Girard SE

Scott, Sandy
"Fountain of Peace" 1989
Central & San Felipe NW

Sebastain
"Variacion Nuevo Mexico"
Sculpture 1989
The Albuquerque Museum

Shows, Andrew
"Kolowisi" Sculpture 1983
Busstop at 8th & Lomas NW

Thomas, David
"Albertosaur Sternbergii"
Dinosaur Sculpture 1987
NM Museum of Natural History

"Pentaceratops Sternbergii"
Dinosaur Sculpture 1985
NM Museum of Natural History

Thompson, Helen and Senior Artists
"Historia de Barelas"
Tapestry 1989
Senior Multi-Service Center
714 7th Street SW

Townsend, Storm
"To Serve and Protect"
Sculpture 1984
NE Heights Police Substation
8201 Osuna NE

Vega, Ed
"Dawn Light" Sculpture 1982
San Mateo Mini Park
San Mateo & Indian School NE

"Modulator" Sculpture 1985
Lawn/Jonson Gallery at UNM

Velhagen, Eric
"A Tradition of Public
Transportation in Albuquerque"
Painting 1989
Transit Department Building
601 Yale SE

Walters, Billie
"The Five Stones of
Elena Gallegos" 1982
Albert Sims Park
East Gallegos Picnic Area

Weissman
Ceramic Tile Mural 1986
Bear Canyon Senior Center
Gutierrez & Pitt NE

Witherspoon
"Mountain Waves" Wall Sculpture 1986
Piedra Lisa Park
Menaul & Punta de Vista NE

"Madonna of the Trail"
Sculpture
Fourth & Marble

Albuquerque International Airport / Art Collection

Adams, Clinton
"Figure in Green" Lithograph 1969
Concourse C

Adams, Ron
"Profile in Blue" Lithograph 1988
Concourse C

Alvarez, David
"Zebra" Woodcarving 1988
Gate E

Anderson, Liz
"Untitled" Ceramic vessel 1988
Concourse B

Antreasian, Garo Z.
"Untitled: 81.2.1 A+B"
Lithograph 1981
Concourse C

Boomer, John D.
"Serenity and Hope" Sculpture
Concourse B

Calcagno, Larry
"Earth Legend Series"
Acrylic on canvas 1975
Concourse A

Carrillo, Charles M.
"La Hueda a Egipto" Retablo 1988
Gate D

Cash, Marie Romero
"Cristo & Mourning Figures"
Mixed media 1986
Gate D

Cate, Joe and Rosey
"Untitled" Necklace 1988
Ticketing-North

Chavez, Richard I.
"Untitled" Necklace 1988
Ticketing-East

Cippy Crazy Horse
"Traditional Pueblo
Concho Belt" 1988
Ticketing-West

Goodacre, Glenna
"The Basket Dance" Sculpture 1987
Security Checkpoint

Curtiss-design Biplane
Built & flown 1911-1915
Ticketing-North

Dominguez, Eddie
Terracotta fish platter/glaze 1987
Gate E

Dehn, Virginia
"Rites" Acrylic/clay on canvas 1986
Concourse C

Ettenberg, Frank
"Deep Sea Falls" Oil on canvas 1985
Concourse A

Foster, Gus
"Central Ave. at Carlisle, Albuq."
Photograph-mural 1988
Concourse C

Fox, Lincoln
"Dream of Flight" Sculpture 1989
Concourse Lounge

Fragua, Clifford
"Guardian of the Fourth World"
Marble/alabaster 1989
Ticketing-North

Gachupin, Laura J.
"Owl Bowl" Ceramic 1988
Ticketing-West

Gandert, Miguel
"Rudolfo Mascarenas-Amalia, NM"
Black & white photograph 1987
Concourse C

Gasper, Dinah & Peter
"Fetish Necklace" 1989
Ticketing-West

Gonzales, Edward
"Hacienda Pan" Oil on canvas 1987
Gate E

Gorman, R.C.
"Storage Jar" Lithograph 1987
Concourse C

Grayson, Ilena
"Untitled" Earthenware 1988
Concourse B

Gutierrez-De La Cruz, Lois
"Polychrome Jar" Ceramic 1988
Ticketing-West

Hahn, Betty
"Botanical Layout: Peony"
Photo color lithograph 1979
Concourse B

Hamilton, Russell
"Yellow Pot" Oil on linen 1987
Concourse A

Hurley, Wilson
"La Cueva Sunset, East"
Oil on canvas 1988
Baggage Claim Area

"La Cueva Sunset, West"
Oil on canvas 1988
Baggage Claim Area

Jennings, Phyllis
"Tewa Motel, Albuquerque, NM"
Color photograph 1984
Concourse A

John, Tina R.
"Untitled" Navajo tapestry 1989
Ticketing-North

Johnson, Yazzie & Gail Bird
"Untitled" Necklace 1988
Ticketing-East

Karp, Aaron
"Caldron" Acrylic on canvas 1987
Concourse A

Kaskalla, Roderick
"Untitled" Bracelet 1988
Ticketing-West

Kloss, Gene
"Song of Creation" Drypoint 1988
Concourse A

Kozikowski, Nancy
"Runways" Tapestry 1988
Above escalators

Laval, Louise M.
"Andean Spirit" Doll 1988
Concourse B

Lee, Bob
"Night on Elk Mountain"
Oil on canvas 1988
Concourse B

Lowney, Bruce Stark
"The Last Hill" Lithograph 1986
Concourse B

Medina, Marcellus & Elizabith
"Jar with Dancers" Ceramic 1988
Ticketing-West

Montoya, Robert B.
"Images in the Pueblo Night"
Casein on ragboard 1988
Ticketing-North

Naranjo, Elizabeth
"Lamp Vase" Ceramic 1988
Ticketing-East

Natseway, Charmae Shields
"Seed Pot" Ceramic 1988
Ticketing-East

Newhall, Beaumont
"Ansel Adams-Ranchos de Taos,
New Mexico" B & W photo 1980
Concourse C

Niblett, Gary
"Guadalupe Sunrise"
Oil on canvas 1987
Concourse B

Ortega, Ben
"San Pascual" Santo 1987
Gate D

Ortega, Paul Andrew
"Untitled" Chimayo weaving 1988
Gate E

Ortega, L Armando
"Lucinda" Chimayo weaving 1988
Gate E

Owen, Angie Reano/
"Untitled" Bracelet 1988
Ticketing-West

Pena, Dora Tse Pe
"Untitled" Ceramic 1988
Ticketing-East

Pesata, Lydia
"Untitled" Basket 1988
Ticketing-North

Chalee, Pop (Merina Lujan)
"Zuni Masked Dancer" Painting c.1945
Ticketing-East

"Navajo Yeibichai" Painting c.1945
Ticketing-East

"Horse Mural" Painting c.1945
Ticketing-East

"Buffalo Mural" Painting c.1945
Ticketing-West

"Mutaciua" Painting c.1945
Ticketing-West

"Apache Crown Dancer"
Painting c.1945
Ticketing-West

"Brown Deer" Painting c.1945
Aviation Offices

"Blue Deer" Painting c.1945
Aviation Offices

"Buffalo Dancer" Painting c.1945
Aviation Offices

"Taos Horsetail Dancer"
Painting c.1945
Aviation Offices

Prythero, Tim
"American" Sculpture 1988
Concourse C

Quandelacy, Stewart J.
"Medicine Bear" Fetish 1988
Ticketing-North

Rippel, Morris
"Corrales" Watercolor on board 1988
Concourse A

Rivera, Elias
"Under the Portal of Santa Fe"
Oil on canvas 1988
Gate E

Rivera, Francis
"Spring Fever" Oil on canvas 1987
Gate E

Roberts, Holly
"Coyote with Woman Inside"
Oil on B&W silver print 1986
Concourse A

Robles, Julian
"San Ildefonso Hunting Dancer"
Oil on canvas 1988
Concourse B

Rodriguez, Mike
"Calico Cat" Woodcarving 1988
Gate D

Rodriguez, Paula
"Popular Santos in New Mexico"
Wooden cross 1988
Gate D

Romero, Senaida & Emilio
"Holy Family" Colcha/tin 1988
Gate D

Roybal, Tanquilino
"St. Francis" Santo 1988
Gate D

Sandoval, Ramoncita Cruz
"Poe Kwinsawin" Skirt 1988
Ticketing-North

Scholder, Fritz
"The Magician" Lithograph 1985
Concourse A

Scott, Sam
"Sun Song" Oil on canvas 1987
Concourse A

Slaymaker, Martha
"La Facade II" Mixed media 1987
Concourse C

Snidow, Gordon
"What the hell are we waiting for
now, Christmas?" Gouache on board
1987, Concourse A

Stroh, Earl
"Quiet Scherzo I" Lithograph 1983
Concourse B

Stuyck, Rosemarie Lopez
"Queen of Rosary, Lady of Guadalupe,
Lady of Sorrows" Retablo 1987
Gate D

Suina, Ada
"Storyteller with Eight Separate
Children" Native clay 1988
Ticketing-North

Sussman, Arthur H.
"Buffalo White"
Oil & mixed media 1984
Concourse C

Tapia, Luis Eligio
"Our Lady of Guadalupe" Santo 1988
Gate D

Teller, Stella
"Storyteller" Native clay 1988
Ticketing-North

Tenorio, Robert P.
"Sikyatki Shaped Bowl" Clay 1988
Ticketing-East

Thomas, Jinni
"Ever Changing"
Acrylic & watercolor 1987
Concourse B

Torivio, Dorothy Valley
"Seed Jar" Pottery 1989
Ticketing-West

Toya, Maxine R.
"Hopi Woman" Ceramic 1989
Ticketing-North

Valdez, Horacio
"San Rafael" Santo 1978
Gate D

Velarde, Pablita
"Why the Coyote Bays at the Moon"
Painting 1989
Ticketing-North

Volkin, Hilda Appel
"All that Surrounds the Earth
Surrounds Me" Sculpture 1987
Concourse B

Yates, Irene Martinez
"Bere de Santa Cruz"
Woodcarving 1987
Gate D

Youngblood, Nathan A.
"Pottery Jar" Ceramic 1989
Ticketing-East

Angel Fire

Shanehouse, Bill
Public Sculpture Garden

Belen

Ruta, Peter
"Pinones" Oil painting
Belen State Office Building

Tijerina, Kathleen
"Hachita," "Manhattan Cafe,"
"Whitehouse Cafe" Oil paintings
Belen State Office Building

Traube, Alex
"Painted Chairs" Oil paintings
Belen State Office Building

Deming

Yazzie, Gary
"Colors of the Dance" Watercolor
Deming State Police Building

Farmington

Barber, Cynthia
"Canon de Maravillas" Sculpture
Harriet B. Simons Building

Hubble, Rod S.
"Legacy of Day" Acrylic Painting
Harriet B. Simons Building

McGuire, Frank
"Song of Welcome" Sculpture
Harriet B. Simons Building

Rivera, Francis
"Rites of Passage" Pastel painting
Harriet B. Simons Building

Strock, Glen
"El Valle" Gouache (painting)
Harriet B. Simons Building

Fort Stanton

Yazzie, Gary
"Stealing Glances" Oil paintings
Fort Stanton Hospital

Grants

Barber, Cynthia
"Untitled" Wall sculpture
New Mexico Museum of Mining
100 Iron Street

Kie, Robert
Desert scene Painted mural 1976
Grants State Bank
824 W. Santa Fe

Meyer, Father Howard OFM
Virgin Mary Lava Rock
Park-St. Theresa's Catholic Church
500 E. High

Montoya, Jerry
Desert & Sky Painting
St. Theresa's Catholic Church
500 E. High

Peters, Bob
Four dimensional triangles Steel
NMSU-Grants campus

Tatkoski, Arthur & Ron Powell
Stained glass windows
First Presbyterian Church
400 Nimitz Drive

Hobbs

Baudoin, Ali
"Earth Cooler" Sculpture
Hobbs State Office Building

Las Cruces

Acosta, Manuel
Historical mural
First National Bank, 500 South Main

Barrick, Ken
Murals projects at Corbett Center,
Jacobs Hall and Hadley Hall
NMSU campus

Carrion, Felix
Mural and Sculpture
Fire Station on Missouri Ave.
Mural at Mesilla Valley Hospital

Flint, Clifford
Sculpture at Young Park
Lee's Drive and Nevada

Kinser, Grant
"The Joy of Learning" Bronze
Branson Hall Library, NMSU campus

Lea, Tom
WPA Mural
Branigan Cultural Center
106 W. Hadley

Lewitt, Sol
"A square within which are
horizontal parallel lines;
outside the square, vertical
parallel lines. On the other
side, a circle within which are
vertical parallel lines; outside
the circle are horizontal parallel
lines." Concrete sculpture
Speech and English Building
NMSU campus

Morales, Danny
Evolution Mural
Branigan Cultural Center
Downtown Mall

Penn, Beverly
Steel piece
Branigan Library, Main and Picacho

Pennock, Tony
Mural NM Boys Ranch
Downtown Mall
Main and Water Streets
Murals on Watertanks, I-25

Schwaiger, Glenn
Mirrored piece
Branigan Library, Main and Picacho

Sundt, Duke
Conquistador, Cowboy, and Indian
Bronze sculpture
Business College, NMSU campus

Las Vegas

Contreras, Susan
"Oaxaca" Oil painting
Las Vegas Medical Center

Ellis, David
"We are the smell of the rain
Sun on the Skin
We are heaven and earth and
Peace in the heart"
Ceramic tile mural
Las Vegas Medical Center
Hot Springs Blvd.

Lincoln

Faudie, Fred
"Billy the Kid" Acrylic paintings
Lincoln County Courthouse

Los Alamos

Brookins, Anita
"The Quarry" Watercolor 1970
Nambe Room, Fuller Lodge

Burciaga, Ernesto V.
Poster/color photograph 1985
Los Alamos Municipal Building

Ennis, Cary
"Red with Black on Black"
Oil painting 1988
Municipal Building Lobby

Gallegos, Mary Beth
"Summer Meadow" Oil Painting 1986
Kiva Room, Fuller Lodge

George, Jean Morgan
"Late Afternoon Light"
Oil painting 1989
Mesa Public Library

Hogan, John
Four panel oil painting 1988
County Municipal Annex
901 Trinity Drive

Jaramillo, D.
"Lotus" Sculpture 1989
Mesa Public Library

Lange, Richard
"Aquatic Pool Figures" Mural 1988
Larry R. Walkup Aquatic Center

McConnell, Joan
"Mesas" Drawing 1970
Nambe Room, Fuller Lodge

"Cliff Dwellings Series #8"
Watercolor collage 1988
Municipal Building Lobby

Messimer, James
"Rock Concert" Oil painting 1987
Los Alamos Municipal Building

Olsen, Hal
"First Snow" Oil painting 1982
Los Alamos Municipal Building

Pate, George
"Las Trampas" Watercolor 1987
Council Chambers, Municipal Building

Prueitt, Mel
"Chromatic Image" Photograph 1990
Municipal Annex

"Contemplating Liftoff"
Photograph 1990
Municipal Annex

"Texture Mapping" Photograph 1990
Municipal Annex

Rigg, Glenn
"Water in Motion"
Stained Glass Windows 1989
Larry R. Walkup Aquatic Center

Sandoval, Secundino
"Good Success" Watercolor 1988
Los Alamos Municipal Building

Seamons, Lillian
"Hopi Tapestry" Watercolor 1987
Los Alamos Municipal Building

"Storytime" Watercolor 1989
White Rock Branch Library

Siri Gian Khalsa
Poster/oil painting 1986
Los Alamos Municipal Building

Suehs, Virginia and Charlie
3-D shadow box 1986
Los Alamos Municipal Building

Tatom, Kirk
"Winter Circle" Sculpture 1989
Los Alamos Municipal Building

Yarnell, Barbara
Art deco ceramic vase
Municipal Annex

"Raphael Presente a Leonard da Vinci" Lithograph 1989
White Rock Branch Library

Raton

Chapman, Manville
Eight murals in oil 1934
Shuler Theatre interior
131 N. 2nd Street

Santa Fe

Bacigalupa, Andrea
"San Francisco de Asis"
Bronze sculpture 1980
Santa Fe City Hall

Favour, Margaret
Fabric Wall Hanging 1980
Sweeney Convention Center
201 W. Marcy

Hicks, Tommy
"Up" Painted metal 1980
Sweeney Convention Center
201 W. Marcy

Hunziker, Robert
"Mesa" Stucco relief 1988
Sandoval parking garage

Hyde, Doug
"Untitled" Sculpture
Museum of Indian Arts and
Culture, Camino Lejo

Kimbal, Celia C.
"Untitled" Mural
Joseph Montoya Building
St. Francis Drive

Klabunde, Tim
"Mother & Child" Sculpture 1988
La Familia Medical Center
1121 Alto

Klingensmith, Laurie
"Prickly Pear" Photo prints
Marian Hall, Palace Avenue

Kraft, Grace
"Higher Up" Printed silk
Marian Hall, Palace Avenue

Leyba, Samuel
"Suenos de Juventud"
Tile mural 1989
Monica Roybal Center
737 Agua Fria

Leyba, Carlos and Samuel
"Herbalism and Medicine
in New Mexico" Mural
Harold Runnels Building
St. Francis Drive

Lipps, Thomas
"Fountainhead Rock"
Stone fountain 1988
Water & Sandoval Streets

Lolas, Carlos
"Passway," and "Compound"
Oil on canvas paintings
State police complex
Cerrillos Road

Maher, Janet
"New Mexico Quilt"
Tile Mural 1989
LaFarge Branch Library
1730 Llano

Patterson
"The New Mexico Calendar"
Wood 1979
Santa Fe City Hall

Rivera, Sonny
"Don Diego de Peralta"
Bronze sculpture 1989
Santa Fe Airport

Southard, Charles
"Homage to the Burro"
Steel sculpture 1988
Sandoval parking garage

Stiha, Vladan
"Artist Walk of Fame"
Bronze plaques 1985
Lincoln & Palace Avenues

Vigil, Frederico
"Acequia Madre" Mural 1989
Acequia Madre School
Acequia Madre

West, Jerry
"Suenos y Recuerdos de Santa Fe"
Interior painted mural
Santa Fe City Hall

Tri-cultural sculpture
Metal sculpture 1977
Sweeney Convention Center
201 W. Marcy

"Untitled" Fountain sculpture
Cornell Park

"Untitled" Oil painting
Harold Runnels Building
St. Francis Drive

Silver City

Barraza, Jose
"El Bailador" (The Dancer)
White cement over metal 1980s
McCray Art Building, WNMU campus

Battenberg, John
"Peace Warrior" Sculpture 1962
Miller Library, WNMU campus

Howard, Cecil
"Heritage" Mural 1969
Fine Arts Auditorium,
WNMU campus

Van Soelen, Theodore
WPA painted murals 1930s
Ranching in Silver City area
Copper mining in Santa Rita
Grant County Courthouse

WNMU Art Students
Painted mural c.1978
Southwest Indian motifs
Rear walls of buildings
Downtown Big Ditch Park

Socorro

Karp, Aaron
"Ledge" Oil on paper/canvas
Socorro State Police Building

Yazzie, Gary
"Untitled" Oil on masonite
Socorro State Police Building

Taos

Chacon, George
"El Santero" Mural 1989
Paseo del Pueblo/E. Kit Carson

Egri, Ted
"Worlds Within" Sculpture 1987
Taos Community Auditorium

Gersh, Bill
"Buckaroo and Fiddler"
Sculpture 1989

Mercer, Gray
"Red Horse" Sculpture 1985
Paseo del Pueblo Sur

"Black Thoroughbred"
Sculpture 1988
Ski Valley Road

**Vasques, Enriqueta and
Juanita Jaramillo**
"Un Puno de Tierra" Mural 1977
El Prado

Truth or Consequences

Martinez, Ernesto
"Untitled" Acrylic on canvas
Veterans Center

Tucumcari

Acosta, Manuel
Mesa with corral Acrylic 1965
Trigg Memorial Hospital

Beville
"Post Parade" Bronze 1989
Tucumcari Area Vocational School

Christofferson, Gerda
Portraits of Indians
Pastel painting 1971
Tucumcari Public Library

Cosner, Bernice
Desert Scene with Indian
Oil painting 1984
Tucumcari Historical Museum

Curry, Bill
Portrait of Gov. John E. Miles
Oil painting 1975
Quay County Courthouse

Portrait of Herman Moncus
Oil painting 1968
Tucumcari Historical Museum

Landscape with wagon
Oil painting 1970
Tucumcari Public Library

Kiowa meeting Onate-1601
Oil painting 1990
Tucumcari Area Vocational School

West meeting settlers-1901
Oil painting 1990
Tucumcari Area Vocational School

Dewey, K.O.
Kachina Wood sculpture 1971
Tucumcari Public Library

Fister, Janette
"Cassandra" Bronze 1988
Tucumcari Area Vocational School

Hallenkremer, Odon
3 portraits Oil paintings 1971
Tucumcari Historical Museum

Hise, William H.
Sandstone sculpture
Tucumcari Historical Museum

Jennings, Janie
Pioneers Mural 1970
Senior Citizens Center

Johnson, Nels, aka Dobie Joe
Portrait of Herman Moncus
Pencil 1948
Tucumcari Historical Museum

Lane, Scott Tyler
Untitled Bronze 1988
Tucumcari Area Vocational School

Mead, Ben Carlton
Coronado Mural 1939
Quay County Courthouse

Mirabal, Mabel
"Little Red Hen" Bronze 1988
"Grace" Bronze 1989
"Monique" Bronze 1989
Tucumcari Area Vocational School

Sinor, Yoni
"Lynx Warrior" Bronze 1988
Tucumcari Area Vocational School

Toy, Janet
Indian on horse and Cowboy
2 Oil paintings 1971
"The Gaulding House"
Pen and Ink 1971
Tucumcari Public Library

Locations of Cultural Resources

Index to Cultural Resources

Arts Associations

Arts & Crafts Fairs/Visual Arts

Community Events

Historic Buildings & Sites

Historical Organizations

Libraries

Museums

Performing Arts